WILEY & SAS BUSINESS SERIES

The Wiley & SAS Business Series presents books that help senior-level managers with their critical management decisions.

Titles in the Wiley & SAS Business Series include:

For more information on any of the above titles, please visit www.wiley.com.

Mobile Learning

*A Handbook for Developers,
Educators, and Learners*

Scott McQuiggan
Lucy Kosturko
Jamie McQuiggan
Jennifer Sabourin

WILEY

Cover image: Tammi Kay George and Lisa Morton
Cover design: Tammi Kay George and Lisa Morton

For general information on our other products and services or for technical support,
please contact our Customer Care Department within the United States at (800)
762-2974, outside the United States at (317) 572-3993 or fax (317) 572-4002.

Wiley publishes in a variety of print and electronic formats and by print-on-demand.
Some material included with standard print versions of this book may not be included
in e-books or in print-on-demand. If this book refers to media such as a CD or DVD
that is not included in the version you purchased, you may download this material at
http://booksupport.wiley.com. For more information about Wiley products, visit
www.wiley.com.

Library of Congress Cataloging-in-Publication Data:

ISBN 978-1-118-89430-9 (Hardcover)
ISBN 978-1-118-93895-9 (ePDF)
ISBN 978-1-118-89428-6 (ePub)

Printed in the United States of America

10 9 8 7 6 5 4 3 2 1

Contents

Preface

Mobile learning is an exciting and important movement, in our opinion. We, the authors, are not in-service teachers. We are all employees at SAS Institute, a prominent statistical software company. We work on Curriculum Pathways, educational software that SAS provides for free to any educator. We work closely with teachers in the development of this web and mobile content, and our research and work provides us with an altogether unique perspective. Like scores of educators, researchers, developers, legislators, and thought leaders, we think that mobile learning holds tremendous promise for our educational system, with the potential to unlock a new world of educational opportunities to today's kids.

We know, foremost, that to have quality educational apps that improve education, developers need teachers, and teachers need developers. This symbiosis is vital to the field of mobile learning, yet we find little written on the topic. In our development practice, feedback from in-service teachers is so valuable, and frequently leads to new features or new apps being created. If there is one takeaway from this book, it'd be that developers and teachers, though their education and talents are likely very different, should work together to make mobile learning tools that accomplish the goals of today's classroom. We believe that mobile learning holds true promise for improving the educational system, the economy, and the future success of our country. But make no mistake; actually delivering on the promise of mobile learning is wholly dependent on having excellent teachers with excellent educational resources, such as apps, at the service of our students. Through this partnership, it is our hope that a shared understanding of what makes a great educational app can take hold, shaping the future of mobile learning.

To facilitate this meeting of the minds, this need for mutual understanding and communication, we've structured this book as a handbook for both teachers and developers. In Section 1: The Mobile Classroom, we offer a pedagogically based discussion of what mobile devices offer in terms of how students learn, fundamentals from the science of learning that apply to mobile devices, as well as logistics and tips for various implementations and technological set-ups that schools might offer. While this section is geared toward educators, the content provides valuable insight into how and why students learn, the demands and limitations of the modern classroom, and the strategies used to integrate mobile devices into education; therefore, there is quite a bit developers can glean from this section to better serve their audience and its needs.

Section 2: Creating the Mobile Learning Experience is designed to provide developers with the information they need to enter the educational app market and develop quality resources for teachers and students. We offer discussions of business models, design principles, best practices for development cycles, the unique team structures that enable educational apps to come to fruition, and how data analytics can optimize learning. We also present the technological features and offer some guidelines on how to include what is necessary to make an app do what it's intended to do and not be unreasonably large. Again, while the intended audience for Section 2 is developers, we feel there is a benefit for educators as well: an awareness of how educators fit into the software development process, the rationale behind business models in the education market, and how developers go about evaluating and refining their product, just to name a few.

One of the exciting things about mobile learning, in a general sense, is the wide-reaching opportunity it presents. In Section 3: Mobile Learning for Everyone, we present three niches that are especially primed for impact from mobile devices: informal learning, preschool, and special populations. The accessibility features that mobile devices offer are unprecedented, and developers and teachers will find valuable information on how to optimize app features and how to choose accessible apps in this section. We finish this section with a discussion of data privacy and digital citizenship, two pressing issues to ensure safe mobile technology use for all of today's students.

In our Appendices section, we provide a list of all the apps mentioned in our book, for easy reference. Additionally, we offer a definitive checklist for educators to use when determining if a new app meets their needs. The Great App Checklist aims to help educators sift through what's out there and determine what makes a good app.

For this book, we've interviewed dozens of in-service educators, to bring their perspective to you, alongside academic research, popular press articles, and our experience as developers of educational resources and apps. The mix of practical advice, experience, academic research and methodology is a unique way to frame the field of mobile learning, but one we feel is essential to fully comprehending the potential and realizing the promise of it.

Acknowledgments

The journey of writing a book is, not surprisingly, long and laborious. When we started our research and writing, we felt well prepared as a team of writers and experts in our fields with cross-disciplinary perspectives. We were excited to fill a void we saw in the field: take the world a step closer to having a theory of mobile learning and create a resource for teachers and developers in the process.

While we trusted our own experience and skills, we knew we'd also rely on others to complete this book. Reviewers, artists, editors, educators, and interviewees give this book a level of credibility and expertise we alone couldn't have. We derived so much value from the folks listed here. We are deeply grateful for the help, insight, and feedback we received along the way. This truly shaped this book into what you hold before you.

First and foremost, we are grateful to Jim and Ann Goodnight for supporting us in this project, and for their generous support of education (mobile and otherwise). We are so appreciative of the leadership and guidance provided by Armistead Sapp. We are thankful for the amazing group of reviewers who were candid and helpful with their feedback: Elliot Inman, Robert Epler, Kristin Hoffmann, and Tim McBride.

We are so grateful for the artwork from the incomparable duo, Tammi Kay George and Lisa Morton, who came up with the cover for the book and so many creative renderings of concepts based on our confusing notes. Thank you so much for the drawings that make this book so unique.

We are grateful to Wiley Business Press and SAS Press for guiding us in our efforts to get the book we were envisioning published, especially Stacey Hamilton. We also are very grateful for the research expertise of Jennifer Evans.

We made efforts to contact as many teachers as we could in our research for this book, and we are very grateful for the following educators who indulged us by giving us a glimpse of their world. They were honest with us about the realities of mobile learning in the classroom, what is lacking, what is amazing, and what they wish was different. These are also, incidentally, the educators and specialists who are shaping the minds of our youngest Americans, which is a comforting thought to the authors. Thanks to: Amy Wilkinson, Julie Stern, Rebecca Goddard, Tara Brooks, and Tricia Hudacek, to the team of teachers at Brentwood Elementary in Raleigh, North Carolina (Sean Russell, Linnea Czerney, John Silverthorn, Emily Hardy), and the teachers at Research Triangle High School in Durham, North Carolina. Thank you to all of the respondents to the online surveys, and the teachers who attended our focus groups. We are also very grateful to the scores of educators who are sharing their experience on blogs and Twitter in the effort to improve others' usage of educational technology.

We'd like to thank the other experts we consulted through our writing: Ed Summers, Diane Brauner, Erica Roberts, Greer Aukstakalnis, Carrie Grunkemeyer, Kelly Stewart, Jamie Hall, and Aaron Massey.

The feedback from countless educators with questions, suggestions, comments, and recommendations regarding the mobile apps from SAS Curriculum Pathways has built, and continues to build, our understanding of what makes a good app. We are particularly grateful for the development partnership with Garrett-Keyser-Butler Community School District, and their leadership from Dennis Stockdale and Tonya Weaver, which continue to inform our own development efforts.

At SAS, we're thankful for the help of our coworkers, specifically Keli Lloyd, Ottis Cowper, Connor Hickey, Ada Lopez, Trena Brantley, and Phil Issler. We are fortunate to work with the SAS Curriculum Pathways team that has fundamentally shaped our understanding of mobile learning development and practice.

And finally, each of us is grateful to our families and significant others for their support and understanding through the writing of this book.

CHAPTER 1

Changing Education with Mobile Learning

We cannot always build the future for our youth, but we can build our youth for the future.

—*Franklin Delano Roosevelt*

n our ever-changing marketplace, today's students are being educated, largely, for jobs that haven't yet been invented. Technology is being created and updated at a frenetic pace, and growing more pervasive and useful with each stride. As schools face dwindling resources and higher stakes than ever, does mobile technology hold the key to improving the educational system and reengaging students? Mobile technology offers a plethora of features and benefits that enable it to break the educational system wide open, engaging students in new ways and making educational experiences more meaningful, if schools can effectively utilize structured, integrated approaches for implementation of this new technology.

This interest in smartphones, tablets, and laptops is a major opportunity to present new and exciting educational experiences. To what extent are schools capitalizing on this, though? And how often are they getting in their own way in reaching students? One teacher notes with frustration that her school has several iPad carts that teachers are encouraged to use, but cellphones are banned categorically. "There are certain times we might be doing a lesson and someone asks a question and I think 'This'd be a great time to all get out our devices and look something up,' but we can't use cellphones and have to reserve our iPad carts in advance, so the moment passes. It's frustrating because almost all of the kids have phones and their parents are paying for data plans anyway, but we can't use them."[1] In effect, schools with policies like these end up ignoring the technology and the skillset necessary to effectively use it in learning and life, leaving students not fully prepared for the real world.

In another school, eighth-grade teachers have access to iPads the school has purchased and encourages them to use in their classrooms. Teachers are excited to have the devices, but don't really know what to use them for, and they often sit unused. When asked what she uses them for, one teacher suggested they can be used as calculators. Clearly handing a device to a teacher with no guidance or training is not a way to make the best use of this expensive, Internet-connected device.

Stories like these, of school policy being dictated to teachers and ineffective mobile technology use, are, sadly, not difficult to find. Policies that categorically ban certain devices that are used in everyday life are lazy, failing to see the possibilities that they have to change and improve pedagogy. However, schools realize boundaries and acceptable uses of mobile technology need to be clearly defined, but they may not know where to begin. Rather than reimagining education and figuring out how to integrate modern technology to effectively reach students, administrators too often ignore and put up walls against new technologies. We present these stories not to discourage or say that there are simply too many hurdles and poor implementations of mobile technology. We offer these examples to illustrate the widespread misunderstandings about mobile learning and our need to address some key challenges.

Ignoring mobile learning because of potential distraction or misuse results in missed opportunities for teaching tomorrow's citizens how to find and use a seemingly limitless source of information at their fingertips. Mobile technology offers a huge opportunity to revolutionize education and learning, if knowledgeable, creative, and open-minded teachers and administrators embrace it.

A BRIEF HISTORY OF EDUCATIONAL TECHNOLOGY: WHAT WILL REVOLUTIONIZE THE SYSTEM?

A new classroom tool promises to improve student learning and enable a more enriching learning experience. In a video promoting this tool, a student is seen answering questions in class at his own pace, and receiving immediate feedback to know if he was wrong or right. An expert notes some benefits of this tool: "There is also a motivating effect. The student is free of uncertainty or anxiety about his success or failure. His work is pleasurable. He does not have to force himself to study … it generates a high level of interest and enthusiasm." This expert notes that technology could enable students to cover more than two times the information when compared to traditional classroom techniques.

B.F. Skinner gave this forecast on the potential for technology to revolutionize learning and classroom procedures in 1954.[2] His teaching machine sounds strikingly similar to predictions today on how mobile technology can revolutionize classroom learning for students, though these were based on Skinner's teaching machine, a clunky early computing machine that offered students a new way to learn independently using targeted, self-paced lessons. Similar predictions have since been made about personal computers, netbooks, and other technologies. So, the question is, why were those predictions wrong in 1954, and subsequently, and why are they different with mobile learning?

While mobile technology offers a distinct difference from other technology, technology itself is hardly a stranger to the educational setting. Computers have been in the classroom and have been promising to revolutionize education for decades, though they haven't changed education much. It's fair to say that while Skinner's teaching machine was novel, it didn't do as much as he imagined it would to shake up the traditional and inefficient classroom structure.

Over the past half century, as computers developed and became smaller, more efficient, and easier to use, they increasingly found their way into the classroom. This technology has changed the experience in schools, as well, as noted in Figure 1.1. Computers have been in

Figure 1.1 Educational Technology Over Time

schools since the 1960s: first to store student data and eventually, for student use. This changed in the early 1980s with the Apple II. Before the Apple II, large mainframe computers had some presence in schools, though they were not very widespread.[3] The first affordable and widely adopted personal computer was the Apple II, which also happened to be a watershed moment for personal computer technology. It offered a computer for everyone, not just the hobbyists and folks who wanted a computer to tinker with. The Apple II was ready to run for anyone, and it was widely adopted by educational markets (which were also heavily marketed to[4]). By the mid-1980s, the Apple II was the predominant computer in K–12 settings.[5] In the 1980s, much of the curriculum surrounding computers in the classroom related to teaching how computers worked (programming languages, for instance) or for games (i.e., Oregon Trail) and less on using them to perform other nontechnical educational functions.

By 1990, most classrooms across the United States had access to computers in some way, and their use in augmenting and supporting classroom instruction grew as the 1990s went on. These systems provided a self-paced learning experience for each user; however each learning experience followed a set trajectory that offered the same help, the same questions and answers, and the same path. In short, there was no customization to the learning, only an individualized pacing. There was often instant feedback, so it did offer many benefits to old systems, though the true potential for an intelligent learning system was not reached.[6] Computers used CD-ROM disks, and with the growth and release of new Microsoft products throughout the 1990s (Windows 95, Windows 98, most notably) and the maturation of the software and hardware industries, computers became commonplace in the classroom.[7] Technological initiatives at the time focused on connecting classrooms to the still very new Internet. As the World Wide Web grew to show its use in homes and offices across America, government initiatives channeled funds to get classrooms wired and students online, as well as to give students technological literacy skills.[8]

Desktop computers, laptops, and netbooks were the most prevalent technologies utilized by schools until early 2010 when Apple released the iPad, which created a new category for mobile devices: the tablet computer. Featuring touchscreen technology, increased portability, Wi-Fi, and an intuitive user interface, the iPad presented a major game-changer for digital learning. Soon after, competing tablets emerged on the Android operating system. Slowly, the tablet stole market share from netbooks, and in early 2013, Acer and Asus, the top two netbook producers, officially phased out production of their netbooks, effectively ending the netbook market.[9]

Computers, and subsequently tablets, began as novelties and eventually went on to create entire markets and ways of functioning that are hard to imagine living without. Have they changed education in the same, fundamental way? Are they being used to enhance instruction and change the way we learn for the better, or are they just another tool in the same old pedagogy? Looking at the past 60 years of computer technology and education, we see a recurring pattern: The belief followed each advance and breakout technology that it would solve all educational problems.[10] Obviously, these promises were not met. While computers have definitely been incorporated into existing structures, their impact hasn't been as great as it has been on other sectors, nor as great as we expect mobile technology to be.[11] The benefits that mobile learning enables—personalized, on the go, and novel learning environments—offer a chance to revolutionize the education system. As Bill Gates noted in 2009, "The world of education is the sector of the economy so far the least changed by technology. Ten years from now, that won't be the case."[12] We're entering a new era for technology and education and mobile technologies. We believe mobile technology with smart implementation and progressive school policies can lead the way.

MOBILE LEARNING: REACHING KIDS TODAY

At Research Triangle High School, a charter school in Durham, North Carolina, the ninth graders are in English class. The BYOD (bring your own device) setup and flipped classroom structure requires that the students watch a lesson the night before, and use their tablet or laptop to supplement the discussion or project that is occurring in the classroom. When you walk in the room, it feels different. It certainly isn't the typical classroom we imagine with desks in a row and students sitting, looking to the teacher with their hands in the air. Indeed, beside that image, it might even feel as if no one is paying attention, as everyone is illuminated by a screen, and no one is watching the teacher. This perception is quickly shattered, however, when the teacher surveys the students to gauge understanding, and it's obvious that they are all paying attention, all are on task. Beyond that, the use of certain mobile devices (this school prohibits cellphones for classroom use) enables and even encourages students to multitask, collaborate, and teach each other—all skills professionals practice daily in the modern workplace. This school, like many across the country, is embracing the mobile technologies that exist, working with them instead of against them, and giving their students a real-world education rather than clinging to previous paradigms of education and learning.[13]

Mobile technologies offer a new paradigm in connectivity, communication, and collaboration in our everyday lives. For education, these are huge opportunities to provide an experience that is relevant and engaging. Using technology in the classroom is not a new idea at all. Computers, laptops, and netbooks have all been added to classroom settings with the hopes of revolutionizing education, promising vast improvements to student outcomes. These technologies, largely, have left education unchanged and in a continual state of need for improvement. All of these technologies can be thought of like crayons, says James Paul Gee, a thought leader in games and learning: "They are just tools that can make and do good things (e.g., art) or make a mess (e.g., crayon all over the walls)."[14] It matters tremendously not only that they be added to the educational process, but that the educational process shift to incorporate new capabilities.

Ultimately, when considering the value of mobile learning initiatives in education, it is most important to consider what is best and most valuable for the students. What initiatives will provide them with the education that sets them up for a lifetime of success? What technologies engage them and help them learn most effectively? Today's students are fundamentally different from those who came before them. Christened as *digital natives* by educational writer Marc Prensky in 2001, "today's students are no longer the people our educational system was designed to teach."[15] If anything, the advent of mobile devices has only served to further solidify these digital natives' different needs and expectations when approaching education.

Mobile learning offers a novel approach to reach them—it offers flexibility in when the learning takes place, personalized content, and teaches relevant skills for the future. It has the potential to create a generation of learners who see the world as their classroom.

Tablets and smartphones have dramatically altered the technology landscape, and transformed the way we as a society communicate and access information.[16] In the workplace and in homes, these technologies have been incorporated and used to change and increase the efficiency of everyday activities, but traditional schools are still relatively resistant to or untouched by these iconoclastic technologies.[17] As schools continue to negotiate acceptable usage, boundaries, and bans with students and parents over mobile devices, many opportunities for educational innovation may be missed.

WHAT IS MOBILE LEARNING?

For the purposes of this book, we believe mobile learning has little to do with the physical devices themselves. Rather, mobile learning is the experience and opportunity *afforded* by the evolution of educational technologies. It is anywhere, anytime learning enabled by instant, on-demand access to a personalized world filled with the tools and resources we prefer for creating our own knowledge, satisfying our curiosities, collaborating with others, and cultivating experiences otherwise unattainable. Mobile learning implies adapting and building upon the latest advances in mobile technology, redefining the responsibilities of teachers and students, and blurring the lines between formal and informal learning. It embodies and facilitates the understanding of what it means to be a lifelong learner and what it takes to thrive in today's workplace. So, while we do talk about technology in this book, it's essential to understand that *mobile learning* is something different than *mobile devices*. It is the outcome that these technologies enable through creative and appropriate use.

At the time of writing this book, the fruition of mobile learning is made possible by the proliferation of portable, Internet-enabled devices. Portability assumes it is a device that can be easily accessed on the go, making this definition not simply any device that can access the Internet. It also requires Internet capability that allows the user to access new content on demand (rather than only what the device holds). In our discussions surrounding how mobile learning can impact education and pedagogy, we primarily discuss tablets, smartphones, and small personal media players. We also discuss Chrome books and laptops to some extent because there are big areas of overlap in pedagogy and implementation strategy. Tablets and smartphones offer substantial differences and benefits, including making mobile learning more accessible and affordable in schools than their predecessors.

BENEFITS AND CHALLENGES OF MOBILE LEARNING

Mobile learning is not a panacea for all the problems that plague our education system; we don't suggest that by simply handing out iPads one can expect increases in student achievement and enthusiasm for learning. Just like the personal computers that came before them, mobile devices hold tremendous potential to change the way students learn and our expectations of what should happen within the classroom walls. The ability of tablets and other mobile technologies to shake up the current status quo of the educational system and improve it is dependent on the pedagogy in which they are woven. It depends on teachers' open minds, creativity, and preparation to integrate them in the curriculum; school budgets and culture to allow for devices in the hands of students; and continued innovation in how devices are used so they remain effective. Further, success also requires banishing the assumption that digital natives, adept though they are with technology, know how to use mobile devices for educational purposes without training. Just like their teachers, administrators, and parents, students require guidance on how to learn with this new educational technology.

There are many benefits and challenges with mobile learning, and many are associated with different learning environments. For instance, a 1:1 mobile environment both addresses and introduces different concerns than a classroom with a mobile-device cart. We dive deeper into these learning environments, their related pedagogies, and how mobile devices affect them in Chapters 4 and 6.

Benefits of Mobile Learning

+ Ability to learn on the go

+ Reach underserved children and schools

+ Improve higher-order thinking skills

+ Support alternative learning environments

+ Enable personalized learning

+ Motivate Students

Figure 1.2 Benefits of Mobile Learning

Benefits

Mobile learning offers many benefits and opportunities to reach students in different ways and to improve and personalize the education they're receiving, as shown in Figure 1.2.

The first major benefit is the ability to learn on the go. Traditionally, sitting in a classroom between the hours of 8 a.m. and 3 p.m. is where and when we expect students to learn. Increasingly, however, learning isn't limited to a predetermined location or time. Learning can occur anytime and anywhere with mobile devices. In reality, given the prevalence of smartphones among adults, this facet of mobile technology for K–12 simply brings the children to the place where adults are, meaning the educational paradigm children experience more closely mirrors the working paradigm. The ever-increasing rate of smartphone usage is truly indicative of the changing norms of our culture in the ways we "communicate, access information, connect with peers and colleagues, learn and even socialize."[18] Educational experiences are meant to prepare students for real life, and as such, should reflect the realities of the modern world.[19] Smartphones and Internet-enabled mobile devices are pervasive in our culture, and education shouldn't ignore this fact.

Mobile learning also is a potential way to reach underserved children and schools. Mobile technology, when compared to other technology initiatives, provides a relatively lower cost per student for a high powered and durable technology. Tablets are often less expensive than computers, so when the inevitable upgrades and technology improvements come along, updating the technology for an entire classroom (or school) is less cumbersome. Indeed, this technological cycle has been a primary reason for resistance to including newer technologies as they come along; the budget for technology easily gets maxed out on maintaining current, secure computers in schools. Mobile devices offer a different financial and technological model altogether, one that is much easier to maintain under tight budgets. Many device manufacturers provide low-cost or even included maintenance plans to insure the continued functioning of the devices. To aid the acquisition of mobile devices many states (such as Indiana[20]) have led the way by redefining what a textbook is and what funds allocated for textbooks can be used for (i.e., purchasing mobile devices). Mobile devices provide excellent, state of the art technology for a relatively affordable price.

Additionally, mobile devices offer substantial power in taking learning opportunities outside of the four walls of the classroom. Virtual museums, online classes, and simulated experiences all come standard with a mobile device and the Internet. Especially for low-wealth school districts or lower-income students, mobile technology could truly level the playing field.

Mobile learning provides a medium that improves higher-order thinking skills. The Partnership for 21st Century Skills has defined four key skills for students to master in school: critical thinking and problem solving, communication, collaboration, and creativity and innovation.[21] The features of mobile learning inherently foster these complex skillsets in students. The ability to easily share information with others, creatively utilize a wide variety of resources and critically evaluate the veracity and value of sources are just a few examples of the activities implicit to everyday use of mobile technology in education. Higher-order thinking skills and mobile learning are explored further in Chapter 5.

Many schools are offering alternative learning environments, such as flipped classrooms or blended learning environments, which allow teachers to use class time more efficiently and even cover more material, among other things. Mobile devices offer tremendous opportunities for facilitating and enhancing these setups. There are, of course, still many ways that mobile learning can enhance the traditional classroom setup as well and improve pedagogy. This concept will be discussed in Chapter 3.

Mobile devices, especially in a 1:1 setup, better enable personalized learning to thrive. Personalized learning environments enable teachers to more easily target which students are struggling with which concepts and assign coursework and homework accordingly. Mobile technology makes this process more seamless, enabling effective implementation and tracking of student growth. Further, if the students have their own devices (or always use the same device in the classroom), it is possible to easily track student data. This provides a rich data set to add to the student record for future reference and research. Mobile data and learning analytics will be discussed in Chapter 10.

And finally, mobile learning provides a new way to motivate students by providing high levels of engagement and novelty, personalization, and autonomy. The ability to constantly use new apps and find new ways to use the device keeps it fresh and interesting for students. The use of cellphones and mobile devices is high among children, and there is value in meeting students where they are rather than limiting them to older learning methods when they clearly have an aptitude and passion for newer technologies. Allowing and encouraging mobile use for academic purposes gives new meaning and excitement to lessons. Julie Stern, a middle school teacher, says, "The kids are pushing mobile (learning.) Some things you can get away with not doing every day but it's hard to get away with not doing mobile once you've given the kids a taste of it."[22]

Challenges

Mobile learning comes with its share of difficulties. Sometimes, even despite the excitement and array of benefits, the challenges facing schools are difficult to overcome. It's our hope that this book provides strategies in addressing these common obstacles, as well as arguments against philosophical oppositions to mobile learning for education. The most common challenges mobile learning faces are listed in Figure 1.3.

One hurdle that mobile learning initiatives can face is the differentiated access to devices and Internet across different audiences. Availability and cost of broadband in schools and homes can be a big hurdle for smaller and low-wealth school districts, presenting a huge disparity among students from different economic backgrounds. Federal and

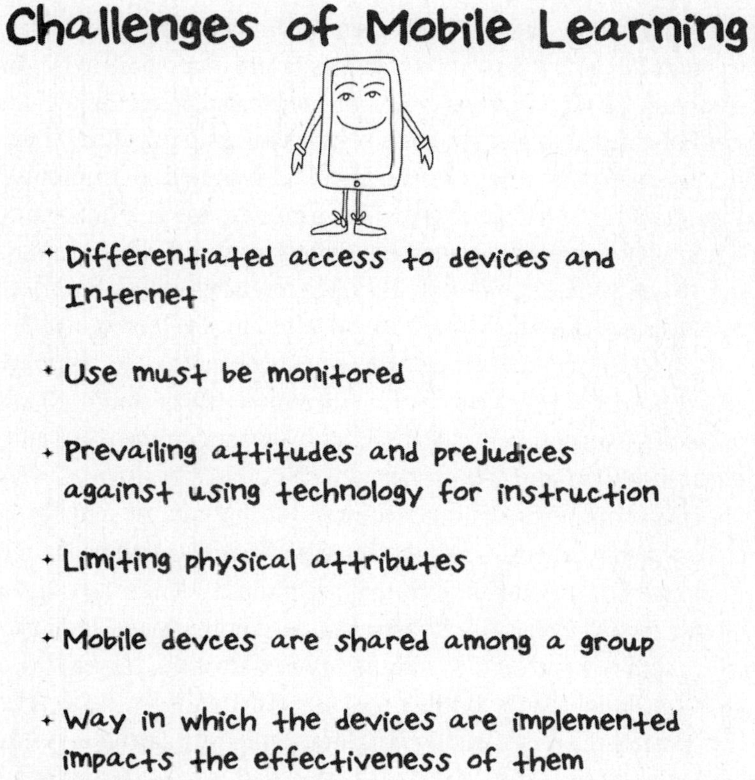

Challenges of Mobile Learning

+ Differentiated access to devices and Internet

+ Use must be monitored

+ Prevailing attitudes and prejudices against using technology for instruction

+ Limiting physical attributes

+ Mobile devces are shared among a group

+ Way in which the devices are implemented impacts the effectiveness of them

Figure 1.3 Challenges of Mobile Learning

state programs are closing the gap to some extent, like the ConnectED initiative that aims to get high speed Internet into 99 percent of schools by 2017. While use of mobile devices offers the chance to level the playing field for underprivileged districts, having wide access to the Internet in school and at home is essential to taking advantage of the many benefits of these devices. Implicit in the challenge of differentiated access is the cost factor, and we acknowledge that a tablet is more expensive than a textbook, and some schools just might not be able to afford them. Though recent studies have shown that the falling costs of electronics has led to higher levels of device ownership among lower income and minority families, there is still a notable (if closing) gap.[23]

When mobile devices are used by students in classrooms or at home, their use must be monitored in some way. While mobile devices can be used for academic enrichment, the opportunity also exists for them to be used for distraction or unethical behavior. There are also health concerns stemming from increased screen time and privacy concerns about students or the device, itself, oversharing personal information. Certainly, these concerns could also be made for adults using mobile devices, and teaching responsible use and digital literacy should become part of any lesson involving mobile technology and children. Schools will need to develop an Acceptable Use Policy (AUP) and think about which sites should be limited. While allowing mobile devices in school will undoubtedly open the school up to increased liability, it is possible to mitigate this risk by teaching responsible use and creating a disciplinary framework to enforce it. This is certainly preferable to, as is often the case, letting the risk of liability lead to overly restrictive policies.[24] A discussion of data privacy and digital citizenship is given in Chapter 15.

There are many prevailing attitudes and prejudices against using technology for instruction, and the system remains structured in a way that reinforces traditional educational methods. Effectively incorporating mobile technologies into K–12 education means abandoning some of these traditional structures, and many stakeholders are resistant to this huge cultural shift.[25] While there are many studies and anecdotal support for the power of mobile learning, there is no accepted theory of mobile learning and, hence, some disagreement among educators, administrators, and legislators on the actual value of the paradigm.

Sometimes these attitudes are reflected in laws prohibiting the use of mobile technologies (including cellphones) in the classroom categorically. In 2006, New York City Mayor Michael Bloomberg enacted a citywide ban on cellphones in the city's public schools, saying they were "a distraction in school and could be used to cheat on exams."[26] Similar bans and severe limitations exist all over the country. It's worth considering: Is this an effective restriction? In a recent study, more than 95 percent of surveyed students admitted to using their cellphones for texting, emailing, social networking, and browsing the Internet during class.[27] The class time that is wasted arguing with students and enforcing rules could be better spent capitalizing on the benefits and opportunities (including teaching responsible use) of what is possible with appropriate device use. Schools in Forsyth County, Georgia reported less in-class texting and off-task behavior on cellphones when the devices were used in their BYOD classrooms for schoolwork.[28] Breaking through these philosophical barriers requires strong leadership and professional development to ensure mobile learning is possible for each school.

While mobile phones and tablets offer many benefits over computers and laptops, there are some limiting physical attributes that make them more difficult to use. For instance, most tablets don't come with a keyboard, making typing more difficult. Typing on a smaller interface, such as a smartphone or iPod Touch, is even more challenging. However, while this sort of limitation might be a major hurdle for some groups, digital natives seem to see it as less of a challenge than the adults who teach them. The need for a device with a physical keyboard, for instance, is usually a preference of the administrator who orders the devices rather than from complaints by students that they're tired of using touch-only devices to type.

In some educational situations where mobile devices are shared among a group, the functionality and benefits are impacted. Often a cart of mobile devices will be provided for the school to share rather than a 1:1 arrangement simply because of budgetary considerations. In this scenario, using them can be more difficult and less engaging.[29] There are many ways that enable student data to be transferred across devices, particularly by storing data and work in the cloud and offering logins for apps. While it's been shown that mobile learning is optimal when students have their own devices and can fully integrate their preferences and resources,[30] having access to shared devices is not going to nullify all of the benefits of mobile learning. In a device-sharing arrangement, however, the lack of ubiquity—the access to devices anytime in the classroom—does compromise some of the benefits of mobile learning. For instance, if teachers want to use *Evernote* to demonstrate digital note taking one day, but don't have the mobile devices the next day, it's hard to have a coherent process, let alone derive educational value from the lesson. Are the kids to print out their notes? Visit them on the cloud? Just wait until they have the devices again? When mobile devices are shared across classrooms or schools, some of the potential for the device to offer personalized and instant access is necessarily lost. While this challenge is worth noting, as it has impacts on how apps are developed and used, we also note that having *some* access to mobile technology is certainly better than none.

And finally, the way in which the devices are implemented impacts the effectiveness of them. Mobile devices shouldn't simply be added to existing curricula and used in place of an old tool—they should be used to change the way lessons are structured to engage students in new ways. In essence, teachers should first make a mobile-learning plan, then get devices; not get devices and subsequently fold them into normal instructional methods. Using the devices in innovative ways will make it so schools can sustain the wow factor that technology currently brings to classrooms over the long term. Though we don't know how students will react to these devices as they become more commonplace, we do know that continually refreshing content and activities will keep the devices shiny and new even after several years of use.

HOW TO MAKE MOBILE LEARNING WORK

While mobile learning indisputably holds promise to change education and give students a better, more valuable experience, the way it is implemented in schools makes a huge difference. In fact, strong implementation is the deciding factor for mobile learning, insofar as a bad implementation can stop a mobile learning program dead in the water. In this book, the programs we discuss and the best practices we share

are all contingent on mobile learning initiatives with strong support, progressive policies, and smart implementation.

The main criterion for a successful mobile learning program is to open the entire system up to the change. By this we mean, administrators can't simply say, "Here's a tablet!" and assume education will change in any fundamental way. Systemic changes need to occur to facilitate the new devices and learning structures, teachers and users need to be educated on new possibilities and paradigms in learning, and boundaries pushed. These systemic changes can facilitate a more relevant and engaging learning experience for today's students.

Professional Development

Teachers and administrators must have or obtain the requisite skills to incorporate mobile devices and technology into their teaching. One theme we discuss in Section 1 is the fallacy that since students are proficient with mobile devices, they're automatically able to use them to learn. Indeed, learning to use mobile devices for education is an adjustment for students, and it will be for teachers as well. Finding good apps, enhancing lessons rather than retrofitting old lessons with an app, and ways to be prepared if the mobile device fails you are all important skills for the mobile teacher. It cannot be assumed that adapting to a mobile classroom will be easy or understood by all teachers, and professional development can provide educators with the means to effectively use this technology. Professional learning communities within the school or online are great resources for teachers looking for mobile learning support and discussions.

Use Data to Personalize Learning

Mobile devices offer tremendous opportunities to harvest data on student usage and knowledge, which can drive smarter decisions and personalized learning plans, among other things. A smart mobile learning strategy will take advantage of this information and use it to enhance the educational process. The flexibility offered with a device enables students to explore content at their own pace, dive deeper into what is most interesting, and reward their curiosity with instant answers.

Based on what engages them most, apps can suggest similar resources, or frame other lessons in terms of what he or she liked in the past. In a 1:1 environment, a student's classwork is even more useful, as it can remain on the device over an extended period of time for reference and analysis. A mobile classroom can also enable instant data collection. For instance, the *Socrative* app enables teachers to poll students during the lesson and instantly gauge understanding on a certain topic.

Change Instruction

While using mobile devices does not require a teacher to completely abandon the way he or she runs a classroom, it may require creative changes in how apps and devices are incorporated to strengthen certain lessons or activities, and creative use of apps (such as app stacking). Reimagining lessons is also necessary; adding an app as an afterthought is not the best way to take advantage of the technology, nor is simply using devices for content delivery. In the end, it's essential to remember that pedagogy still matters and technology won't replace good teachers, ever. Adding new and engaging technology to the classroom is a learning experience for all parties and often gives rise to more teachable moments and opportunities to learn together. Tricia Hudacek, a reading specialist and teacher reflected on her experience using iPads with her students: "If there are problems, oftentimes the class as a whole can figure it out. This provides awesome teachable moments."[31] Good teachers will be able to see the potential in mobile learning and adapt their classroom structure accordingly.

Flexible Policies

While some schools and school districts have quickly, perhaps without much careful consideration of the consequences, moved in the direction of bans and censorship, we advocate creating more lenient policies to support a mobile learning plan—policies that more closely resemble real-world usage. Digital citizenship is a key skill today's students will need when they graduate, and teaching them how to participate in social media responsibly, how to evaluate information found online, how to search using appropriate criteria and act in a respectful way online are all skills that need to be cultivated. Teaching these skills as part of an integrated mobile learning curriculum rather than completely restricting use of certain sites, apps, or devices is important.

It's also important for schools to update and provide well-thought-out policies regarding student privacy. There must be a balance between protecting student data and enabling student data use by entitled individuals to enhance the learning process. Privacy is a significant, and largely uncharted, area that is central to mobile learning. We discuss it at length in Chapter 15.

Good Apps

Finally, a strong mobile learning plan cannot function without good apps to scaffold the lessons. Teachers must figure out how to locate good content and tools, and how to incorporate them into curriculum and lesson plans. Similarly, app developers must focus on addressing the needs of the audience and tailoring app development to the educational market. The best educational apps present necessary information in a fresh way and are in tune with schools' needs. In essence, developing a quality educational app is not just making a textbook into an ebook, and it's also not using all the available functions on the mobile device just because they're there. Good educational apps, like all parts of mobile learning, require a sense of balance to make them appropriately interactive and impactful. We offer many examples of good educational apps and their classroom uses in APPendix A.

CONCLUSION

The skills that used to be demanded of children upon the completion of school were good handwriting, math fluency, and reading literacy, with education's focus being on creating a consistent product: a similarly prepared student.[32] The skills required today are less concrete, and entail more critical reading and evaluation of material and the ability to seek answers effectively using the technology available to them at any given time.[33] Mobile devices offer a tremendous opportunity to make education more engaging and relevant to the next generation of learners. Digital natives don't want to have to power down during school—they want to use the technology to make their experience more relevant.[34]

The key for successfully channeling the mobile learning revolution will not simply be about digitizing current educational systems. The real appeal will be allowing people to choose their own paths, leverage their talents, and pursue subjects of interest. Mobile learning has huge business potential, but the most exciting and rewarding aspect of these solutions is that students of any age or background might have the chance to pursue knowledge that is meaningful and relevant to them. Integrating technology, and specifically mobile technology, early and often prepares students for the new reality.

NOTES

1. Anonymous, North Carolina Middle School, interview with authors, April 22, 2014.
2. Idea Learning Group, "History of eLearning: 'E' is for 'Evolutionary,'" October 11, 2012, www.idealearninggroup.com/blog/history-of-elearning-e-is-for-evolutionary.
3. Everett Murdock, "History, the History of Computers, and the History of Computers in Education," www.csulb.edu/˜murdock/histofcs.html.
4. Walter Isaacson, *Steve Jobs* (New York: Simon & Schuster, 2011).
5. Murdock, "History."
6. Beverly Park Woolf, *Building Intelligent Interactive Tutors* (Burlington, MA: Morgan Kaufmann Publishers, 2009).
7. Murdock, "History."
8. "Educational Technology Timeline: Highlights During the Clinton Administration 1993–2000," U.S. Department of Education, www2.ed.gov/about/offices/list/os/technology/reports/timeline.pdf.
9. Charles Arthur, "Sayonara Netbooks: Asus (and the Rest) Won't Make Any More in 2013," *The Guardian*, www.guardian.co.uk/technology/2012/dec/31/netbooks-dead-2013.
10. Alena R Treat, Ying Wang, Rajat Chadha, and Michael Hart Dixon, "Major Developments in Instructional Technology: During the 20th Century," www.indiana.edu/~idt/shortpapers/documents/ITduring20.html.
11. Isaacson, *Steve Jobs*.
12. Kathy Matheson, "Bill Gates: Better Data Mean Better Schools," *Seattle Times*, July 21, 2009, http://seattletimes.com/html/localnews/2009511088_apusbillgates education2ndldwritethru.html.
13. Research Triangle High School, Durham NC; authors' notes from visit, April 15, 2014.

14. James Paul Gee, *The Anti-Education Era: Creating Smarter Students through Digital Learning* (New York: Palgrave Macmillan, 2013).

15. Marc Prensky, "Digital Natives, Digital Immigrants," *On the Horizon* 9, no. 5 (2001), www.marcprensky.com/writing/Prensky%20-%20Digital%20Natives,%20Digital%20Immigrants%20-%20Part1.pdf.

16. Fabio Sergio, "10 Ways That Mobile Learning Will Revolutionize Education," *Fast Company*, May 31, 2012, www.fastcodesign.com/1669896/10-ways-that-mobile-learning-will-revolutionize-education.

17. Ibid.

18. L. Johnson, S. Adams, and M. Cummins, *NMC Horizon Report: 2012 K–12 Edition* (The New Media Consortium: Austin, Texas, 2012), www.iste.org/docs/documents/2012-horizon-report_k12.pdf?sfvrsn=2.

19. Ibid.

20. Kyle Stokes, "How State Dollars Could Fund Your District's Next Tech Initiative," StateImpact Indiana, http://indianapublicmedia.org/stateimpact/2012/05/11/how-state-dollars-could-fund-your-districts-next-tech-initiative/.

21. Partnership for 21st Century Skills, www.p21.org. Accessed June 7, 2013.

22. Julie Stern, East Cary Middle School, interview with authors, May 2014.

23. Victoria Rideout "Learning at Home: Families' Educational Media Use in America," The Families and Media Project (New York: Joan Ganz Cooney Center, January 2014), www.joanganzcooneycenter.org/publication/learning-at-home/.

24. Jennifer Fritschi and Mary Ann Wolf, "Turning on Mobile Learning in North America: Illustrative Initiatives and Policy Implications," UNESCO Working Paper Series on Mobile Learning, 2012.

25. Johnson, Adams, and Cummins, NMC Horizon Report.

26. Celeste Katz, "Mayoral Hopefuls Vow to Lift Cell Phone Bans in Schools," *New York Daily News*, April 26, 2013, www.nydailynews.com/new-york/mayoral-hopefuls-vow-lift-school-cell-phone-ban-article-1.1328874.

27. Lauren Barack, "High School Students Use Cell Phones in Class—but Not for Schoolwork, Says Study," *The Digital Shift/School Library Journal*, January 7, 2013, www.thedigitalshift.com/2013/01/k-12/high-school-students-use-cell-phones-in-class-but-not-for-schoolwork-says-study/.

28. Forsyth County Schools, "BYOT Frequently Asked Questions," www.forsyth.k12.ga.us/Page/34766. Accessed May 19, 2014.

29. Tanya Roscoria, "The Impact of the iPad on K–12 Schools," *Converge*, February 9, 2011, www.convergemag.com/classtech/impact-ipad-k12-schools.html.

30. Project RED, The Research (summary), 2010, www.projectred.org/about/research-overview.html.

31. Tricia Hudacek, Teacher and Reading Specialist, online survey response, March 2014.

32. Sugata Mitra, "Build a School in the Cloud," TEDTalks, February 2013, www.ted.com/talks/sugata_mitra_build_a_school_in_the_cloud.html.

33. Ibid.

34. Prensky, "Digital Natives, Digital Immigrants."

SECTION 1

The Mobile Classroom

When schools add mobile devices to their classrooms, how can educators and administrators ensure they actually enable mobile learning and do not simply retrofit lesson plans and create more stress for teachers? How can teachers make smart use of devices in a small-scale implementation or in a 1:1 setup? In what ways do mobile devices cultivate higher-order thinking skills in students and offer a more engaging way to experience lessons? The mobile classroom offers many new and exciting promises, but it also calls up many questions for educators faced with the reality of using mobile devices for learning. In this section we answer these questions and many more to create a roadmap for educators who use mobile technology to improve education.

In this section, we offer a thorough discussion of the research and theory behind the science of learning as it applies to mobile devices and digital learning. We break down what makes mobile devices unique and more promising than the technologies that have preceded them. How does the standard pedagogy that prevails in today's classroom support the use of mobile technology? We explore the ways classrooms and schools can make smart use of technology, integrating it in lessons to enhance them rather than simply adding it as an afterthought, or transferring old ideas into digital format.

There are many practical and theoretical discussions regarding mobile devices that help us to better conceptualize the opportunities and overcome the challenges they present. This section is designed to provide educators and developers with just that: a framework to comprehend the wide range of possibilities within the lens of established educational theory, and a roadmap to navigate the practical implementation of mobile devices in the classroom. Mobile devices can enable mobile learning, but if they're used without thoughtful strategy, they are no more revolutionary to our students than any other technology.

CHAPTER **2**

The Science
of Learning

INTRODUCTION

Before determining how to appropriately use mobile learning in the classroom to enhance and personalize learning, it is important to consider what we know about how we learn. Many established theories of learning offer insights that apply to the use of mobile technologies in particular. This chapter provides a theoretical framework for discussions about educational app creation and evaluation, as well as use of mobile technology in the classroom and pedagogy.

The science of learning describes the cognitive processes surrounding why and how we learn. Historically, theoretical shifts in psychology have defined such processes in different ways, consequently changing the study of learning over time. The majority of late-nineteenth to mid-twentieth century education was dominated by behaviorists who argued that empirical psychological research can only be conducted by measuring observable behaviors and treating mental processes and the mind as a black box. Studies of learning, such as Pavlov's famous salivating-dog conditioning experiments, concluded that the construction of knowledge occurs through external conditioning and reinforcement of behaviors from the environment.

However, concurrent with the behaviorist and other movements in the mid-twentieth century, studies were being published that showed that learning could occur without strict conditioning or external reinforcement. Learning often occurred after a single experience, as in an animal that becomes unwell after eating something and never eats it again (one-trial learning). Research accumulated showing that people used language in ways they had not been formally taught.[1] Learning could occur by one person simply watching another person experience something, as in Bandura's social learning experiments, without any direct reinforcement at all. People developed associative networks of related ideas, even when they had not been strictly trained to do so.[2] The human mind was more than just a pre-programmed machine that has been taught to do a limited number of fixed operations. The human mind was flexible, self-adapting, and, in many respects, self-taught. That research reflected a paradigm shift from a behaviorist perspective to a cognitive perspective; it is called the *cognitive revolution*.

Today, cognitive perspectives on learning represent the majority view and "explain learning by focusing on changes in internal mental processes that people use in their efforts to make sense of the world."[3] The dawning of the cognitive era yielded quite a few innovative theories of learning that have been widely used to inform K–12 education practices: Piaget's constructivist perspective, which emphasizes the roles prior knowledge and experience have on learning, and Vygotsky and Bandura's more social-cognitive theories of learning, which acknowledge the importance of social interactions and the components of one's environment for learning.[4,5] Therefore, within this book, we define learning as long-term construction of and/or modifications to one's existing knowledge structures in an effort to create personal understanding of incoming information and experiences.

In this chapter, we provide evidence for how and why mobile technologies develop a learner-centered approach that supports the way in which we learn. We present an overview of the science behind learning in terms of both the how (the involved cognitive processes) and the why (the metacognitive and motivational constructs that dictate our actions). Throughout this discussion, mobile technologies are used as a lens for expanding upon the educational implications of the way in which we go about constructing knowledge. We highlight certain educational opportunities for capitalizing on the features of mobile technologies as well as identify considerations for optimizing learner-centered design.

INFORMATION PROCESSING AND LEARNING

We have defined learning as a construction and/or modification to the knowledge structures of long-term memory. However, what defines a knowledge structure? What processes generate the construction or modification of knowledge structures? What aspects of the material and the student affect or determine the quality of learning? In the following section, we dissect this definition by clarifying certain terms and phrases. To explain the way we process new and incoming information and, consequently, learn, we turn to the modal model of memory.[6]

Modal Model of Memory

As seen in Figure 2.1, the modal model divides memory into three main components: sensory, working, and long-term memory. Long-term memory denotes the most typical representation of memory—an

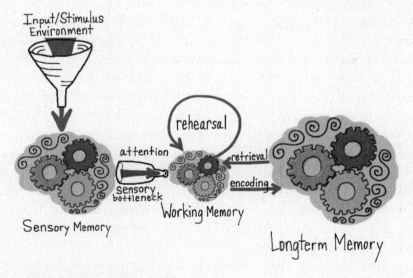

Figure 2.1 Modal Model of Memory

Table 2.1 Types of Knowledge

Type	Definition
Declarative	Episodic: Autobiographical memory of information pertaining to personal experiences.
	Semantic: General factual, world knowledge (e.g., vocabulary, facts).
Procedural	Knowledge of how to carry out behaviors (e.g., riding a bike).
Conditional	Knowledge of when or why to perform a particular action (e.g., when one should take notes).

unlimited storage unit housing everything an individual knows and has experienced during a lifetime. Such experiences and acquired information constitute what we previously referred to as knowledge structures. Knowledge structures can take on one of three forms— declarative, procedural, or conditional knowledge (see Table 2.1)—and are purposefully organized through meaningful connections within long-term memory. Pieces of information that are closely related receive stronger connections than more disparate information, and the more connections a knowledge structure attains, the more path-ways an individual can take to retrieve, or remember, the information in new situations.[7]

Amendments to our long-term memory, or learning events, occur as we perceive and reason about new, incoming information based on our existing knowledge and previous experiences. In terms of the modal model, this process begins in sensory memory. Everything we see, feel, smell, hear, or taste at any given time is placed in this large memory store for a brief period of time—even information we are not necessarily concerned with. For instance, think about a time when you have attended a noisy social event. Due to certain cognitive limitations (more on this later), we cannot process all incoming sensory informa-tion, but we can, with minimal mental effort, filter out other voices to allow you to focus on a particular conversation. In doing so, you are strategically allocating attention toward the most important infor-mation in sensory memory, a concept known as selective attention. Consequently, only sensory information receiving attention is then transferred to working memory—the cognitive workbench and gate-way to long-term memory.

Working memory houses the crux of a learning event. As informa-tion is filtered and transferred from sensory memory, it is temporarily placed in working memory; however, working memory is theorized to be limited in both capacity and duration.[8] As noted previously, we cannot attend to all of the information placed in sensory memory. In other words, we are constrained in the amount of information that can transfer from sensory to working memory. One common rule-of-thumb for estimating the capacity of working memory is Miller's "Magic Number," approximately 7 +/– 2 units of information at any given time,[9] and for younger children, the magic number is believed to be closer to 4 units.[10] Additionally, information in working memory will only remain there for about five to twenty seconds before dissipating unless it is being actively processed by the individual.[11] Purposefully repeating the information—a process known as maintenance rehearsal—or elaborating by forming connections with other information in working memory, prior knowledge, and/or prior experiences, can mitigate the time constraints of working memory, but also affect the quality of learning.

Quality of Learning

While the underlying cognitive processes involved in most learning events are generally similar, not all learning events are created equal. For example, it is generally much easier to recite the full names of our immediate family members than to recite the full names of elementary school teachers who taught us 30 or more years ago. Differences in how easily we can recall information and/or transfer that knowledge to new situations depends on how often we use this information and the quality in which it was encoded. As mentioned, information held in working memory is subject to fading, or forgetting, if not actively retained in working memory and subsequently encoded into long-term memory. Thus, the manner in which we handle information while in working memory dictates the degree of learning.

Consider a time when you needed to memorize a phone number. You may have had this experience when a cell phone battery had run low or you were simply someplace where you could not just tap the digits into some computing device. To remember the number, you probably did what many of us do: repeated the digits over and over again until you were able to write the number down. This is a strategy known as maintenance rehearsal—we are rehearsing the information and actively maintaining it in working memory in an attempt to not forget. Although learners often use maintenance rehearsal to memorize information for a test (e.g., vocabulary words, steps in a process), this technique is a very shallow method of learning known as rote learning. Unless we continue to access information learned via rote (i.e., multiplication tables), the information can be harder to retain over time or to apply to new situations.

However, information in working memory can be processed through elaborative rehearsal. With elaborative rehearsal, we actively reason about incoming information by generating connections with prior knowledge or assigning some degree of practical organization. As a result, meaningful learning occurs as the newly constructed knowledge structures are encoded in long-term memory in a more robust, integrated manner. In the most abstract terms, rote and meaningful learning describe the difference between memorizing and understanding or comprehending information. For instance, one might use an analogy to previously learned material to foster understanding of the novel information. Or, instead of simply mechanically memorizing a list, one might organize the information into a matrix or concept map. Even associating the material with a visual image can foster meaningful learning.[12] By deliberately assigning structure and/or comparing and integrating new information with prior knowledge, we engage with the material at a much deeper level. Although this process is more cognitively taxing than rote memorization, it is ultimately more engaging, and it more readily ensures ease of remembering and the likelihood of applying the information in new situations.

Optimizing Working Memory

Although it would be ideal if all students could engage in meaningful learning at all times and make as many connections with prior knowledge as possible, cognitive load theory suggests this goal is dependent upon the limitations of working memory. While some cognitive tasks seem extremely simple or even automatic (e.g., solving the problem 2+2), more complex activities can be quite difficult due to the demands on working memory as it approaches capacity. Therefore, what must educators and developers consider when developing instruction designed to effectively challenge the student while designing within the constraints of working memory?

Above we noted Miller's magic number that defines the capacity of working memory as approximately 7 +/− 2 units, or chunks, of information at any given time for adults (approximately 4 chunks for children). The terms unit and chunk are intentionally vague, yet have critical educational implications. For now, consider a chunk to be a single piece of information like a digit or word. If we attempt to memorize a random list of letters or solve a complex math problem that requires holding more than 7 +/− 2 numbers in working memory, we often have great difficulty. However, when information is organized into meaningful units or chunks, the capacity of working memory quickly increases. For example, when memorizing a random list of 20 numbers and letters such as the one below, the task is nearly impossible.

C I A F B I U S A 9 1 1 S O N Y 1 2 3 4

However, the following list also contains the same 20 numbers and letters, but is far more manageable:

CIA FBI USA 911 SONY 1234

This is because while the second list is also 20 numbers and letters, it is really six meaningful chunks of information. Similarly, mnemonics are another strategy for increasing the capacity of working memory—memorizing the colors of the rainbow becomes much easier when remembered it as the name Roy G. Biv (red, orange, yellow, green, blue, indigo, and violet). It should be noted, however, the efficacy of utilizing mnemonics and meaningful chunks is dependent upon the individual—the chunking scheme used above would be useless to an individual unfamiliar with the acronyms CIA, FBI, or 911. Again, the more we know about what the learner already knows, the better able we will be to position appropriate content. But in general, by organizing larger pieces of information into meaningful units, we allow for greater processing capacity in working memory, which allows the individual to engage in more complex thought or retrieve additional information from prior knowledge, thereby increasing their depth of learning.

Another way in which we optimize the capacity of working memory is through automization. With respect to cognitive processing, automization refers to practicing or overlearning information or skills such that they become automatic and require very little mental effort.[13] Consequently, information and skills that have been automatized can be accessed or enacted without requiring working memory resources, allowing for more complex operations to occur without experiencing cognitive overload. Think about driving from your home to the neighborhood grocery store. This seemingly complex task can usually be done while engaging in other cognitive processes, such as listening and singing along to the radio and thinking about what you will have for dinner. Your experience with driving the familiar route has allowed for this skill to be automatized—you do not need to actively think about hitting the brakes, pressing on the gas, turning the wheel, or reading street signs. When you get home, you might not even remember all the details of the drive. Now, think about driving a common route and finding a sudden detour forcing you to travel along unfamiliar streets. As the same task of driving is now no longer automatized, you immediately turn down the radio, forget about dinner plans, and focus on navigating the unfamiliar streets all due to the limitations of working memory.

While automatized operations foster our ability to multitask, they also facilitate deep, meaningful learning. For instance, compare a beginning reader to a fluent reader reading this sentence: All square objects have four straight sides of equal length. A beginning reader deciphers and sounds out the words individually and then holds each word in working memory in order to derive the meaning of the sentence. However, the sentence is quite long, likely generating an impossible cognitive load. In contrast, the fluent reader has automatized the skill of decoding, reserving the majority of working memory capacity for simply comprehending the sentence. The fluent reader can easily understand and learn from this sentence, and she has cognitive resources to access information from long-term memory and even think about times in which she has come across square-shaped objects. In sum, the automatization of information and operations is what allows us build upon our prior knowledge in order to acquire more complex information and skills when encountering new information.

Finally, social cognitive perspectives of learning emphasize the importance of extending working memory by utilizing external sources.[14] Sources of external support range from pieces of paper for taking notes to expert tutors, and encompass any resource that can be used to scaffold, or assist, learning. By offloading information currently held in working memory to external sources, capacity can be allocated to complex, critical thinking and/or the integration of additional information from prior knowledge.[15] Similarly, concepts such as Vygotsky's zone of proximal development and distributed cognition suggest knowledge acquisition can be optimized through collaboration by distributing cognition across two or more individuals.[16,17] Therefore, external extensions of working memory are a common and beneficial way to reach the potential of working memory.

OTHER CRITICAL FACETS OF LEARNING

While we have described the how of learning in terms of underlying processes, the why still needs to be considered. Factors such as motivation, interest, and metacognition also play a pivotal role in the way we learn and help to explain why we approach learning activities in many different ways. For example, why do we process certain information at a nominal level while engaging in more higher-order thinking such as problem solving, critical thinking and reasoning, and creativity for other material? Why might we observe differences in performance between two equally well-prepared students?

Motivation

Motivation is an abstract term for the control center of our behavior. Motivation prescribes our willingness to engage in tasks, determines the amount of cognitive effort we put forth while participating in an activity, and dictates our persistence. In the previous section, we distinguished the difference between rote and meaningful learning and highlighted the benefits meaningful learning has for long-term retention and transfer. However, we also emphasized all learning is *not* created equal. Although higher-level processes such as critical thinking, creativity, and reasoning yield deeper understanding, such tasks require additional effort on behalf of the learner—an effort mediated by motivation.

Academic motivation has been found to stem from a variety of sources and is commonly categorized as either intrinsic or extrinsic.[18] Intrinsic motivation refers to our inherent inclination to engage in a task simply because of personal enjoyment, satisfaction, or feelings of importance.[19] Intrinsically motivated learners readily put forth the requisite effort for deeper learning; consequently, intrinsic motivation has been associated with increased academic achievement.[20] On the other hand, extrinsic motivation stems from the potential for external reward (e.g., praise, money, grades). Often, extrinsically motivated students are not simply learning to learn, but rather learning to receive something in return. Therefore, often when extrinsically motivated, there is little reason to go above and beyond a required threshold, and, thus, has been shown to yield shallow processing and minimal cognitive effort.[21]

However, a notable aspect of motivation is its malleability over time. Individuals who are extrinsically motivated to complete a task can develop intrinsic motivation through, for example, positive experiences that raise one's self-efficacy and nurture an individual's beliefs about their own competencies.[22] Therefore, carefully crafted instruction that fosters confidence, appreciation, and autonomy can generate intrinsic motivation over time. However, the malleability of motivation can also shift from intrinsic to extrinsic given certain circumstances. In fact, overall trends suggest academic motivation declines as students progress through school, especially in mathematics and science.[23,24] Through middle and high school, external rewards such as grades are more heavily weighted as measures of performance and sources of recognition, and they make students more focused on getting the grade than mastering the material. Although we generally strive for students to be intrinsically motivated, extrinsic motivation is not necessarily bad. For example, helping students to realize the importance of deeply processing and understanding academic material for achieving their extrinsically-motivated goals (e.g., college admission) can serve to stabilize the presence of intrinsic motivation over time.[25]

Interest

Although generally categorized within the larger umbrella of motivation, the concept of interest has unique and important cognitive implications worth noting here. Due to the frequency of its use in everyday conversation, connotations associated with the term "interest" are vast; nonetheless, interest is often associated with conditions—internal or external to the individual—that yield inclination for engaging in an activity. With respect to education, a forefather of educational psychology, John Dewey (1859 to 1952), suggested the degree to which a student learns is dependent upon effort he puts forth, and effort is regulated by interest in the task.[26] More recently, research has extended Dewey's hypothesis and produced two significant findings:

1. The state of being interested manifests as heightened cognitive and affective processes and, consequently, influences what and to what extent students learn.[27]

2. The instantiation of interest is highly dependent upon the interaction between person and context.[28]

Related to the first point, interest in an activity or to-be-learned information appears to have a powerful impact on cognitive processing. Previous research with reading comprehension suggests we seem to automatically allocate attention toward segments of text we perceive as interesting.[29] In doing so, more cognitive capacity is available for deeper, more complex thought. Consequently, several studies have found students highly interested in the topic of an expository text performed better on high-level questions requiring inferences, transfer, and synthesis than those reporting low levels of interest independent of prior knowledge, cognitive ability, reading ability, and interest for reading.[30,31,32] Moreover, individuals, in general, are more motivated to engage in activities that align with their existing interests,[33] and this interest-based inclination has been shown to foster academic achievement.[34]

The second notable implication of interest lies in the way we become interested. Interest researchers differentiate between individual or personal interest and situational interest.[35] Personal interests are what we typically think of when we refer to interest—an interest that is "relatively stable and … usually associated with increased knowledge, positive emotions, and increased reference value."[36] These are topics and activities that we enjoy and habitually engage in because of the content, not the context or other task features.[37] For instance, a student might be more interested in math or a reading passage if it is taught using baseball as a backdrop, as that is one of her personal interests. In contrast, situational interest arises irrespective of personal interest in a topic due to components of one's environment that that we find inherently stimulating.[38] For example, while sitting in a waiting room, a person might pick up a magazine and read an article on a topic of little interest simply because the headline was surprising or relevant to our life—the article itself, not previous experience or personal preferences, stimulated interest. Therefore, we can experience the cognitive benefits of being interested without necessarily having previous experience or preference for the material. Providing students with prerequisite information, situating learning within a meaningful context, and activities such as hands-on learning have all been shown to stimulate situational interest regardless of personal interests.[39]

Interest can serve an integral role for both motivating students to engage in a task as well as optimizing the functionality of working memory during knowledge construction. Moreover, the concept of situational interest provides unique opportunities for generating interest and learning for individuals less than enthusiastic about the material itself.

Metacognition and Strategy Use

In the most basic sense, metacognition refers to thinking about our own thinking. Therefore, metacognition refers to an awareness of what we know (and what we do not know) as well as a control for regulating, and optimizing, our thinking through the use of strategies.[40] Have you ever read a book or reached the bottom of the page and realized you do not remember anything you just read? (We hope that doesn't happen in this book!) Such a realization demonstrates metacognitive monitoring, and, as you go back to re-read the page, you are implementing a strategy to compensate for your lack of understanding. Similarly, recognizing our own cognitive limitations as students, we might write down important information during a lecture as a strategy for remembering key points. Metacognition has been described as the mission control of cognition, as it is this control that regulates behaviors such as when and where we need to direct our attention or assessments of progress toward a goal.[41] Metacognition plays an extremely important role across one's lifetime, as we are less often learning in a formal setting and more often expected to take on the majority of responsibility for our own learning.

While this might seem simple, metacognition and strategy use are skills developed over time and generally do not begin to emerge until late elementary school.[42] Even through middle and high school, and throughout college, there are distinct differences in students' abilities to monitor and control their own learning.[43] Thus, it cannot simply be assumed that students who say they understand a lesson are making an accurate assessment. As educators, it is important to develop these skills by helping students become more metacognitively aware of their learning and develop effective strategies for coping with cognitive limitations, filling holes in their current understanding, and identifying personal learning preferences. For example, teaching students methods for self-testing on material to ensure mastery, techniques for taking organized notes that facilitate meaningful learning, procedures for knowing when and how to seek help, properties of a productive study environment, and even ways to manage time wisely can all help to foster metacognitive growth, efficient strategy use, and ultimately effective independent learning.[44]

IMPLICATIONS FOR MOBILE LEARNING

Although the way in which we process information can be modeled and generalized across the population, this should not undermine the dependencies brought about by the unique characteristics of an individual. Throughout this chapter, we have outlined the role certain cognitive, metacognitive, and motivational factors play in the process of learning. Central to the properties and behaviors of all of these components is their dependence on characteristics of the individual learner. A learner's existing knowledge, previous experiences, developmental level, and personal preferences are just a few of the many variables

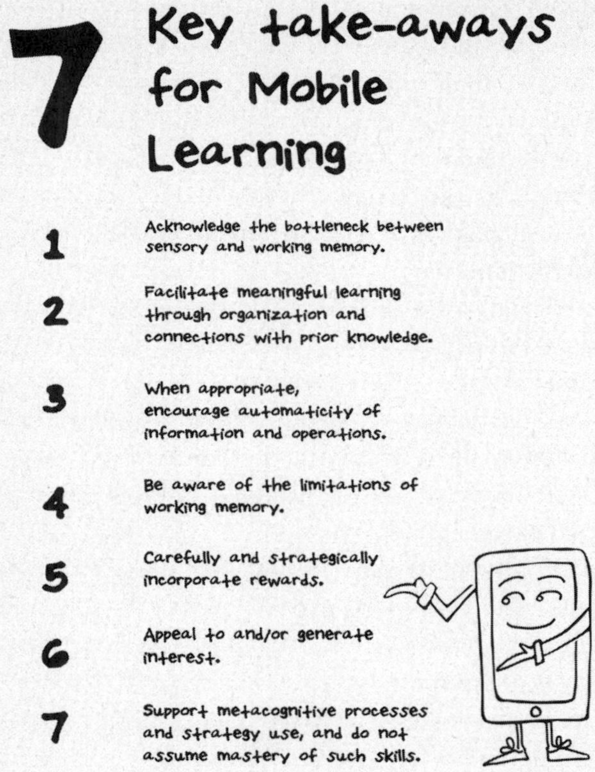

7 Key take-aways for Mobile Learning

1 Acknowledge the bottleneck between sensory and working memory.

2 Facilitate meaningful learning through organization and connections with prior knowledge.

3 When appropriate, encourage automaticity of information and operations.

4 Be aware of the limitations of working memory.

5 Carefully and strategically incorporate rewards.

6 Appeal to and/or generate interest.

7 Support metacognitive processes and strategy use, and do not assume mastery of such skills.

Figure 2.2 Seven Key Takeaways for Mobile Learning

one must account for when designing effective instruction. Therefore, we propose seven essential implications that the science of learning has on the design of mobile technologies for learning (Figure 2.2), and we give several tips for apps to accommodate these well-established learning principles.

Acknowledge the Bottleneck between Sensory and Working Memory

Although we may be able to register all the sensory information provided at any given moment, we simply cannot attend to every sight, sound, smell, touch, and taste at every moment. Consequently, while mobile learning designers can present students with all of the information they might need, the subset of information that actually reaches working memory is dependent upon the memory constraints common to all people and, in some cases, the unique characteristics of each learner. Information deemed critical and important enough to receive attention by one student might not necessarily overlap with that of another. For example, the information categorized as essential or important by an instructor might be meaningless to a low-performing student or negligible to a high-performing student. At the same time, erroneous information in sensory memory threatens to distract learners by drawing attention away from elements of the task. This can include sensory information from the environment, but also, without careful mobile design, sensory information from the mobile learning device or app that distracts the learner from the main point. Ensuring that every student in a classroom is attending to appropriate information is an extremely difficult task for traditional classroom settings, especially with larger classrooms. But effective mobile learning design may be able to overcome many of those distractions, filtering out irrelevant sensory information and directing students to the target content.

With the personalization enabled by mobile technologies, we can better traverse the bottleneck between sensory and working memory. Formative assessments, or knowledge checks, designed into the mobile learning device or app, can encourage on-track performance and productivity, taking advantage of the principles of learning originally discovered by the behaviorists. At the same time, mobile-learning devices can create a context for the naturally occurring, elaborative, or enhanced interactions of students with content, taking advantage of the kinds of learning principles discovered by the cognitive psychologists. Personalized feedback and guidance further ensure that students are attending to the information appropriate for them. Therefore:

- Direct the learner to the most relevant content, taking advantage of multiple sensory systems to attract attention.
- Plan for cases in which important information is initially overlooked or neglected, allowing that content to be re-presented or easily re-accessed.
- Encourage effective allocation of attention by limiting the quantity of content presented in one section, interaction, or app experience.

Facilitate Meaningful Learning through Organization and Connections with Prior Knowledge

The ease and likelihood of retrieval of information stored in long-term memory is dependent upon how often the information is accessed, and the quality and quantity of associations it has with other existing knowledge structures. Therefore, true understanding and comprehension of material does not occur through simple memorization of facts, but rather by developing a sense of how such facts integrate with other information. Students must actively transact with the material and create their own meaning rather than sit passively and hope for the transmission of knowledge.

Techniques for encouraging such behavior include priming relevant prior knowledge, providing partially-completed concept maps and matrices, utilizing visual information, or creating analogies with familiar information. For example, teaching electrical circuits might be easier to comprehend when compared to the properties of a water circuit. This allows students to connect new learning to knowledge structures already in long-term memory, thus increasing the likelihood that new learning will be transferred to long-term memory. Given the uniqueness of any individual student's prior knowledge, in a traditional classroom, it can be difficult to scaffold meaningful learning for a class of 25 or more learners. With mobile technologies, learning can easily be more personalized. Students without much prior knowledge can work at their own pace by first filling in their gaps in prior knowledge necessary for mastering the task at hand, while students with high levels of prior knowledge can go beyond the current assignment by researching and elaborating on the material. When planning for or designing mobile learning:

- Provide several levels of the same lesson to accommodate individual differences in knowledge and ability.

- Create lessons in which the student, not the teacher, is constructing meaning.

- Utilize visual, auditory, and text information without overloading the student to facilitate even more robust encoding.

- Demand active construction of knowledge by encouraging interaction while recognizing the difference between observable activity and cognitive activity—provoking critical thinking in a student might manifest as internal thought, yet this yields better learning than a student charged with actively filling in the blanks on a worksheet.

When Appropriate, Encourage Automatization of Information and Operations

Expanding upon the previous section, automatized information and operations significantly reduce an individual's cognitive load, as well as allow for mastery in a given area. For example, by automatizing number fluency and operations, students can handle more complex math problems. By automatizing word decoding and text parsing, reading becomes a modality by which new learning can take place. However, automaticity does not come immediately, as it requires diligent practice over time. In a traditional classroom, a teacher might not have time to accommodate the necessary practice for essential skills. It might be particularly challenging to provide each individual learner with careful feedback. But the ubiquitous nature of mobile technologies allows for practice anytime, anywhere. Therefore, to encourage automatization:

- Identify essential, foundational skills that can be practiced independently, and design exercises within the app to allow for practice.
- Provide multiple, interesting ways to practice the same skill so as not to compromise motivation.
- Accommodate practice anytime, anywhere—with consideration for the audio and visual constraints presented by certain settings.

Be Aware of the Limitations of Working Memory

Unfortunately, the limitations of working memory can inhibit the depth of cognitive processing; however, there are techniques for overcoming this obstacle. Aggregating information into meaningful units, and automatizing information and operations, significantly expands the capacity of our mental workbench for the meaningful construction of knowledge. Moreover, peers, teachers, parents, books, worksheets, technology, and other resources can also act as external extensions to working memory. For example, actions as simple as offloading information (e.g., taking notes, drawing pictures) can free up resources in working memory. Moreover, discussing topics with peers and essentially pooling together everyone's prior knowledge and current understanding—a process known as distributed learning—can reduce cognitive demands. Lastly, utilizing technology as a means for presenting information to students visually and/or interactively can be more effective than having students mentally visualize how a process works on their own.[45]

Mobile technologies easily provide and facilitate an external extension of working memory. For example, mobile technologies seamlessly take on the role of a multimedia simulation, an interactive, organized note-taking space, or gateway to collaborative learning scenarios. Acknowledge and cope with the limitations of working memory with these ideas:

- Know the developmental level of your user. Consider what skills and information are likely automatized to facilitate higher-level thinking.

- Facilitate opportunities for distributed cognition and collaborative learning via multiuser apps, electronic sharing (with teacher or peers), and other methods for sharing personal content (presentation projections, email, text messaging, etc.).

- Display relevant information in a meaningful way and allow for user offloading.

Carefully and Strategically Incorporate Rewards

While some research suggests the use of rewards is detrimental to intrinsic motivation, carefully and strategically implemented rewards can be viable instructional aids.[46] Typically, there are quantitative and qualitative differences in the quality of learning between a student who is intrinsically motivated and one who is extrinsically motivated; ultimately, we want students to learn because they want and love to learn, not because they are forced to or incentivized by some external reward system. Unfortunately, reality is far from a world of intrinsically motivated students across all domains making the use of rewards a strategic, yet complicated, tool.

Research-based best practices suggest tangible rewards should only be utilized when absolutely necessary and should be reduced over time.[47] Moreover, students should receive rewards for productive behavior as opposed to a final product, and students should be made explicitly aware why they are receiving the reward.[48] Therefore, to effectively implement a reward system, classroom teachers must pay close attention to the needs and actions of each student—a problem solved by the use of mobile technologies. The personalization of a mobile experience can effectively provide extrinsic motivation for productive behavior, as opposed to a final product. As a result, students are encouraged to try hard, transact with the material, generate connections with prior knowledge, and implement effective strategies—the characteristics of an intrinsically motived student—and high performance more likely becomes a by-product of these behaviors. When utilizing rewards in the classroom:

- Allow for flexible, personalized reward structures. In other words, reward only those students who might benefit from rewards—refrain from rewarding students already intrinsically motivated to complete the task.
- Reward students for productive learning behaviors, not final products.
- Adhere to best practices for reinforcement learning by devising a reward structure that systematically fades as students approach mastery.

Appeal to and/or Generate Interest

When learners are interested, cognitive processes become more effective, effort increases, and, consequently, the quality of learning goes up.[49] However, it is safe to assume that not all topics and activities mandated by a school's curriculum are as flexible, and we can expect the cognitive advantages of interest will only manifest occasionally, even for the best students. In order to work around lack of personal interest, we can achieve situational interest by manipulating attributes of a learning task. For example, research suggests a student that dislikes reading will put forth more effort if the topic of text aligns with her interests.[50] Integrating choice, novelty, surprise, narrative, hands-on activities, technology, cohesion, social interactions, and personal relatedness are just some of the many ways in which we can achieve situational interest in the classroom.[51] Care should also be taken to maintain situational interest for the entire class over the course of an activity.[52] In other words, be prepared for the novelty to wear off.

Several of the aforementioned sources of situational interest are easily attained through the use of mobile technologies. For example, simply using technology has been shown to trigger students' situational interest for a task.[53] Similarly, the nature of mobile is very accommodating to incorporating hands-on activities, providing choice and autonomy, fostering social interaction, and presenting information in a novel manner. In fact, Mitchell found interactivity through social interaction and hands-on activities to be one technique for maintaining situational interest over time.[54] To trigger and maintain interest in the classroom:

- Consider ways in which learning objectives can incorporate student personal interests (e.g., reading about topics of interest).
- Strategically incorporate other sources of situational interest. Do not assume that simply presenting information via mobile technology will maintain interest over the course of an activity.

Support Metacognitive Processes and Strategy Use, and Do Not Assume Mastery of Such Skills

Metacognition and strategy use highly influence the efficiency and effectiveness of learning and directly impact long-term academic success.[55] As students progress through middle and high school and prepare for the demands of college and careers, more responsibility for learning is placed on the student. Students are charged with independent learning and taught strategies for doing so. However, regulating one's own learning is a learned skill developed over time through instruction and practice and typically does not begin to emerge until late elementary or early high school.[56] Even so, the rate of development and proficiency of these skills can be vast from student to student.[57] Teaching and supporting students' metacognition cannot be done through a one-size-fits-all approach, as the best strategies for learning are developed through learner preference and previous experiences.[58]

The ubiquity of mobile technologies in modern life facilitates independent learning as users are free to utilize this instructional method anytime, anywhere. Therefore, mobile technologies serve as a unique venue for supporting metacognition and strategies in the form of tools as well as opportunities for practice. However, given varying degrees of student metacognitive competency, completely independent learning can be particularly challenging, even detrimental, for some. When integrating mobile technologies into pedagogy:

- Consider the role mobile learning can play as a tool for supporting metacognitive skills and strategy use (e.g., note taking, organization, time management, goal monitoring).
- Scaffold metacognitive behaviors, such as progress monitoring and concept mastery.
- Support the use of various strategies for learning by providing opportunities for self-assessment to reinforce the student's understanding of what he or she does and does not know.

CONCLUSION

In this chapter, we highlighted the ways in which the science of learning should be considered when designing and implementing instructional methods, especially app development for mobile devices and mobile learning. Because we believe the learner must be central in the development of mobile learning environments, we will refer to these points throughout the book as we discuss what makes a good app, best practices for integrating mobile into the classroom, and considerations for special populations. By adhering to the cognitive, metacognitive, and motivational needs of the learner, a good mobile app aligns with and supports the way in which we construct meaningful knowledge—knowledge that represents true understanding, comprehension, and mastery.

NOTES

1. Noam Chomsky, *Knowledge of Language: Its Nature,Origin, and Use* (Westport, CT: Praeger Publishers, 1986).

2. J. Alba and L. Hasher, "Is Memory Schematic?" *Psychological Bulletin* 93, no. 2 (1983): 203–231.

3. P. D. Eggen and D. P. Kauchak, *Educational Psychology*, 4th ed. (Upper Saddle River, NJ: Prentice-Hall, 1999): 242.

4. Lev Vygotsky, *Mind and Society: The Development of Higher Mental Processes* (Cambridge, MA: Harvard University Press, 1978).

5. Albert Bandura, "Human Agency in Social Cognitive Theory," *American Psychologist* 44, no. 9 (1989): 1175–1184.

6. R. C. Atkinson and R. M. Shiffrin, "Human Memory: A Proposed System and Its Control Processes," *Psychology of Learning and Motivation* 2 (1968): 89–195.

7. J. E. Ormrod, *Educational Psychology: Developing Learners*, 6th ed. (Upper Saddle River, NJ: Pearson, 2008).

8. J. Sweller, "Cognitive Load during Problem Solving: Effects on Learning," *Cognitive Science* 12 (2006): 257–285.

9. G. Miller, "The Magic Number Seven Plus or Minus Two: Some Limits on Our Capacity to Process Information," *Psychological Review* 63, no. 2 (1956): 81–97.

10. N. Cowan, "The Magical Number 4 in Short-Term Memory: A Reconsideration of Mental Storage Capacity," *Behavioral and Brain Sciences* 24 (2001): 87–185.

11. A. D. Baddeley, "Is Working Memory Still Working?" *American Psychologist* 56, no. 11 (2001): 851–864.

12. M. Sadoski and A. Paivio, *Imagery and Text: A Dual Coding Theory of Reading and Writing* (Mahwah, NJ: Lawrence Earlbaum Associates, 2001).

13. W. Schneider and R. M. Shiffrin, "Controlled and Automatic Human Information Processing: I. Detection, Search, and Attention," *Psychological Review* 84, no. 1 (1977): 1–66.

14. Vygotsky, *Mind and Society*.

15. J. Sweller, "Cognitive Load During Problem Solving."

16. Vygotsky, *Mind and Society*.

17. Edwin Hutchins, *Cognition in the Wild* (Cambridge, MA: MIT Press, 1995).

18. P. R. Pintrich and D. H. Schunk, *Motivation in Education: Theory, Research, and Applications* (Upper Saddle River, NJ: Merrill Prentice-Hall, 2002).

19. E. Deci, *Intrinsic Motivation* (New York: Plenum Press, 1975).

20. A. E. Gottfried, J. S. Fleming, and A. W. Gottfried, "Continuity of Academic Intrinsic Motivation from Childhood through Late Adolescence: A Longitudinal Study," *Journal of Educational Psychology* 93, no. 1 (2001): 3–13.

21. E. L. Deci, R. Koestner, and R. M. Ryan, "A Meta-Analytic Review of Experiments Examining the Effects of Extrinsic Rewards on Intrinsic Motivation," *Psychological Bulletin* 125, no. 6 (1999): 627–668.

22. B. J. Zimmerman, "Self-Efficacy: An Essential Motive to Learn," *Contemporary Educational Psychology* 25, no. 1 (2000): 82–91.

23. Gottfried, Fleming, & Gottfried, "Continuity of Academic Intrinsic Motivation."

24. M. R. Lepper, J. H. Corpus, and S. S. Iyengar, "Intrinsic and Extrinsic Motivational Orientations in the Classroom: Age Differences and Academic Correlate," *Journal of Educational Psychology* 97, no. 2 (2005): 184–196.

25. Ormrod, *Educational Psychology.*

26. J. Dewey, *Interest and Effort in Education* (New York: Houghton Mifflin, 1913).

27. G. Schraw and S. Lehman, "Situational Interest: A Review of the Literature and Directions for Future Research," *Educational Psychology Review* 13, no. 1 (2001): 23–51.

28. S. Hidi and K. A. Renninger, "The Four-Phase Model of Interest Development," *Educational Psychologist* 41, no. 2 (2006): 111–127.

29. M. McDaniel, P. J. Waddill, K. Finstad, and T. Bourg, "The Effects of Text-Based Interest on Attention and Recall," *Journal of Educational Psychology* 92, no. 3 (2000): 492–502.

30. U. Schiefele, "Interest and Learning From Text," *Scientific Studies of Reading* 3, no. 3 (1999): 257–279.

31. K. Renninger, L. Ewen, and A. K. Lasher, "Individual Interest as Context in Expository Text and Mathematical Word Problems," *Learning and Instruction* 12, no. 4 (2002): 467–490.

32. V. Clinton and P. van den Broek, "Interest, Inferences, and Learning from Texts," *Learning and Individual Differences* (2012), www.academia.edu/5565152/Interest _Inferences_and_Learning_from_Texts.

33. J. J. A. Denissen, N. R Zarrett, and J. S. Eccles, "I Like to Do It, I'm Able, and I Know I Am: Longitudinal Couplings Between Domain-Specific Achievement, Self-Concept, and Interest," *Child Development* 78, no. 2 (2007): 430–447.

34. J. I. Rotgans and H. G. Schmidt, "Situational Interest and Academic Achievement in the Active-Learning Classroom," *Learning and Instruction* 21 (2011): 58–67.

35. K. A. Renninger and S. Hidi, "Revisiting the Conceptualization, Measurement, and Generation of Interest," *Educational Psychologist* 46, no. 3 (2011): 168–184.

36. A. Krapp, S. Hidi, and K. A. Renninger, "Interest, Learning and Development," in *The Role of Interest in Learning and Development*, eds. A. Renninger, S. Hidi, and A. Krapp (Hillsdale, NJ: Erlbaum, 1992): 3–25.

37. U. Schiefele, E. Schaffner, J. Moller, and A. Wigfield, "Dimensions of Reading Motivation and Their Relationship to Reading Behavior and Competence," *Reading Research Quarterly* 47, no. 4 (2012): 427–463.

38. Hidi and Renninger, "The Four-Phase Model of Interest Development."

39. J. T Gutherie, A. Wigfield, N. M. Humenick, K. C. Perencevich, A. Taboada, and P. Barbosa, "Influences of Stimulating Tasks on Reading Motivation and Comprehension," *The Journal of Educational Research* 99, no. 4 (2006): 232–245.

40. L. Baker and A. Brown, "Metacognitive Skills and Reading," 1980, http://files.eric .ed.gov/fulltext/ED195932.pdf.

41. B. J. Zimmerman, "A Social Cognitive View of Self-Regulated Academic Learning," *Journal of Educational Psychology* 81 (1989): 329–339.

42. J. Alexander, M. Carr, and P. Schwanenflugel, "Development of Metacognition in Gifted Children: Directions for Future Research," *Developmental Review* 15 (1995): 1–37.

43. Ibid.

44. B. J. Zimmerman, "Becoming a Self-Regulated Learner: An Overview," *Theory into Practice* 41, no. 2 (2002): 64–70.

45. R. E. Mayer, *Multimedia Learning* (New York: Cambridge University Press, 2001).

46. J. Brophy, *Motivating Students to Learn* (Boston: McGraw-Hill, 1998).

47. Deci, Koestner, and Ryan, "A Meta-Analytic Review of Experiments."

48. Brophy, *Motivating Students to Learn*.

49. Rotgans and Schmidt, "Situational Interest and Academic Achievement."

50. U. Schiefele, "Interest, Learning, and Motivation," *Educational Psychologist* 26, no. 3/4: 299–323.

51. D. A. Bergin, "Influences on Classroom Interest," *Educational Psychologist* 34, no. 2 (1999): 87–98.

52. Hidi and Renninger, "The Four-Phase Model."

53. M. Mitchell, "Situational Interest: Its Multifaceted Structure in The Secondary School Mathematics Classroom," *Journal of Educational Psychology* 85, no. 3 (1993): 424–436.

54. Ibid.

55. B. Zimmerman, "Self-Regulated Learning and Academic Achievement: An Overview," *Educational Psychologist* 25, no. 1 (1990).

56. Zimmerman, "Becoming a Self-Regulated Learner."

57. B. Zimmerman and D. Schunk, *Self-Regulated Learning and Academic Achievement: Theoretical Perspectives* (Hillsdale, NJ: Erlbaum, 2001).

58. Zimmerman, "Becoming a Self-Regulated Learner."

CHAPTER **3**

What Is It About These Devices?

There just seems to be something different about learning with mobile devices. In interviews with classroom teachers, a persistent theme was clear: mobile devices add a level of engagement to any activity, and seem to captivate those students who are often otherwise disengaged. We've come across comments like "Some days, I have kids 100 percent on task, all day," and "Students played games to prepare for final tests. Their test scores have improved significantly."[1] Almost any task is more engaging on a device, be it watching a video clip or using flashcards or taking notes in class.[2]

But what is it about these devices? We believe the answer lies in a synergy of characteristics that yield a ubiquitous experience unmatched by other technologies. Based on our research, interviews and experience, we've tried to unpack the familiar "there is just *something* about these devices!" by positing 10 distinguishing factors that set the mobile experience apart from other technologies (such as laptops) and the absence of electronic technology altogether (i.e., books).

Many of the factors overlap to some degree, and the examples may cover one or more of the factors (which we attribute largely to the ubiquity of mobile devices), but this list (shown in Figure 3.1) provides a foundation for understanding mobile technology's impact on students today.

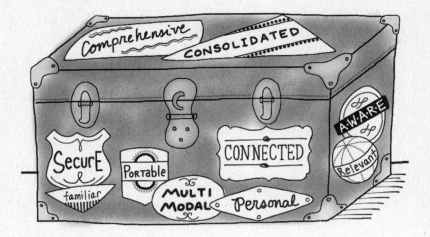

Figure 3.1 Distinguishing Factors of the Mobile Learning Experience

CONNECTED

The on-demand, perpetual connectivity of mobile devices changes the way we communicate with one another, gather and store data, and indulge our curiosity—all of which have great implications for education. Mobile devices enable users to not only be constantly connected to their data and resources, but also to always be connected to one another. Learning is no longer tethered to the teacher, classroom, or textbook; instead students are connected to educational opportunities from virtually anywhere, making almost every situation a potential learning environment. This anytime, anywhere access is also popular among students, with a recent ECAR study showing that 78 percent consider Wi-Fi "extremely valuable to their academic success."[3]

Always Connected

Standard features such as email, text messaging, and video and voice calls allow educators to maintain lines of communication with students outside of school. "Kids who never speak would speak up. I have a better relationship with students," one teacher commented.[4] Students can easily contact their teachers if they get stuck on a homework assignment, and teachers can send out reminders and other resources after the school day ends. In a recent interview, one high school student complimented her teachers for helping her stay on track by sending out reminders, quizzes, and exercises during an extended snow storm that closed her school for multiple days.[5] Targeted apps, such as *Remind*, allow teachers to communicate with students and parents without having to actually share personal phone numbers or emails. This can be especially useful for younger students and for communicating details about field trips or assignments to parents.[6] Aside from providing assistance day to day, "students who feel their teachers care and support them are more likely to perceive themselves as successful and valued in their jobs later in life."[7] Furthermore, bringing mobile devices home has been associated with an increase in parental involvement in students' education.[8]

Similarly, networking components like Bluetooth and Wi-Fi simplify group work and collaboration. Discussing requirements, plans, and goals; sharing research and resources; drafting documents, creating presentations, and generating other projects no longer require face-to-face meetings or USB thumb drives. Collaboration and sharing apps—*Google Drive, Dropbox, NearPod, Padlet, Join.Me, Showbie*, to name a few—furnish excellent platforms for working together both in and out of class. Using mobile devices "has increased our collaboration," one student commented. "We look for information and form groups to solve problems together."[9] An online lesson planning resource outlines the following activity: for vocabulary lists, assign each student one word and have them find a picture that represents the term using *Safari* or the camera on the device, mark up the image using *Comic Touch, Thinglink*, or *SAS Gloss*, and share the image using *AirDrop*; therefore, at the end of the activity, each student has a detailed flashcard deck filled with text and images of the entire vocabulary list.[10] Similarly, social apps, such as *Twitter*, allow teachers to facilitate conversations outside of the classroom. "During the State of the Union address I ... offered them a variety of pathways to have a dynamic and connected conversation ... [via chat rooms, instant messaging, or a hash-tagged Twitter chat]."[11] Therefore, students are able to virtually discuss current events that occur after school hours.

The connected experience also dismantles acknowledged constraints of the classroom. Virtual field trips, 3-D maps, simulations, and communication with individuals around the world transform schools from brick-and-motor facilities to limitless spaces. Without leaving the confines of the classroom, students can tour the Louvre in Paris, visit laboratories around the world, design wind turbines,[12] virtually walk around the Coliseum in Rome, or interview experts, entrepreneurs, and other key individuals in their particular areas of interest. For example, in a lesson about campaigns for the public good and bravery, an eighth-grade class had the opportunity to tweet and video conference with General John Michel of the U.S. Air Force who was deployed 8,000 miles away in Afghanistan.[13]

Instantly Connected

Unlike laptop and desktop computers, mobile devices have the unique advantage of instant connectivity. Many classroom teachers praise tablets and smartphones for their lack of boot-up time allowing more time for on-task engagement. A ninth-grade geography teacher noted, "Today I met the kids at the door, they signed in and took the iPads. By the time the bell rang, they had the iPads and were ready to go; whereas in the media center, you have to [finish up] five minutes earlier."[14] Likewise, Linnea Czerney, a technology coordinator, argues that being able to Google something at any moment and find the answer allows students to be more inquisitive and self-directed.[15] Similarly, in an interview about educational technology, a middle-school student cited his iPod Touch as a more time-efficient way to find the definition of unknown words saying, "if I don't know a word, I'll just say *define* whatever the word is so instead of using the dictionary and taking that […] time, I just use the Internet [or the *Dictionary.com* app]."[16] Other teachers note the ease of looking up a word's meaning or pronunciation by simply highlighting it within an ebook app.[17]

AWARE

The myriad of sensors available on many devices—such as a camera, microphone, touchscreen, gyroscope, and geolocation—combine to give the mobile experience a unique quality. Devices can see what you see, know where you are, hear what you hear, and consequently, respond accordingly. While this might feel overly intrusive, this information can enhance the user experience. Information presented on your device is contextualized and personally relevant. Additionally, several companies offer add-on *appcessories* to further enhance the device's awareness by giving it more information (e.g., heart rate monitor, blood sugar monitor, blood alcohol test attachment, carbon monoxide, light intensity, thermometer, pressure sensor, iBeacons, and microscope). The multitude of sensors and the variety of applications enable mobile devices to become much more than a communication vehicle. Many integrated actions can be enabled through these embedded sensors and add-ons—like geolocation-based scavenger hunts or authentic experience with real-world equipment, such as stethoscopes and blood sugar monitors. Here, however, we will focus on three key common tablet and smartphone features: the built-in microphone, camera, and touchscreen.

Developers have taken advantage of the simple microphone to create ingenious experiences. One student identified the robust speech-to-text engine available on many iOS devices as particularly useful for dictating notes as opposed to typing or writing them by hand.[18] Also, several teachers note great advantages of allowing students to record and listen to themselves reading aloud (e.g., *SAS Reading Records*).[19] Sean Russell, a second-grade teacher, had a student who typically struggled with reading-aloud activities, which in turn affected his confidence. To record students reading a passage, they were using an app that offered the ability to redo words if they stumbled, which Russell attributed as a "huge factor," enabling this student to show improvement in his overall performance and have a more gratifying experience.[20] Nature apps, such as *Cicada Hunt*, process ambient noise to identify animals and other species in the student's vicinity. Devices are even being used in music class with apps that simulate instruments (e.g., *Ocarina, Pocket Trumpet, Real Clarinet*) by blowing into the microphone and pressing keys on the touchpad.

The camera has proven similarly powerful beyond providing the ability to document information by taking pictures and video. Image-processing apps allow students to take pictures of objects in their environment and instantly receive relevant information. A popular example of this technology is the ability to scan QR codes, a classroom shortcut that avoids having students enter long URLs.

More complex systems leverage the portability of mobile devices to let students snap images of everyday artifacts. For example, students learning about their local flora and fauna in school can use *Leafsnap* to immediately identify plants in their community. Some teachers even use the screenshot functionality as a tool for students to turn in assignments, simply capturing a picture of what they've created and emailing it to their teacher.[21]

The camera has also afforded the rapidly growing arena of augmented reality (AR) apps that bring new meaning to learning in context. Similar to a tour guide, several apps utilize location-detecting sensors and the camera to provide students with additional information as they navigate around a particular space. Companion apps to the Smithsonian museums, the American Museum of Natural History, and other popular venues offer immersive experiences that let students angle the devices' camera toward exhibits in order to see a display of bones render into a living dinosaur or a picture of a plant change into a 3D model. Apps like *acrossair* permit users to create their own AR worlds by tagging specific locations with images and text; thus, students become the curator of a space that can be shared with other users. User-generated AR worlds affords alternatives to dangerous, expensive, or otherwise unattainable experiences. The simulation app—*Elements 4D*—turns 2D representations of the elements of the periodic table into 3D manipulatives, which allow students to visualize their various properties and experiment with chemical reactions.

Direct manipulation on a touchscreen appears to be more intuitive than input devices such as a mouse or keyboard, as it more closely mimics our existing behaviors. With mobile devices and gesture support like pinch to zoom, grab and rotate, and lasso, interactions come naturally, and we are not charged with learning keystroke combinations or click sequences. For example, a recent study found significant learning advantages for direct gesture manipulation when learning scientific concepts.[22] To determine best practices for teaching challenging concepts like astronomical scale, students in the study were provided the opportunity to navigate the universe using a simulation displayed on the iPad. Results found the pinch to zoom and expand gestures helped students to better comprehend the enormity of space and size differences between Earth and other planets and stars.[23] The *Google*

Earth app allows for a similar experience by offering students a 3D, scale model of the traditional, often-criticized 2D map of the world.

Finally, logging and analyzing sensor activity expands the options for assessment. Instead of more traditional forms, such as tests or quizzes, apps can instead provide feedback about user-interaction patterns. This might include how and when the student tapped on the screen (touch screen), where the student was located or how she moved around a certain space (geolocation, Bluetooth, and iBeacons), or a recording of students' collaboration (microphone). State Farm's *Driver Feedback* app provides a great example.[24] Using the built-in gyroscope of the iPhone, the app monitors the driver's behaviors and logs risky actions, such as sharp turns, speedy acceleration, and hard stops. This information is then analyzed, for example, to assess the skills of young adults learning to drive. Ultimately, the awareness of the mobile device can enable students to be evaluated on authentic behaviors as opposed to a regurgitation of knowledge.

MULTIMODAL

Mobile device sensors create rich, interactive learning environments that seem to outshine the engagement inspired by other educational resources—the feeling that anything is more interesting on a mobile device is prevalent among the teachers we interviewed.[25] Although common desktop and laptop computers can appeal to our auditory and visual senses, mobile apps additionally support touch and movement for enhanced, immersive multimodal experiences that adapt and respond to our commands and movements.

The multimodal space of mobile devices also expands the realm of possibilities for student-generated work. Projects, presentations, study guides, and homework assignments are no longer confined to what you can create with tangible materials. Instead, students can easily integrate multimedia elements like, images, songs, and videos. As one student said, "it's really cool."[26] While certainly novel and cool, these multimedia and interactive elements often force students to think more creatively and critically about the subject matter, thereby making a more meaningful learning experience. For instance, in a kindergarten class at the Park Tudor School in Indiana young students were given iPads and asked to create a video about the life cycle of butterflies. At first, students commented about how they did not know how to make a video or use video-editing apps.[27] With a little guidance from their teacher, students were researching online, reading books, drawing pictures, photographing butterflies and plants in their school garden, documenting their research in the field with short videos, and finally, cutting the aggregated movie filled with images, video clips, titles and subtitles, voice overs, and music.[28] Beyond learning more about butterflies, students were given the opportunity to practice using mobile devices for research, collaboration, and communication, but also learned some new skills along the way.

FAMILIAR

The proliferation of mobile devices has yielded a particular advantage for the classroom. According to a 2013 Pew survey, 77 percent of families reported having at least one smartphone in their household, and 46 percent reported having at least one tablet. According to this same survey, 43 percent of all children use a mobile device regularly. Among teens, 74 percent use mobile devices to access the Internet on a regular basis.[29] Devices are so familiar to students in their home and personal lives that teachers don't need to spend lots of class time teaching basic functionality. Many students enter kindergarten well versed in the use of devices, oftentimes to the amazement of their teacher. Rebecca Goddard, a technology facilitator, recently watched in awe as classes of kindergarteners made videos using green screening for their career fair. "It was amazing to watch, they really *get* how to film each other and splice it together," she said. While the adults administering the education might feel otherwise, for the youngest students who have been exposed to this technology since birth, Goddard notes, "they don't know any other way of learning."[30] Thus, cognitive processing is not needed for simply using the app, and more resources can be allocated to learning. Similarly, educators are quick to note students' familiarity with mobile devices has given unexpected students the opportunity to be leaders and experts. "One student does something, another asks how—soon that student is teaching the class," one teacher at Brentwood Elementary noted.[31]

Remarkably, familiarity with one device can often transfer to being well-acquainted with a different mobile platform—something not necessarily true between other devices (e.g., computers running Mac versus Windows operating system). For example, both iOS and Android operating systems use a similar application structure, where apps are programs downloaded independently to the device, represented by an icon on the main screens, and easily accessible with a simple touch. Touch devices also tend to use the same gestures for common tasks, such as pinching to zoom.

Similar standards and conventions are apparent between apps themselves as well. For example, Apple produces a set of guidelines for designing for iOS.[32] This ensures that apps behave in a similar and predictable way even between different developers. For example, these guidelines propose a set of common navigation strategies and the UI elements that are designed to support them. When app developers follow these guidelines (which many do) the result is a set of applications that are consistent with one another, making them easier to learn and reducing error.[33]

Educators are also finding ways to take advantage of the apps students are already using outside of school to leverage both familiarity and motivation. *Twitter, Instagram, Facebook* and other social apps have proven to be great resources for engaging students in conversation both in and outside of class. Additionally, creativity and problem-solving game apps are making their way into the classroom. One popular and cross-platform app, *Minecraft*, has scores of associated lesson plans from geometry to ancient history.[34]

PERSONAL

Mobile devices are also personal, especially if students have their own. Unlike other technologies, mobile devices are designed to be a personal assistant carried with users wherever they go. It is something that is brought along as opposed to something you go to, like with personal computers. Many adults report feeling that their devices are an extension of themselves, and younger users may feel the same way. This is especially true when students have the opportunity to customize what is on the device. The variety and placement of apps on a mobile device are unique to its user, tailored to his or her specific preferences, interests, and needs.

The strategies we use and the scaffolding we need to optimize learning are unique to each individual. For example, the way we take notes or the background information we need to make sense of a particular concept can vary significantly from student to student. Personalized mobile devices that can accommodate these individual differences are consequently the perfect companion to education. Fortunately, the app stores provide a range of apps for accomplishing almost any task. A search for note-taking or time-management apps will return a plethora of resources, each offering different experiences or features that distinctively appeal to different users; thus, educators do not need to necessarily dictate the choice of apps but rather teach the more abstract skills and let students adapt their learning environment to match their needs.

Likewise, mobile devices offer a private and safe space for working. Many educational apps are designed to allow for differentiated instruction. Educators can also easily assign different work to each student in order to deliver an appropriate level of challenge. When all students are engaged with their own device, differentiation becomes less overt. It is not necessarily noticeable that one student is working on a different activity or with a different rubric from another student.

Another important benefit of a personal device is that mistakes are kept personal as well. Many educational experts will agree that taking risks and overcoming failures are critical for higher-order thinking skills such as creativity.[35] However, nervousness or fear over the possibility of mistakes often stifles students. When working independently in a classroom setting, it is not necessarily noticeable if students make mistakes. Teachers can notice and address mistakes with students, but these mistakes won't be obvious to the student's peers. The safe-place nature of mobile devices is very valuable.

Having a personal device also means not having to split time with other students, thereby reducing periods of inaccessibility. Compared to shared technologies, mobile-based activities and projects can more easily straddle multiple days, weeks, or even academic years. After learning with mobile devices, a student compared learning with tablets versus learning in the computer lab by stating that with tablets, "We can do more assignments. In the past, we [could] do only one project in the computer lab. For example, the environment project, we could spend two days researching and type right away."[36] Through a personal device, students now have around-the-clock access to resources (e.g., online textbooks), notes, work and projects, and class portals and webpages (e.g., learning management systems, class websites). Not surprisingly, this constant access has been shown to increase average study time.[37]

COMPREHENSIVE

In 2013, the number of apps available in Apple's app store reached the 1 million mark (adding great validity to the catchy tagline, "There's an app for that"). Through this comprehensive access to apps, mobile devices transitioned from a simple cellphone to a seemingly universal tool that fits in your pocket. Mobile devices become your watch, camera, video camera, phonebook, calendar, filing cabinet, novel, notebook, textbook, navigator, calculator, flashlight, compass, wallet, pedometer, media player, diary … the list goes on. Therefore, investing in a single mobile device for students reduces the need for additional expenses (for instance, textbooks, calculators, and laboratory equipment) while providing access to a burgeoning arena of educational resources (environmental sensors, augmented reality, and simulations, to name a few).

However, while the proliferation of apps might tempt one to scour the app store in search for the perfect app, pedagogy should always precede technology or, in this case, pedagogy should always be the primary consideration, rather than focusing only on the content of an app. For example, instead of searching for an app that teaches students about the water cycle, a more meaningful use of technology might be to use a video creation or annotation app that allows students to *demonstrate* their understanding. Therefore, being aware of the variety of apps, as seen in Table 3.1, can be beneficial as educators outline teaching objectives and begin to design a lesson. For more app ideas, check out APPendix A.

Table 3.1 Types of Educational Apps

Type	Definition	Example
Game	Offers educational information in an entertaining way, usually through drills or competition-based environments.	*Math Chomp, Pocket Law Firm, Stack the Countries, Rocket Math*
Utility	Has no specific educational value, but offers a basic function and can be combined in ways to accommodate projects, lessons, and learning.	*Notes, iBooks, SAS Gloss, Camera, Voice, Animoto Video Maker, DropBox, Evernote*
Administration	Allows teachers to more efficiently administer education and manage their job responsibilities.	*Poll Everywhere, Class Dojo, Too Noisy*
Tool	Designed for education, but offers a blank slate. They provide scaffolding to common education actions but require the student or teacher to supply the content.	*SAS Flash Cards, Explain Everything, Google Drive, SAS Reading Records, SAS Gloss, SAS Data Notebook, Popplet*
Content Specific	Provides a large amount of information on one topic.	*To The Brink, Elements 3D, EcoMobile, SAS Math Stretch, DuoLingo, companion apps for Smithsonian American Museum of Natural History.*
Reference	Provides basic information in a connected, searchable format.	*Dictionary.com, Wolfram Alpha*
Social	Enables the connection and easy sharing.	*Edmodo, Twitter, Edublogs*

CONSOLIDATED

When asked what is the best device for conducting research and writing papers, one student cited tablets because he could consult a variety of resources including download books, search the Internet, and watch YouTube videos.[38] With all the sensors and apps that make mobile devices so flexible and comprehensive, consolidation makes productivity seamless and efficient.

App stacking, also known as app smashing, is the process described by the student above: easily switching between apps within the same activity. Activities are easily streamlined by consolidating all the relevant resources on one device—which can also curb related classroom management difficulties. Also, app stacking is a wonderful tool for designing mobile learning experiences that directly align to teaching objectives. Instead of searching for the *one* app that perfectly accommodates a lesson or need in the classroom, educators can instead group several apps into a single folder and plan classroom activities around them. For example, teachers can challenge students to determine the best location for a wind turbine by analyzing wind data from multiple cities across the country using *Wolfram*, graph their results using *Numbers*, and present their argument using *Keynote*.[39]

By having their own device, students are left with little excuse for not having class materials, and the consolidated space is also a great resource for helping students stay organized. Holding students accountable for coming to class prepared is much easier when everything lives on their device. No pencil? No calculator? No book? No paper? No problem. Additionally, features such as cloud storage and cross-platform apps make work completed using any technology, whether at home, school, or otherwise, accessible.

PORTABLE

As the name suggests, mobile devices make the aforementioned benefits available anytime, anywhere. On-demand answers to any of your questions, problem-solving resources, creativity spaces, data collection and documentation tools, vehicles for communication and sharing, and much more reside easily in your pocket.

While learning has traditionally occurred with students sitting at desks in a classroom, mobile devices change this. Inside the classroom, apps like *Fetch! Lunch Rush!* put students in motion while applying their math skills. However, sturdy cases, extended battery life, and connectivity let students learn in the field as never before. For example, *Merlin Bird ID*, helps students identify birds outdoors by asking students a series of questions.

Also, by capitalizing on the portability of mobile devices, what is taught in school can easily be transferred outside, blurring the lines between formal and informal learning. In essence, "Mobile technologies bring the real world into the classroom and they bring the classroom into the real world."[40] For example, instead of using mobile technology to teach students how to research, educators must teach them how to use mobile devices to acquire, analyze, and synthesize information. Activities like having students take pictures of their vocabulary or spelling words as they come across them in their daily lives help contextualize and draw connections between home and school. Or, extend an astronomy lesson by showing students how to use *StarWalk* or a related app to identify and observe the differences between stars and planets at night.

Parallel to many of the benefits working adults experience from using a mobile device, students gain on-the-go access to homework and communication with classmates and teachers. In short spells of time (such as car trips, bus rides, or before soccer practice starts), students can read a few pages of a novel that was assigned or check in with group members on an assignment. These multitasking and time management skills are crucial to success in our hyperconnected world.

RELEVANT

When students observe their parents or other adults in the workplace, they likely see mobile devices being used for much more than games, social media, and communication with friends. They see mobile devices being used for research, collaboration, data collection and analysis, and a myriad of other applications. Therefore, when mobile devices are integrated in the classroom, we are provided with the opportunity to teach students how to use them productively and in ways that are relevant for thriving in today's workplace. So, instead of 59 percent of working individuals reporting that "they developed most of the skills they use in their current job outside of school,"[41] we might see more students entering the workforce with relevant and in-demand skills (and keep pace with new skills as they're demanded.)

By giving students access to and experience with the exact devices that are used in the real world at that point in time, we can teach them readily transferrable knowledge about how to use tools to manage time and multitask, support creativity, communicate, offload information to help solve problems, study, acquire information and research, among other things. John Silverthorn, an elementary school teacher, notes his students seem "more intrinsically motivated" when they use devices in class, empowered by seeing the connections between the material they're currently studying and other things they've learned, or connections to their nonacademic lives.[42] Certainly, as today's students grow, mobile devices will continue to evolve and improve; fluency with mobile devices is a vital skill to succeed in the future.

The information presented on a mobile device is also more likely to be up-to-date than sources such as a textbook. By refreshing content as necessary, apps are better positioned to offer the most current information. Consider using *Google Maps* versus a printed atlas. Aside from allowing students to virtually roam through streets (and even inside some buildings) and zoom in and out at will, Google updates and expands their images and data constantly. For example, *Google Maps* proved to be a useful tool to analyze current events during the recent border crisis between Ukraine and Crimea. Seemingly in sync with the debate, Google updated their maps with a line delineating the disputed border.[43]

SECURE

There are many concerns about the security of mobile devices. Their portability makes them easy to leave behind, and they often contain large amounts of personal or sensitive data—a significant threat to student privacy. However, for this reason mobile platforms have been designed to be even more secure than traditional desktop computers.[44]

For example, many mobile devices ship with specific protections against loss and theft. It is easy for IT staff and app developers to require that users set up a password on the device before they are able to use features that would make sensitive information available. Requiring a password before a student can even enter sensitive information ensures that once the information is stored on the device, it cannot be easily accessed by any other individual. Additionally, GPS tracking can help locate devices (*Find My iPhone* does just this), and device management systems can be set to identify atypical or malicious activities.

In general, mobile devices tend to also mitigate concerns regarding malware attacks as compared to desktop and laptop computers. One reason for this is that mobile devices are often updated more regularly, meaning they have the latest security protocols to protect users and their information. By utilizing device management systems, school technology specialists can force operating system and app updates for school-issued devices. Apple's iOS is particularly secure; it is estimated that only 0.7 percent of all mobile malware poses a threat to Apple devices.[45] For schools managing many devices, this is a huge benefit.

CONCLUSION

As most teachers we've interviewed have suggested, we agree that there certainly is something different about mobile devices. While mobile devices enable the above 10 factors, the biggest perk is something bigger than any device: mobile learning. Sure, the devices are shiny, exciting, and state of the art, but what we think is the most exciting thing about them is all of the realities they bring to the classroom. Instead of *learning about* classroom material and the world around us, mobile devices afford students the opportunity to *learn within*, using the device in new and unprecedented ways every day. Today's classrooms are patently different from what classrooms were even 10 years ago, and updating pedagogy, classroom practices, and expectations is necessary. There are myriad ways to make mobile devices tools in the modern classroom, and even more ways to make education more relevant and engaging for students. Ultimately, it's not about what the devices offer; it's about how they change the learning environment and experience for the student.

NOTES

1. C. C. Chou, L. Block, and R. Jesness, "A Case Study of Mobile Learning Pilot Project in K–12 Schools," *Journal of Educational Technology Development and Exchange* 5, no. 2 (2012): 11–26.
2. Amy Wilkinson, kindergarten teacher, Washington GT Elementary, Raleigh, NC, interview with authors, April 9, 2014.
3. Eden Dahlstrom, Tom de Boor, Peter Grunwald, and Martha Vockley, *ECAR National Study of Undergraduate Students and Information Technology, 2011*, EDUCAUSE Center for Applied Research, October 2011, www.educause.edu/library/resources/ecar -national-study-undergraduate-students-and-information-technology-2011%C3 %A2%E2%82%AC%E2%80%9Dslide-presentation.
4. Chou Block, and Jesness, "A Case Study of Mobile Learning."
5. Project Tomorrow, "National Release of Speak Up 2013 National Findings: 2014 Congressional Briefing Recording," April 8, 2014, www.tomorrow.org/speakup/2013 StudentFindings_CB_recording.html.

6. Julie Stern, sixth grade language arts teacher at East Cary Middle School, Cary, NC, interview with authors, April 22, 2014.

7. Jenna Levy and Preety Sidhu, "In the U.S., 21st Century Skills Linked to Work Success," May 30, 2013, www.gallup.com/poll/162818/21st-century-skills -linked-work-success.aspx.

8. Project K-nect NC, www.projectknect.org/Project%20K-Nect/Home.html. Accessed June 26, 2014.

9. Chou and Jessness, "A Case Study of Mobile Learning," 20.

10. Apptivities, "Social Learning with Digital Trading Cards and Bump," August 30, 2013, www.apptivities.org/?p=143.

11. Katherine Schulten, "What 'Connected Education' Looks Like: 28 Examples From Teachers All Over," *New York Times* online, The Learning Network, October 1, 2013, http://learning.blogs.nytimes.com/2013/10/01/what-connected-education-looks -like-28-examples-from-teachers-all-over/.

12. National Geographic, "Harness the Power of Wind," environment.national geographic.com/environment/global-warming/wind-power-interactive/.

13. Schulten, "What 'Connected Education' Looks Like."

14. Chou, "A Case Study of Mobile Learning," 19.

15. Linnea Czerney, STEM K–1 coordinator, technology coordinator, Brentwood Elementary, Raleigh, NC, personal interview, August 22, 2013.

16. Project Tomorrow, "National Release of Speak Up 2013."

17. Stern, interview.

18. Project Tomorrow, "National Release of Speak Up 2013."

19. Jamie Hall, interview with authors, May 2, 2014.

20. Sean Russell, second grade teacher, Brentwood Elementary, Raleigh, NC, interview with authors, August 22, 2013.

21. Rebecca Goddard, technology facilitator at Rowan-Salisbury Schools, NC, interview with authors, May 5, 2014.

22. M. Schneps, J. Ruel, G. Sonnert, M. Dussault, M. Griffin, and P. Sadler, "Conceptualizing Astronomical Scale: Virtual Simulations on Handheld Tablet Computers Reverse Misconceptions," *Computers & Education* 70 (2014): 269–280.

23. Ibid.

24. State Farm Insurance, www.statefarm.com/customer-care/download-mobile-apps/ driver-feedback-for-iphone.

25. Brentwood teachers' interview, Brentwood Elementary, Raleigh, NC, interview with authors, August 22, 2013.

26. Chou, "A Case Study of Mobile Learning," 20.

27. Park Tudor School, "Learning and Creating with iPads in Kindergarten," www .youtube.com/watch?v=Y5b6y7DJuYk.

28. Students' Video, "Metamorphosis," www.vimeo.com/32850366.

29. Mary Madden, Amanda Lenhart, Maeve Duggan, Sandra Cortesi, and Urs Gasser, *Teens and Technology 2013*, Pew Research, March 13, 2013, www.pewinternet.org/ 2013/03/13/teens-and-technology-2013/.

30. Rebecca Goddard, technology facilitator, Rowan-Salisbury schools, interview with authors, May 5, 2014.

31. Brentwood interview.

32. Apple, iOS 7 Design Resources, 2014, https://developer.apple.com/design/#//apple _ref/doc/uid/TP40013289.

33. Sakshat Virtual Labs, "Consistency and Inconsistency in Interaction," http://iitg .vlab.co.in/?sub=72&brch=170&sim=862&cnt=1.

34. MinecraftEDU, www.minecraftedu.com. Accessed 6/26/14.

35. Ken Robinson, "How Schools Kill Creativity," February 2006, www.ted.com/talks/ ken_robinson_says_schools_kill_creativity.

36. Chou, "A Case Study of Mobile Learning," 19.

37. Project K-nect NC.

38. Project Tomorrow, "National Release of Speak Up 2013."

39. Apptivities.org.

40. Carly Shuler, "Pockets of Potential: Using Mobile Technologies to Promote Children's Learning," The Joan Ganz Cooney Center, New York, January 2009, www .joanganzcooneycenter.org/wp-content/uploads/2010/03/pockets_of_potential_1 _.pdf.

41. Gallup, "21st Century Skills and the Workplace."

42. Brentwood interview.

43. Tess Vigeland, "With Crimean Borders in Dispute, Google Maps Has It Both Ways," *National Public Radio*, April 12, 2014, www.npr.org/2014/04/12/301795703/with -crimean-borders-in-dispute-google-maps-has-it-both-ways.

44. Chad Udell, "10 Reasons Why Mobile Learning Is More Secure Than Desktop Learning," *Float Learning*, June 10, 2013, http://floatlearning.com/2013/06/10-reasons -why-mobile-learning-is-more-secure-than-desktop-learning/.

45. Department of Homeland Security, "Public Intelligence Bulletin: Threats to Mobile Devices Using the Android Operating System," July 23, 2013, http:// publicintelligence.net/dhs-fbi-android-threats/.

CHAPTER 4

Creating the Mobile Classroom

rguments for the educational use of mobile devices are abundant. They have been credited for inspiring motivation, promoting self-confidence, supporting science, technology, engineering, and mathematics (STEM) learning, and overall academic achievement.[1,2] However, mobile devices are not magic bullets, and putting mobile into practice should not be done hastily. A truly mobile classroom does not treat mobile devices as an add-on or supplement but rather as a fully integrated necessity for instruction and learning. And mastery of technology integration is not universal, as there are stark differences among teachers when it comes to technology integration and even technology tolerance.[3] In this chapter, we discuss considerations for optimizing the use of mobile by redefining traditional instructional methods in a variety of settings.

Education expert Michael Horn offers a good baseline for the implementation of a mobile learning program within a school. Acknowledging that devices are not the solution in and of themselves, he argues technology is simply a single component among a host of other fundamental changes for improving learning. In fact, Horn's model suggests that when implementing a blended learning environment, schools should first conceptualize the rally cry and measurable learning outcomes. From there, identify the team—leadership, stakeholders, agents, and so on—and quantify current levels of student and teacher experience related to this initiative. *Then*, consider technology as a potential aspect of the overall solution. Purchasing and distributing devices should never mark the beginning of a mobile learning initiative; successful technology integrations occur only after careful planning, strategy, and continuous refinement.[4] In this chapter we explore how mobile learning implies diligent reconstruction of learning theories and what this looks like across various settings.

THEORETICAL FOUNDATIONS

Successful technology integration does not happen overnight. From professional development to daily instruction, curricula must not be simply modified, they must be reimagined. Knowing how to simply use a mobile device does not necessarily mean one can effectively use a mobile device to teach. Educational Psychologists Punya Mishra and Matt Koehler suggest successful technology integration hinges on a combination of teachers' technology, pedagogy, and content knowledge (TPACK), as outlined in their popular TPACK framework.[5] As seen in Figure 4.1, when it comes to designing instruction, knowledge of technology, pedagogy, and content can interplay at various levels. For example, teachers' technological pedagogical knowledge (TPK) implies creativity in the way technology is used for instruction; however, this intersection omits the role content plays on lesson planning—for instance, consideration of the constraints the content might have on how technology can be used for instruction.[6] At the heart of the TPACK model lies "the basis of effective teaching with technology, requiring an understanding of the representation of concepts using technologies, pedagogical techniques that use technologies in constructive ways to teach content, knowledge of what makes concepts difficult or easy to learn, and how technology can help redress some of the problems that students face, knowledge of students' prior knowledge and theories of epistemology, and knowledge of how technologies can be used to build on existing knowledge to develop new epistemologies or strengthen old ones."[7] Therefore, when designing mobile learning lessons, teachers should consider how they have integrated each of these areas and refine accordingly.

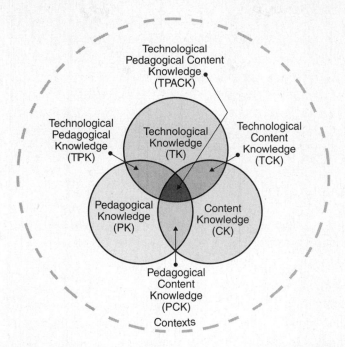

Figure 4.1 The TPACK Model. Source: *Reproduced by permission of the publisher,* ©2012 by http://tpack.org.

Similarly, the educational technology guru, Ruben Puentedura, uses the SAMR (substitution, augmentation, modification, redefinition) model, which provides another nice theoretical framework for technology integration (see Figure 4.2). On one end of the spectrum, technology is used to enhance the lesson by capitalizing on various components of the device (e.g., using a digital textbook or utilizing a multimedia presentation). For the most part, technology is retrofitted into previously designed lessons that are used as either a substitute or slight augmentation of a previous resource. At the other end, technology is used to transform learning by fostering deep understanding and engagement through higher-order thinking and constructivist-style activities (e.g., having students create a video to demonstrate their understanding)—lessons that would not be possible without the mobile device. In these cases, technology is used to fundamentally modify a lesson or redefine a lesson altogether. All the while, however, pedagogy and content are equally weighted in terms of

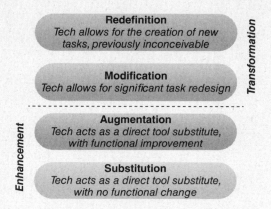

Figure 4.2 The SAMR Model. Source: *Image created by Dr. Ruben Puentedura, www.hippasus.com/rrpweblog/archives/2014/08/22/SAMRInPractice.pdf.*

value and importance. Through his analysis of educational technology implementations, Puentedura argues that as lessons shift along the spectrum—for example, from augmentation to modification—there are greater opportunities for learning.[8]

INSTRUCTIONAL METHODS

As presented through the theoretical models of technology integration, a great benefit of mobile technology is the ability to complement instructional methods, but this benefit comes only through careful consideration. Based on the content and available technologies, certain instructional methods might prove better than others. Moreover, using a variety of teaching styles not only keeps daily activities from becoming stale, but also provides students with the opportunity to develop a repertoire of strategies for learning in any environment—a valuable skill for life-long learning and success. In the following section, we will discuss advantages of and methods for implementing mobile into several common instructional methods.

Traditional Instruction

For centuries, lecture-based, teacher-led instruction has dominated the world of education. Think early twentieth-century schoolhouse:

the teacher is speaking up front, occasionally scribbling on the chalkboard, as the students write frantically at their desks. While this method has been supplemented with more active, student-centric approaches, a quick walk down the hallways of many schools today will tell you the traditional lecture still has a presence in education. Since there is still a place for direct instruction, this old-school style can at least be made more effective and engaging with some mobile enhancements.

Digital note-taking is perhaps the most obvious application of mobile for lecture-based instruction. Popular apps such as *Evernote*, *Google Drive*, and *inClass* are great for taking digital notes and provide tools beyond the traditional notebook, such as adding voice/video recordings and images/photos. By aggregating all your work into one space, a bulky collection of notebooks with ripped and missing pages is no longer necessary, and cross-discipline connections and analyses are more easily prompted. Additionally, these cloud-based systems eliminate the "I forgot my notebook" excuse by providing immediate access across platforms and devices. More importantly, cloud-based functionalities allow teachers to share templates and examples and provide feedback to students learning how to take efficient, organized notes without collecting a pile of notebooks.

Audio/video recorders or conferencing apps are also great supplements to a lecture. Conferencing and screen-sharing apps are especially advantageous for students with visual or hearing impairments. For example, the *Join.Me* app allows the teacher to share a Smart-Board screen with the students' mobile device. Instead of looking back and forth between the board and notes, students can keep their focus on the mobile device. Students with visual impairments can zoom in on the content or increase the contrast while students with hearing impairments can increase the volume of the lecture through the use of headphones. Moreover, creating a recording of a lecture allows absent students and those with questions during homework to refer back to the in-class material.

Lastly, mobile devices can easily be integrated to promote student participation and assess levels of understanding. Nonverbal response systems, such as Twitter, are wonderful tools, especially for the more introverted student. For example, second-grade teacher Sean Russell remembers using the *GoSoapbox* application in a lecture, which allows for students to send questions during a video using their iPod touch devices. For him, it helps to raise the levels of engagement in the class. It can be transformative for some students, though. He mentioned Erin, a child who was a selective mute. He was amazed when one day she asked her very first question in class, using *GoSoapbox*. For her, the forum made the difference and literally gave her a voice.[9] Many systems also allow for back channeling that encourages class participation without the intimidation or humiliation associated with speaking in front of the class. Polling or quizzing apps, like *Poll Everywhere* or *Socrative*, present students with questions posed by the teacher during the lecture. Similarly, discussion platforms, such as *Padlet*, provide students with an online, collaborative discussion space. The benefits of such back channeling are threefold:

1. Students can monitor and calibrate their current level of understanding.

2. Students take on a more active role and are more likely to remain engaged and attentive.

3. Teachers can use the data to make informed reflections about the lecture (e.g., specific trouble areas, variance in affect throughout the lecture).

Blended and Flipped Classrooms

Blended learning is an overarching, categorical term for instruction that incorporates, at least to some degree, online content. The theoretical benefit of a blended approach is the opportunity for student-led, personalized learning. Moving away from the one-size-fits-all model for education, supplementing instruction with online content allows students to engage with concepts of interest at their own pace and find resources that fit their needs and interests. And, with the proliferation of high-quality online and open learning resources, blended instruction is rapidly growing in popularity. In fact, in 2009, over 3 million K–12 students took an online class, and it is projected that by 2019 approximately 50 percent of high school courses will be delivered online.[10]

Similarly, flipped classrooms, a trending and empirically proven[11] subset of blended learning, focus on integrating technology in order to capitalize on the higher-level learning that can occur during student-instructor time. After surveying 403,000 K–12 students, teachers, and other stakeholders, Project Tomorrow and the Flipped Learning Network found one out of six math and science teachers have implemented a flipped classroom model, and 75 percent of students feel it is a good way for them to learn.[12] Using learning theories as a foundation,[13] flipped learning occurs when classroom structures are switched so the student is presented with foundational material outside of school and takes part in more collaborative, interactive, and creative exercises during actual class time. According to the Flipped Learning Network, flipped classrooms can be characterized with four pillars that manifest as:

1. Flexible environments that support a wide variety of instructional and assessment methods that easily adapt to leverage the dynamics of the classroom activity.

2. A shift in learning culture that positions students as the driving force of learning with teachers taking on a more supportive role.

3. An active learning environment that utilizes classroom activities as a vehicle for engaging deeply with content beyond surface-level presentations of skills and concepts.

4. Pedagogy proctored by trained, professional educators with experience and expertise in optimizing conceptual understanding and promoting higher-order cognitive processing.[14]

Under this paradigm, a typical homework assignment would involve students watching an instructional video (e.g., prerecorded teacher lecture, prerecorded expert lecture, educational video, lessons from resources like Khan Academy). This allows each student to learn at their own pace and repeat sections if needed. They can also skip over material they have already mastered, creating a more efficient, personalized environment. An added benefit to this method is the opportunity for inclusion of the parents, giving them a greater understanding of the subject their child is learning about and opportunity to help, and even learn something new. Also, this method keeps the teacher as the center of the content delivery (as opposed to outsourcing with open resources online), preserving the teacher–student relationship and trust.

In class, students work with their instructor and classmates on activities that require students to generate their own understanding by engaging deeply with the material and guiding their own learning—lessons that involve skills beyond those outlined by the curriculum, such as collaboration, creativity, problem solving, and critical thinking. Moreover, as students demonstrate their understanding through classroom activities, the instructor is present to quickly catch and clarify any misconceptions or trouble areas, thereby ensuring a productive use of time. By flipping the class, time with the instructor becomes more opportune than the more passive presentation of information that has traditionally occupied class time. In Figure 4.3, the differences in homework and classwork are illustrated.

Figure 4.3 The Flipped Classroom

While blending and flipped learning demonstrate unique opportunities for transforming education, these styles of instruction rely
heavily on technology—a requirement that yields a host of challenges.
Flipping the classroom, at least initially, requires a lot of work on the
teacher's part. Teachers have to rework their entire set of lesson plans
and method of teaching. It can also feel like a dramatic departure
from the way they are used to doing their job.[15] However, the built-in
functionalities of mobile devices and a flood of handy apps available
for download serve to mitigate these limitations making this style of
instruction far more feasible.

Creating, Deploying, and Viewing Videos

Perhaps the most time consuming component of deploying a flipped
classroom model is finding or creating videos for at-home instruction.
However, the features of mobile devices can significantly reduce
this effort. Apps such as *ShowMe*, *Knowmia Teach*, and *Educreations*
are useful tools for creating videos. Using the built-in microphone
and touch screen, teachers can quickly make videos on the fly by
narrating a lesson and recording a screen capture of themselves
writing on the provided whiteboard. Some systems utilize the camera
feature and allow teachers to record a video of themselves teaching to
simulate the personalization of face-to-face instruction. Cloud-based
backup makes saving and sharing videos simple, taking much of the
difficulty of sharing large files away. Finally, another practical option
for deploying videos is utilizing open educational resources—reduce,
reuse, recycle. Highly reputable, mobile-friendly web resources, such
as Khan Academy, have a wealth of short, single-topic lectures that
can be easily linked to for home access.

Students' mobile devices also mitigate the limitations of accessing
videos at home. Built-in audio and video capabilities and general portability make viewing videos an anytime, anywhere activity. Students
are not constrained to a specific location and can view videos in their
typical studying location. Additionally, 71 percent of teens say "the
computer they use most often is shared with other family members,"[16]
but 71 percent of children (ages 2 to 10) have access to a smartphone
at home, and 74 percent of teens (ages 12 to 17) report using mobile
devices to access the Internet at home;[17] therefore, mobile devices

provide a solution to watching videos at home for students fighting for access to home computers.

Other great mobile tools for students are video annotation apps that allow students to take notes while watching videos—all within the same space. Tools such as *Video Note* automatically sync with *Google Drive* as an added level of convenience. Using this feature, teachers can view students' comments prior to class and use them to inform lesson plans. Video annotations are also a great way to ensure students are completing their homework assignments. Experienced flipped classroom teachers suggest easing students into the flipped process by viewing a few videos in class and teaching students how to engage with the video lectures. These tutorial videos create opportunities for teaching students how to effectively use note-taking tools and prepare for classroom activities. And, with mobile, students can directly apply instruction since they learn on the same device they will use later.

Classroom Activities/Simulations/Tools

With an abundance of high-quality, technology-based interactive lessons available, mobile devices are a great tool for facilitating active classroom activities that encourage automatizing skills and processes, the construction of knowledge, and the application of content while also increasing motivation. In a flipped classroom model, class time is reserved for developing and inspiring higher-order thinking and engaging deeply with the targeted material. Furthermore, as discussed in Chapter 5, mobile learning is highly equipped for accomplishing this type of instruction. From moderating effective collaboration to field-based, experiential learning, mobile devices support the active learner.

Also, the proliferation of simulation and tool-based apps available for mobile devices has significantly stretched the boundaries of in-class activities. Apps like *Frog Dissection* allow students to participate in laboratory-like sessions in a more practical manner—especially for low-income schools with minimal budgets, equipment, and space. Moreover, *3D Brain*, which allows users to explore the brain, and other simulation apps let students experiment with concepts otherwise unattainable in the classroom. Social studies tools like *Time Maps* and *Google Maps* give students access to relevant maps to help visualize concepts. Also, tools such as *Things to Think About, SAS InContext, SAS*

Writing Reviser, and *Popplet* make brainstorming and planning more efficient; therefore, time with the instructor can be more focused on constructive feedback on student-generated material.

PROBLEM-BASED, INQUIRY-BASED, AND EXPERIENTIAL LEARNING

For teachers designing lessons for inquiry or experiential learning, the portability and features of mobile provide a powerful supplement. As discussed in Chapter 2 and later in Chapter 5, learning is optimized when students generate and construct their own knowledge.[18] As opposed to surface-level, rote memorization, inquiry-based learning encourages students to engage deeply with the material, by analyzing and synthesizing the foundational components that allow for transfer of the material to new situations, authentic scenarios, and across domains.[19] While this style of instruction can be quite time-consuming and difficult to administer, mobile devices serve to eliminate some of the outstanding barriers.

One prominent concern with inquiry-based instruction is the dependency on appropriate, just-in-time scaffolding. Posing an open-ended, problem-solving scenario can be extremely inefficient, if not detrimental, if the student does not have the prerequisite knowledge and skills to solve the problem.[20] Moreover, limitations of the classroom, such as access to tools or materials, can impede the authenticity of the inquiry process. For example, challenging students in chemistry to experiment with various chemical compounds is not only impractical, but highly dangerous.

Instead, instructors can utilize apps such as Harvard's *EcoMOBILE*, *Leafsnap*, and apps for geocaching. *EcoMOBILE* puts the power of inquiry at students' fingertips as they explore actual pond ecosystems around their school. Posed with a scientific mystery prompt, students can document their exploration and gather clues on the go using the built-in GPS, camera, and microphone. Using mobile-compatible environmental probes, students can collect data on the water composition and quality. Similarly, *Mentira*, a Spanish-language learning activity, provides an authentic learning experience for students. Utilizing an augmented reality mobile app, students are tasked with solving a murder mystery in a Spanish-speaking neighborhood in Albuquerque, NM. Students must gather clues by interviewing native language speakers and translate written resources. In sum, these apps serve as inquiry scaffolds aiding the student in forming a hypothesis, collecting relevant evidence, analyzing the data, and drawing conclusions. The experience becomes an explicit application of abstract concepts fostering connections between educational material and the real world.

Augmented reality apps like *Elements 4D* and *StarWalk* provide access to otherwise unattainable experiences. With *Elements 4D* students can safely see the visual representation of each element, but more importantly, they can combine elements, view the resulting chemical equation, and see how they react. Similarly, *StarWalk* presents visual support for the generally hard-to-grasp, abstract concepts of space. Without the use of expensive telescopes, each student can simply hold their device up to the sky and see the location, physical attributes, and movement of planets, stars, and satellites.

Through creative app stacking, almost any problem-based activity can be accomplished efficiently with a single mobile device. Want students to make a movie? They can shoot, edit, narrate, and annotate an entire short film on the same device. Want students to experiment with Newton's laws? Give them a soccer ball and a GPS-enabled mobile device, and they can run experiments, collect data, and document their findings in the palm of their hand. Unbound by the restrictions of paper and pencil and computer cables, mobile learning juxtaposes the power of technology with our innate knack for exploration to produce irreplaceable opportunities for deep, meaningful learning.

ALTERNATIVE LEARNING ENVIRONMENTS

Referring back to the TPACK framework, the dotted line surrounding the model implies that "technology, pedagogy, and content do not exist in a vacuum, but rather, are instantiated in a specific learning and teaching contexts."[21] Therefore, a successful mobile implementation strategy must also consider where it is being deployed. The majority of our discussion is centered on the common, brick-and-mortar school setting; however, mobile integration also fits nicely into alternative learning environments such as home and virtual schools. Aside from the benefits for supporting learning and higher-level engagement discussed throughout this chapter and book, there are specific ways to leverage mobile for alternative environments.

Virtual School

Virtual schools, where students learn exclusively using online classes and curricula, have seen increasing prominence. With greater access to technology and online educational resources, virtual schools provide a viable alternative to traditional school for students with disabilities, students with demanding schedules such as semi-professional athletes and musicians, and students seeking greater challenge through higher-quality school districts or college-level courses. Again, mobile devices provide great promise in mitigating the current limitations of virtual schools.

For students with disabilities, the conventions of brick-and-mortar schools—noisy classrooms, sitting quietly for long periods of time, and so on—can trigger certain behaviors that might be disruptive and make learning challenging for everyone. However, the feasibility of virtual schools as an alternative solution is highly dependent on the accessibility of the curriculum.[22] As discussed in depth in Chapter 14, mobile affords several unique accessibility functionalities for special populations—support for screen readers, Braille input, and nonverbal communication just to name a few.

Also, through the combination of mobile integration and virtual schools, ruining a weekend or cutting into a summer break with school make-up days is no longer necessary. Instead of cancelling school due to adversities such as weather, students can attend virtual school from the safety of their home via home technologies or school-issued devices. Devastating storms such as 2012's Hurricane Sandy, 2009's Hurricane Katrina, and even 2013–2014's unusually snowy winter, quickly use up a school district's allotted inclement weather days; therefore, 1:1 technology schools like Pascack Valley Regional High School in New Jersey have implemented virtual school days to avoid the dreaded make-up days.[23] Teachers can easily facilitate lessons, assign and collect work, and provide feedback using online resources and mobile apps just as they would in the classroom.

Finally, the portability aspect of mobile makes these devices a great tool for both students and parents. For most students, the success of virtual school relies heavily on parental involvement. With mobile devices, parents can stay up-to-date on progress and performance in real-time without sitting next to the student as they complete class-work. Also, students can easily communicate with teachers, parents, and academic coaches through mobile communication for immediate feedback and support with features such as video conferencing, phone calls, and text messaging. Lastly, mobile technologies provide anytime, anywhere access to virtual school curricula for students with demanding schedules and travel constraints, so students on the road can stay caught up on their studies.

Homeschool

Similar to virtual schools, homeschool settings provide a useful alternative to traditional school for many students—approximately 1.77 million American students in 2011–2012.[24] Homeschooling can be controversial. Arguments surrounding issues such as socialization, instructor expertise for higher-level subjects, and underrepresentation of subjects and teaching styles are often voiced when discussing the pros and cons of homeschooling. While people often refute these claims with effective solutions, mobile technologies can also serve to alleviate such concerns and perhaps enhance a homeschool environment. For those who choose to homeschool their children, mobile devices can provide a valuable opportunity to access extensive critical content, use standardized appropriate learning resources, and engage in collaborative learning.

Arguably, mobile devices have made us more social than ever before. Although not face-to-face, many of us are in constant communication with others in one form or another. By establishing connections with other students through homeschool networks, mobile devices and their various apps are a great way to develop collaboration and communication skills. Moreover, through apps such as *FaceTime* and

Table 4.1 Integration Levels by Environment

Environment	Task	Substitution	Augmentation	Modification	Redefinition
Traditional, direct instruction	Note Taking	Students take notes on their device.	Students use a note-taking app or guide to scaffold their note taking.	Students use cloud storage to take their notes so they can access them anywhere.	Students create and share mind maps using *Showbie* to demonstrate their understanding of the material.
	Lecture	Present PowerPoint slides with the device.	Students follow along by pulling up the presentation on their own device.	Teacher uses *Poll Everywhere* to access students' understanding and refine the presentation accordingly.	Students live tweet during a presentation using *Twitter*.
Flipped	Remote Lecture	Watch videos at home on their mobile devices.	Watch videos and take notes in a different app.	Students use app to collaborate on their annotations in real time from their own home.	Students collaborate to create their own videos for one another.
Problem Based	Problem Solving	Students use digital textbooks for research.	Students use the Internet to research.	Students collect real data around the classroom or outside and share their results.	Students create a multimedia presentation using their device.
Virtual and Homeschool	Student Presentation.	Students create a final project presentation on their device.	Students present their final project presentation to other students using Skype.	Students create presentations collaboratively.	Students make their own multimedia websites that provide an overview of the project.

Join.Me, homeschool students can practice the art of public speaking by presenting projects to a virtual audience, participating in live debates with other students, and delivering speeches. Similar to the flipped classroom approach, homeschool parents from across the country can also team together and co-teach to take advantage of individual areas of expertise while also exposing students to a variety of teaching styles.

CONCLUSION

Using theoretical models as a guide, successful integrations of mobile devices do not mean retrofitting existing lessons but, instead, redefining them in terms of student participation and scope. Therefore, mobile learning does not mean having students complete the same worksheet as before on their devices; it means creating innovative lessons that would otherwise be impossible without mobile devices by taking advantage of their many capabilities and features. As shown in Table 4.1, enhancing and transforming lessons with mobile devices—as defined by the SAMR model—is possible in all of the environments discussed in this chapter. However, this does not mean teachers need to abandon proven, effective instructional methods. Pedagogical knowledge is instead juxtaposed with creativity with technology and content expertise to define new ways of promoting active participation. As discussed throughout this chapter, mobile devices create new opportunities to enhance traditional methods in order to further engage students with the content in a variety of formal learning environments.

NOTES

1. Joshua Bolkan, "Report: Middle School Students Using Smartphones More Interested in STEM," *The Journal* (November 29, 2012), http://thejournal.com/articles/2012/11/29/report-middle-school-students-using-smartphones-more-interested-in-stem.aspx

2. Project Tomorrow, "Project K-Nect Mobile Learning Initiative Creates Personalized Learning Environments for Math Students in Onslow County School System," April 2012, www.tomorrow.org/publications/ProjectKnect.html.

3. "2014 National Survey on Mobile Technology for K–12 Education," *Amplify*, http://go.amplify.com/2014-mobile-report.

4. Michael B. Horn presentation at iNacol conference, November 7, 2014. Slides at www.slideshare.net/DreamBoxLearning/blended-learning-in-k8-schools-expert-advice-from-michael-horn.

5. P. Mishra and M. J. Koehler, "Technological Pedagogical Content Knowledge: A New Framework for Teacher Knowledge," *Teachers College Record* 108, no. 6 (2006): 1017–1054.

6. M. J. Koehler, P. Mishra, and W. Cain, "What Is Technological Pedagogical Content Knowledge (TPACK)?," *Journal of Education* 193, no. 3 (2013): 13–20.

7. Ibid.

8. Ruben Puentedura, "SAMR: An Applied Introduction," January 31, 2014, www .hippasus.com/rrpweblog/archives/014/01/31/SAMRAnAppliedIntroduction.pdf.

9. Sean Russell, Brentwood Elementary School, Raleigh, NC, interview with authors, August 22, 2013.

10. Knewton, "Blended Learning Infographic," www.knewton.com/blended-learning. Accessed July 17, 2014.

11. N. Hamdan, P. McKnight, K. McKnight, and K. M. Arfstrom, "A Review of Flipped Learning," Flipped Learning Network (2013), www.flippedlearning.org/cms/lib07/ VA01923112/Centricity/Domain/41/LitReview_FlippedLearning.pdf.

12. Project Tomorrow, "Speak Up 2013 National Research Project Findings: A Second Year Review of Flipped Learning," 2014, www.tomorrow.org/speakup/2014 _FlippedLearningReport.html.

13. Hamdan, McKnight, McKnight, and Arfstrom, "A Review of Flipped Learning."

14. Ibid.

15. Associated Press, "Teachers Flip for 'Flipped Learning' Class Model," *USA Today*, January 29, 2013, www.usatoday.com/story/tech/nation/2013/01/27/flipped -learning-class/1868733/.

16. Mary Madden, Amanda Lenhart, Maeve Duggan, Sandra Cortesi, and Urs Gasser, "Teens and Technology 2013," www.pewinternet.org/2013/03/13/teens-and -technology-2013.

17. Ibid.

18. John D. Bransford, Ann L. Brown, and Rodney Cocking, eds., *How People Learn: Brain, Mind, Experience, and School* (Washington, DC: National Academies Press, 1999).

19. R. D. Anderson, "Reforming Science Teaching: What Research Says About Inquiry," *Journal of Science Teacher Education* 13, no. 1 (2002): 1–12.

20. P. A. Kirschner, J. Sweller, and R. E. Clark, "Why Minimal Guidance During Instruction Does Not Work: An Analysis of the Failure of Constructivist, Discovery, Problem-Based, Experiential, and Inquiry-Based Teaching," *Educational Psychology* 41, no. 2: 75–86.

21. MJ Koehler, P. Mishra, and W. Cain, "What Is TPACK?," 13–20.

22. Katie Ash, "Educators Weigh Benefits, Drawbacks of Virtual Special Ed.," *Education Week* (2010), www.edweek.org/dd/articles/2010/06/16/03speed.h03.html.

23. Al Baker, "Snow Day? That's Great. Now Log in. Get to Class," 2014, *New York Times*, www.nytimes.com/2014/02/14/nyregion/snow-day-thats-great-now-log-in-get-to -class.html?_r=0.

24. A. Noel, P. Stark, J. Redford, and A. Zuckerberg, "Parent and Family Involvement in Education," National Household Education Surveys Program of 2012, National Center for Education Statistics, 2013.

CHAPTER **5**

Higher-Order Thinking Skills and Digital Fluency

Higher-order thinking skills encompass behaviors associated with how we productively utilize our knowledge. Productive, real-world skills such as thinking critically about information, applying factual and procedural knowledge to efficiently solve problems, effectively communicating and collaborating with others, and conceiving creative ideas are ways to engage in deeper learning. However, after surveying over 400 employers, the Partnership for 21st Century Skills found a frightening consensus that the majority of high-school graduates are deficient in writing, mathematics, and reading comprehension as well as skills such as critical thinking and problem solving.[1] In a recent poll by Microsoft, 59 percent of employed Americans aged 18 to 35 agree that the majority of the skills they use every day were learned outside of school.[2] In sum, there exists an alarming gap in the ideal and reality when it comes to preparing our students for today's workforce.

Higher-order thinking skills are critical for thriving in today's digitally-connected society. The Assessment and Teaching of 21st Century Skills (AT21CS) is a research project that advocates for greater adoption of teaching higher-order thinking skills. They categorize these skills as ways of thinking (e.g., creativity, problem solving); ways of working (e.g., communication, collaboration); tools for working (e.g., content knowledge, digital fluency); and living in the world (citizenship, cultural awareness).[3] While it is important, arguably obligatory, to acquire content knowledge (i.e., a business leader might study economics or marketing), the way in which it is constructed and, consequently, how it is applied to new situations are the skills that make us marketable. In fact, according to a recent ranking by *Forbes*, the most desirable skills of today's workforce are critical thinking, complex problem solving, judgment and decision-making, and active listening. These skills beat out sales and marketing experience, programming fluency, and proficiency with computer and electronics.[4] What separates experts from innovators is not content knowledge, but rather their fluency in higher-order thinking.

However, despite the demand and utility of higher-order thinking skills, results from the 2012 ACT indicate only 25 percent of tested high-school students demonstrated sufficient mastery in English, reading, mathematics, and science for success in college and beyond.[5] Moreover, after surveying over 400 employers, the Partnership for 21st Century Skills found employers agreed. In sum, there exists a significant gap in the ideal and reality when it comes to preparing our students for today's workforce.

Demand for deeper engagement with classroom material is in the heart of educators as well. In a recent *New York Times* interview regarding the state of science education in America, a group of 19 scientists, educators, and students almost unanimously pointed to the need for authentic, active learning.[6] Some made comments such as, "They should learn how to be an applied problem solver, which is not the same thing as being a fantastic book-based equation solver," "Real science happens when you are immersed in a question," and "We want [students] to see what science and math can do when they are used by a creative mind"; others praised the value of internships within the community, mentorships, and bringing in experts for exposure to potential careers and real-life applications for classroom material. One high school senior dreamed of "more hands-on projects where I would learn something about what I'm doing instead of just memorizing things from a textbook." Another senior complained, "One of the problems I have during math class is not understanding the reasoning behind what we are doing. The teacher will put something on the board and say, 'This is how you do it,' and I'm thinking, 'Why does that make sense?'"[7]

Digital fluency is a facet of higher-order thinking. We believe experience with the popular technologies of today and the more traditional representation of higher-order thinking skills have a bidirectional relationship. Technologies such as mobile devices can serve as a digital assistant for optimizing our problem-solving, critical-thinking, creativity, and communication efficacy. Furthermore, effectively utilizing technology often requires a great deal of complex cognitive processing, such as critical thinking. Given this interconnectivity and the ever-increasing pervasiveness of technology in our lives, we would be missing a critical learning opportunity by instructing twenty-first-century students without such devices. Yet, technology in the classroom has always implied great risk from off-task behaviors to more serious disciplinary infractions, which has created a great deal of apprehension and even zero-tolerance policies in schools.[8] However, we are doing students a great disservice when we restrict access to mobile devices. We should be teaching students how to leverage their devices for creative thought, problem solving, and collaboration as opposed to treating them simply as a nuisance only valuable for texting and non-educational social networking.

In this chapter, we highlight the cognitive processes underlying higher-order thinking and identify suggestions for capitalizing on mobile technology for developing these skills. Through this discussion, we pinpoint the disconnection between the traditional, lecture-style classrooms and those positioned to realize the efficacy of new, innovative curricula. Finally, we discuss strategies for mitigating the threats that come with implementing a mobile-enhanced classroom so that students graduate comprehensively prepared for college and the workforce.

HIGHER-ORDER THINKING SKILLS

When we reflect on the great innovators of the past and present, we can often apply such adjectives as creative or analytical, and categorizations such as great problem-solver or effective communicator. Innovators make their mark not only by mastering the content of a particular domain but, more importantly, by questioning, expanding upon, and/or applying such information in novel ways. The origins of everyday tools such as Liquid Paper and the stethoscope highlight this point.

> *Liquid Paper.* Bettie Nesmith Graham, an aspiring artist of the mid-twentieth century, found herself working as a secretary when the fruits of her artistic labor fell short of the needs of supporting her family. During this time, Graham inevitably made several typing errors, which at the time had no practical solution. Frustrated, Graham resolved the issue by applying her love for painting. By mixing water-based paints to match the hue of paper, Graham simply placed a dab of paint on the page effectively erasing the mistake and continued typing error-free. Ultimately, Graham went on to found her own company, Liquid Paper, which she later sold for $47.5 million in 1980.[9]
>
> *The stethoscope.* "Nineteenth-century French physician, Rene Laënnec, was confronted with an uncomfortable situation. A patient arrived in his office complaining of chest pains. At this time, physicians often employed the percussion technique, which involves tapping the chest and listening for sounds that might indicate a buildup of fluid around the heart or lungs. Unfortunately, Laënnec's patient was overweight rendering the tapping method, as you could imagine, ineffective. The young physician's second option was immediate auscultation, or pressing his ear directly to the patient's chest. However, Laënnec's patient was also female. Polite and embarrassed, Laennec began brainstorming alternatives. He quickly recalled a time when he "observed two children sending signals to each

other using a long piece of solid wood and a pin. With an ear to one end, the child received an amplified sound of the pin scratching the opposite end of the wood." Laënnec's account explains, "I then tightly rolled a sheet of paper, one end of which I placed over the precordium [chest] and my ear to the other. I was surprised and elated to be able to hear the beating of her heart with far greater clearness than I ever had with direct application of my ear."[10] Through a moment of uncomfortable panic, Laënnec's domain expertise and previous experience laid the foundation for one of the most pervasive medical innovations."[11]

Although the utility of higher-order thinking skills might seem to trump that of factual knowledge, this should not undermine its importance. A closer look at our example innovators reveals a key commonality: expertise in a particular domain. There is a reason why you do not read of Laënnec's great literary works or Graham's scientific endeavors—thinking critically or creatively demands content knowledge to think and reason about. Previously acquired knowledge and experiences provide the foundation for higher-order thinking. Cognitive scientist Daniel Willingham uses the following example to illustrate this point:

A treasure hunter is going to explore a cave up on a hill near a beach. He suspected there might be many paths inside the cave so he was afraid he might get lost. Obviously, he did not have a map of the cave; all he had with him were some common items such as a flashlight and a bag. What could he do to make sure he did not get lost trying to get back out of the cave later?
The solution is to carry some sand with you in the bag, and leave a trail as you go, so you can trace your path back when you're ready to leave the cave. About 75 percent of American college students thought of this solution—but only 25 percent of Chinese students solved it.[12] The experimenters suggested that Americans solved it because most grew up hearing the story of Hansel and Gretel, which includes the idea of leaving a trail as you travel to

an unknown place in order to find your way back. The experimenters also gave subjects another puzzle based on a common Chinese folk tale, and the percentage of solvers from each culture reversed.[13]

Therefore, while often referred to as separate entities, factual knowledge and higher-order thinking skills are highly dependent upon one another. The term "higher-order thinking skill" is derived from the additional cognitive effort it entails; effort that can require significant working memory capacity (for a review of working memory, see Chapter 2). Looking back on the discussion from Chapter 2: The Science of Learning, automatizing knowledge structures and procedures through practice creates a cognitive advantage by reducing cognitive load. Consequently, we can actively incorporate more pieces of information or process information at a deeper level—in other words, engage in higher-order thinking. For this reason, these complex cognitive skills are generally domain specific.[14] Any educator can relate to the student who demonstrates great scientific reasoning, but has difficulty when charged with critically evaluating bias in two historical documents. Therefore, as we delve into the details of specific higher-order thinking skills, keep in mind the necessity of sufficient domain expertise.

Problem Solving

Most people are faced with solving a problem every day. Sometimes problems are simple and well defined, such as solving the math problem $2 + 2$. Other times, we are tasked with more difficult, ill-defined problems like choosing a career or drafting a manuscript. Nonetheless, problems can often be solved by repeating this general model: identify the problem, define the problem, identify a strategy, implement the strategy, and evaluate the results;[15] familiarizing students with the generality of these steps can foster the development of this higher-order skill.[16] However, as concise as those five steps might seem, problem solving can be quite complicated. Effective problem solving often requires an individual to consult and apply prior knowledge and previous experiences while also attending to and evaluating progression toward the overall goal (i.e., metacognitive awareness). Furthermore, the same constructs enlisted to benefit our problem solving can also impede the process. A closer look at each step in the problem-solving process sheds light on these issues.

The Problem-Solving Process

Identify and Represent the Problem. To effectively solve a problem, you must first identify what will qualify as a solution and deconstruct the problem into concrete subproblems. With well-defined problems, the goal state is explicit; however, devising the goal state of an ill-defined problem requires additional effort. For example, completing a jigsaw puzzle has a very clearly defined goal state while the goal state is less explicit when asked to write an essay. Nonetheless, defining what will suffice as a goal state affects the remaining steps in the problem solving process.

Once the goal state has been identified, we must then represent the problem. This involves understanding the specifics of the problem. For complex problems, this might involve dissecting the problem into smaller, more manageable subproblems and synthesizing how different components of the problem interact. Also, this step entails understanding any constraints associated with the problem. Therefore, even when a problem is well defined, incorrectly representing a problem can significantly impede one's ability to reach the goal state. Take a try at solving the following scenario:

> A man standing in a room is tasked with tying together the free ends of two cords that are hanging from the ceiling. However, the cords are far enough apart that the man cannot reach the two cords at the same time. On a chair in the corner of the room lies a pair of scissors and tape. How will he tie the two cords together?

> Adapted from Birch and Rabinowitz, 1951[17]

The two-cord problem, as pictured in Figure 5.1, delineates a very explicit solution: connect the two strings. However, solvers often short-sightedly represent the objects involved in the problem—an oversight known as functional fixedness. In the two-cord problem, we often

Figure 5.1 The Two-Cord Problem

view the scissors as a tool for cutting objects, but the weight of scissors could also be used as a pendulum. To solve this problem, place the chair under one of the cords, tie the scissors to the end of the other cord, set the scissors cord in motion, run stand in the chair, catch the traveling cord, and successfully tie the two cords together. Therefore, similar to other higher-order thinking skills, problem solving requires a comprehensive understanding of the components and constraints of a problem and oftentimes, a touch of creativity and critical thinking.

Identify and Implement a Strategy. Once we have accurately understood and represented the problem at hand, we then must select and implement a strategy for solving the problem. To do so, we commonly rely on familiar heuristics and algorithms that have been successful in past experiences. Algorithms involve following a proven, finite process that ultimately leads to the desired goal state, such as mathematical theorems or cooking recipes. When problems are less defined or quantitatively represented, we often utilize heuristics as a mental shortcut or rule-of-thumb for attempting to solve a problem.

Regardless of the problem, we must be aware of strategies for solving it. When solving a novel problem, awareness of and experience with similar problems can help us transfer potential solutions; however, transferring information to new situations is generally a difficult task especially for younger children.[18] For example, we are often slow to apply complex theories and formulas learned in math class to solve real-world situations (e.g., the Pythagorean theorem); therefore, teaching concepts in context by making explicit references to authentic problems can support students' problem-solving skills (e.g., showing how the Pythagorean theorem can be used when building a tree house).

Evaluate the Results. After implementing a strategy, how do we know if the problem has been solved? With well-defined problems, evaluating results is generally less taxing. With a clearly defined goal state, comparing our results can be trivial. However, this process might be more complicated with ill-defined problems. If the problem is "write a Haiku," then judging the result involves evaluating the quality of your work by comparing it to the problem constraints (i.e., the syllable and line definitions of a Haiku) and making relative comparisons to similar results.

LEVERAGING MOBILE LEARNING

Researchers of problem-solving behaviors have identified several difficulties students face while solving problems in the classroom as well as potential solutions to these shortcomings. Such solutions often involve fostering meaningful associations between the problem and previous experiences, prior knowledge, and interests. Others attempt to reduce students' cognitive load by providing relevant resources and teaching strategies for offloading and organizing information (for a review of cognitive load, see Chapter 3). Fortunately, many of these solutions are offered through the affordances of mobile technologies.

Using external representations (e.g., graphic organizers) is an effective method for helping students define the problem space, gather and organize information, and evaluate results by significantly reducing cognitive load,[19] and they also provide a space to organize and evaluate results. The problem-solving literature often points to gestalt psychologist Karl Duncker's Monk Problem for highlighting the benefits of diagrams. In this problem, a Buddhist monk travels from his village at the base of a mountain to a temple at the top of the mountain.[20] The next day, the monk travels back down the mountain to his village, but obviously at a much faster pace. The problem is to identify a specific point in the journey where the monk was at the same place on both days. Arriving at a solution to this problem mentally is quite taxing; however, drawing a picture of the monk's journey up and then back down the mountain—the solution is more easily found. Graphing out problem constraints, creating diagrams, and building charts to analyze data are all exercises that can be performed by hand, but mobile devices make them more readily available. As demonstrated in the Monk Problem in Figure 5.2, knowing how and when to leverage such tools can dictate problem solving efficiency.

As emphasized in the previous section, students should be provided opportunities to practice problem solving in authentic scenarios. Simulations of real-world environments and/or tools attainable through mobile technologies provide an excellent platform for authentic problem solving. In controlled, simulated spaces, students are free to develop and test hypotheses without great effort (e.g., travelling to a laboratory or setting, investing in equipment) or risk. For example, researchers at Harvard have produced *EcoMOBILE*, a virtual experience for learning about pond ecosystems.[21] Through the augmented reality interface, students get to go out in the field and view data about the environment through the lens of their mobile device that would not otherwise be available in the natural environment. Also, with the device, students can take samples from the environment and run simulated analyses on the artifacts similar to the procedures followed

Figure 5.2 The Monk Problem

by actual biologists and conservationists. Likewise, mobile allows immediate access to meaningful data. Relatable information like weather patterns and census data or interest-aligned information such as record sales, Twitter analytics, and other pop culture applications are readily available for making problem solving more meaningful.

Managing and Reducing Cognitive Load Is Critical for Successfully Solving Complex Problems

- Encourage students to offload information stored in working memory and use mobile devices to create external representations when solving complex problems.
- Take advantage of mobile devices' ability to connect students to authentic, meaningful problem solving scenarios and tools.

Creativity

Left-brained, artsy, unstructured, free—on the surface, these are adjectives one might use to describe the term *creativity*. In terms of domain, people often associate creativity with the arts: painting, dance, music, or writing. Using this conceptualization, teaching and encouraging creativity in the classroom is limited to certain activities and applies only to those students with artistic talent. However, a quick survey of revolutionizing innovations reveals creativity applies to all domains and all students. Therefore, in order to effectively foster our students' creative aptitude, we must first understand the concept, which education and creativity expert, Ken Robinson, claims is clouded by three main misconceptions.[22]

First, what actually defines creativity? Einstein stated, "Creativity is seeing what others see and thinking what no one else has ever thought."[23] To generalize this definition, creativity encompasses productive, novel ideas or behaviors.[24] Therefore, an important defining feature of creativity is practicality. Randomly striking keys on a piano might fulfill the requirement of novelty, but the composition might have little meaning and add little value to society. Robinson explains "creativity is a disciplined process that requires skill, knowledge and control … It's a process, not a single event, and genuine creative processes involve critical thinking as well as imaginative insights and fresh ideas."[25] Therefore, the creative process encompasses a variety of components including content knowledge, background information, problem solving and critical thinking skills, and motivation.[26]

Second, creativity is applicable to all domains, not just the humanities. For example, consider this example from Daniel Saunders and Paul Thagard's chapter "Creativity in Computer Science"[27] —a discipline commonly associated with structured, logical thought.

> Another example of [creativity] is the invention of the first high-level language, FORTRAN, by John Backus in 1953, which allowed computer programs to be written in comprehensible, algebra-like commands instead of assembly code.[28] Assembly code consists of lists of thousands of inscrutable three-letter commands, designed to communicate with the machine at its lowest level. …

The layer of abstraction that FORTRAN placed between the underlying electronics and the human was very important to the subsequent development of computer science.

Thus, students should be encouraged and equipped with strategies to think creatively across the content areas. Teachers should encourage students to attain the common prerequisites for creativity, such as gather background information and create a safe space for creative thought. As demonstrated in the example above, students should be primed to think about how information and processes can be integrated across disciplines or challenged to understand how domain content can be applied outside of the classroom. Furthermore, it is well documented that creativity is often preceded by a series of failures, and classrooms should allow for trial and error without negative consequences.[29]

Third, everyone can be creative. Just as a talented young artist can create a beautiful, original masterpiece, a budding scientist can transfer and apply information or processes in a novel way. Although there are interesting cases of accidental creativity that have generated great innovation, generally, the most creative minds are simply experts within a domain, which allows them to critically reason about and integrate various components in a novel way.[30] Therefore, what differentiates an expert from a creative expert is not talent, but rather disposition and awareness of resources. Creativity requires a passion for a particular area that generates motivation to push the limits by thinking critically, taking risks, utilizing strategies, and to constructively benefit from failures. Robinson recalls his experience while consulting with a Native American tribe.[31]

They wanted me to talk to them about how they could promote innovation across their tribe. We sat around a board room table for the first hour, and I guess they were expecting me to get some flip charts out and show them some techniques. We did a little of that, but what I actually got them to do was to get into groups and draw pictures of some of the challenges they were facing as a community. Well, the minute you get people to think visually—to draw pictures or move rather than sit and write bullet

points—something different happens in the room ... So
you can teach people particular skills to free up their own
thinking ...

In sum, creativity should be conceptualized as a content-specific
skill, not a trait someone has or doesn't have. Any student can be
encouraged and taught to think creatively. Using the above characteri-
zation, educational psychologist Jeanne Ellis Ormrod suggests fostering
creativity in the classroom involves ensuring requisite prior knowledge, demonstrating relevant strategies, appealing to individual students' interests and passions, and generating an appropriate mindset by
encouraging risk taking and allowing for failure—some of which defy
the capabilities of a single instructor and other constraints of a classroom. Through mobile devices, however, adhering to these suggestions
becomes more reasonable.

Applications for Mobile Learning

Mobile devices afford a resource for encouraging creativity through
individualized instruction and seemingly unlimited access to background information. First, the personalization of mobile allows one
teacher to create lessons that appeal to the individual interests of each
student. Research suggests we are more creative when working within
our personal areas of expertise and/or interest because of the intrinsic
motivation that transpires and likelihood of content knowledge mastery. For example, a recent study found professional artists working
under commission—an extrinsic source of motivation—produced
significantly less-creative pieces than those artists painting on their
own accord—an indication of intrinsic motivation.[32] Therefore, from
essay writing to creating geometric tessellations to devising an empirical research study, teachers can personalize lessons by transitioning
from whole class to individualized instruction through the use of
mobile devices.

Second, when the structure of a lesson cannot be tailored to
one's interests, mobile devices allow students to compensate for
deficits in prior knowledge according to their individual needs. A
certain degree of mastery can facilitate creative thought; however,
students often come to a lesson with different levels of expertise.

Instead of boring the more knowledgeable students or confusing those less informed, teachers can lean on mobile's wide-reaching access to relevant information for differentiating instruction. This serves a dual purpose of engaging the student in challenging material, as well as teaching him how to evaluate source validity and content on the Internet. Also, mobile technologies are an excellent platform for external representations, known to promote brainstorming and cognitive offloading as students gather and organize information.[33]

Third, to be creative, students must be able to take risks. Utilizing mobile as a venue for simulations is a great way to mitigate the potential costs of failure. Simulation apps such as those offered by *Exploriments* provide a space where students can experiment with physics and chemistry concepts without the risk of injury or chemical combustion or the need for a vacuum space. Similarly, students also must feel safe taking such risks, and in this case, we see mobile as a powerful tool for overcoming the social anxiety surrounding failure. Apps like *Socrative* or *Padlet* allow students to make comments or ask questions within the app, which can take a large part of the intimidation factor of contributing in class away from shy students. With mobile, students are free to experiment and brainstorm within the privacy of their device, mitigating fears of looking dumb or being overpowered by more eager, outgoing students. For example, when teaching young students to write letters, mistakes using a writing app, as opposed to paper and pencil, feel like less of a failure when being able to undo, erase, or start over is a simple button press, not throwing away the paper.

Creativity Is Neither Person Nor Domain Specific— Everyone Is Capable of Creative Thought

- To foster creative thought, create lessons that allow students to work individually or in small groups on activities and projects that appeal to their personal interests.

- Creativity is often dependent upon background knowledge; therefore, encourage students to use mobile devices as a research tool to supplement their current level of expertise.

- Use mobile to provide students with a safe space that does not penalize or publically embarrass students as they explore through trial and error.

Communication and Collaboration

Communication and collaboration skills are vital for success in the modern workplace. Communication extends the higher-order skills outlined above as it is the vehicle for translating thoughts into words and actions. For example, in a group project, a student might have a creative idea to share, but without the means to present those thoughts in a coherent, persuasive way, the group may not understand her vision. Effective communicators are often concise, using common, appropriate language. Such individuals avoid slang and less-common words that might not be clear for the majority of the intended audience. Similarly, complex information should be deconstructed and presented at the lowest level in order to accommodate the listeners' limited attention and working memory capacity. In this case, effective communicators leverage analogies, simulations, and visual displays to scaffold listeners' understanding.[34] Contrast the following methods for teaching students about the circulatory system.

> Using a traditional method, teacher A uses a textbook as a guide and presents the circulatory system using a picture and the following description: "With each heartbeat, blood is sent throughout our bodies, carrying oxygen and nutrients to every cell. ... The circulatory system is composed of the heart and blood vessels, including arteries, veins, and capillaries. ... Arteries carry blood away from the heart. They are the thickest blood vessels, with muscular walls that contract to keep the blood mobbing away from the heart and through the body. ... Veins carry blood back to the heart. They're not as muscular as arteries, but they contain valves that prevent blood from flowing backward. ... A network of tiny capillaries connects the arteries and veins. Though tiny, the capillaries are one of the most important parts of the circulatory system because it's through them that nutrients and oxygen are delivered to the cells."[35]

> Teacher B teaches the same concept, but uses a picture and a familiar analogy: a delivery truck delivering packages around a city. "The process starts with individual homes,

or tissue cells, placing orders for the oxygen stored in a large warehouse (the lungs). ... From the center, the oxygen-rich blood cells hop on bodily highways, or arteries, to deliver their packages ... When they near their destination, the delivery trucks exit the highways and enter capillaries. Capillaries, similar to narrow roads in a neighborhood, allow the trucks to reach homes in need of the oxygen shipments. As a way of signing for the oxygen delivery, tissue cells hand over cellular waste like carbon dioxide to the red blood cells. ... Order fulfilled, the blood cells get back on the capillary roads and exit onto a second set of highways called veins, which lead the cells back to the heart. From here, the minute-long cycle begins anew: red blood cells take a trip to the lungs, pick up an oxygen shipment while dropping off their carbon-dioxide signature, travel back to the distribution center, then go off to the tissue cells for delivery."[36]

In this example, both teachers deconstruct the circulatory system into manageable pieces and use illustrations to help articulate their point. However, teacher B also leverages background knowledge and experience to help communicate ideas more clearly. While students might not initially compare the circulatory system to a delivery truck, given the similarities, the analogy helps to convey the concept.

However, articulating our own thoughts is only one half of the process of communication; listening, receiving, and interpreting incoming information are also included.[37] Effective communication, then, transcends engaging in conversation since the skills associated with receiving information are also applicable to acquiring knowledge in a variety settings such as a classroom lecture. Therefore, aside from comprehending the explicit message, a good communicator makes inferences about "knowledge, values, attitudes and intentions," summarizes and prioritizes incoming messages, and synthesizes information from multiple sources.[38] When the demands of listening overwhelm the limits of attention and working memory, skilled communicators rely on note taking for offloading and organizing information.[39] Such careful analysis can more confidently yield an accurate representation of the intended message, which can then benefit the production of an informed response, if appropriate.

That being said, collaboration skills extend a student's ability to communicate well. Good collaborators not only effectively speak and listen, but do so respectfully and deliberately. Members of a successful team thoroughly understand the demands of the project as well as the strengths of each individual and, consequently, allocate work in an informed and balanced manner. Therefore, beyond communication, collaboration skills include valuing the role of each teammate, accommodating the challenges of working with a diverse team, maintaining a flexible work ethic, respecting scheduling conflicts, and graciously allowing for compromise.[40]

Like other higher-order thinking processes, students develop communication and collaboration skills through practice and guidance. Students should be encouraged to practice verbally communicating their ideas across domains using a variety of resources. Students should be exposed to resources for aiding communication, such as instruments for visually presenting complex information or processes (e.g., charts, graphs) or techniques for drawing attention toward main ideas (e.g., posters, PowerPoint presentations). For becoming more attentive listeners, students should be instructed on methods for generating useful notes and/or organizing information, as well as strategies for monitoring comprehension. Furthermore, instructors should be prepared to provide constructive feedback on areas in need of improvement.

In terms of collaboration, charging students with group work allows practice and exposure to the demands of working together. Instructors can facilitate the dynamic by providing tools and techniques for mitigating the challenges of collaboration. Moreover, integrating explicit rubrics or systems (e.g., the Jigsaw method, Student Teams-Achievement Divisions[41]) have been shown to help students work more cooperatively by overcoming stereotypes and ensuring a balanced division of responsibility such that students can ultimately understand the benefits of teamwork. For instance, the Jigsaw method involves assigning each student a specific subtask or concept related to the problem. Once each student has mastered or completed their task, the group reconvenes, presents their individual findings, and, collaboratively aggregates their work to complete the assignment.[42]

Applications for Mobile Learning

Mobile technologies provide a great deal of utility in terms of communication and collaboration. For communicating information, students can utilize apps such as *Keynote* to supplement verbal communication with visual aids. Moreover, video and audio recording functionalities can be employed as students prepare and practice assignments that require speaking in front of an audience. When acquiring skills associated with attentive listening, *Evernote* and *Google Drive* provide excellent cloud-based, note-taking facilities.

Mobile also has a reputation for solving many of the challenges surrounding effective collaboration. For instance, *Skype* facilitates video conferencing anytime, anywhere, allowing face-to-face communication among members. This overcomes one of the main arguments against mobile that is often made, that it lacks the personal touch of face-to-face communication. Cloud-based resources like those provided by the *Google Drive* suite or screencast applications (e.g., *Screenr*) extend video conferencing by allowing several users to view and edit documents in real time. In fact, a recent study found middle school students are 50 percent more likely to collaborate and communicate with their fellow classmates and teachers when using a tablet to complete school projects.[43] Along this line, mobile technologies can connect students with collaborators around the world. Whether it's students interacting with peers in another country to gain a different perspective or students interviewing real-world experts for a project or paper, mobile technologies allow us to connect with practically anyone, anywhere. Furthermore, shared calendars and scheduling tools provide an accessible platform for monitoring and maintaining productivity and member accountability. Lastly, file-sharing tools, like *Dropbox*, make sending and receiving even large files seamless and simple.

Nonetheless, fluency in leveraging mobile for communication and collaboration hinges on awareness and practice. Unfortunately, data from a recent Gallup poll found 86 percent of students say they often used computers or technology to complete assignments or projects, but only 14 percent reported using technology for video conferencing or other collaboration tools.[44]

Harness Students' Motivation to Socialize and Connect with Peers by Guiding, Not Limiting, Communication and Collaboration

- Use familiar media such as texting, text-based chat, and email to teach students the difference between formal and informal communication.

- Remember when teaching communication, listening skills are just as important as speaking skills; therefore, show students techniques for utilizing mobile technology for offloading and organizing information.

- Foster students' understanding of the limitations of attention by encouraging the use of analogies, examples, and external representation when communicating complex ideas.

- Utilize collaboration methods (e.g., Jigsaw) and shared, cloud-based, mobile work spaces to scaffold productive team work.

CRITICAL THINKING

Critical thinking expert Diane Halpern defines critical thinking as "the use of those cognitive skills or strategies that increase the probability of a desirable outcome. It is used to describe thinking that is purposeful, reasoned, and goal directed—the kind of thinking involved in solving problems, formulating inferences, calculating likelihoods, and making decisions, when the thinker is using skills that are thoughtful and effective for the particular context and type of thinking task."[45] Others have more generally categorized critical thinking as being comprised of both dispositions and abilities.[46] So, critical thinking involves a magnitude of contexts and is applicable to several other higher-order thinking skills. When communicating with others, we think critically as we draw inferences about attitudes and dispositions from tone and language. We think critically anytime we thoughtfully apply our knowledge and experiences creatively to new situations as well as when we analyze information and use evidence to inform judgments or decision making for problem solving.

In a society that consumes information for an estimated average of 12 hours per day, effectively analyzing information has never been more relevant.[47] Discriminating between opinion and fact, comparing opposing perspectives, and developing logically sound, compelling arguments all revolve around scrutinizing the foundational components or information units. In the classroom, critical thinking is taught by inquiring beyond the surface level. Teachers encourage the development of sophisticated epistemological beliefs by having students question even the most renowned sources. Bloom's taxonomy outlines a well-known framework for creating questions that assess a wide range of cognitive skills, pictured in Figure 5.3. Specifically, Bloom's taxonomy recommends asking students questions from the top three levels of the framework that involve verbs for analysis, synthesis, and evaluation: for example, analyze, correlate, combine, generalize, compare,

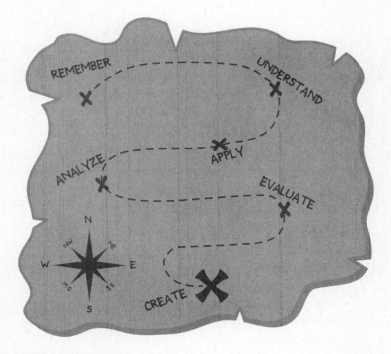

Figure 5.3 Bloom's Revised Taxonomy

support, persuade.[48] To do so, students must be exposed to a variety of information and instructed on relevant strategies. While these levels can be difficult to measure in a controlled laboratory setting, the distinctions are so face valid that the framework has been used for decades to encourage test-item writers to measure a wide variety of skills.

Prompting elementary students to think beyond a text or analyze bias by presenting high school students with first-hand accounts of the Civil War as told by a slave, a politician, and a soldier encourages critical thought.[49] Consider a task as simple as having students critically analyze advertisements, something they encounter every day. From understanding the intended audience to parsing out fact from far-reaching claim, several critical-thinking lessons are embedded within the world we live in.

Applications for Mobile Learning

Mobile learning and critical thinking go hand in hand. Although mobile devices can serve as critical thinking assistants, the advent of these technologies has escalated the importance of critical thinking skills. While mobile technology grants access to a variety of sources and perspectives, the Internet is filled with compelling, yet false, information, so critically analyzing the credibility of sources instead of taking information at face value is extremely crucial. Therefore, from analyzing an argument in an English language arts class to making inferences in social studies, these technologies provide a beneficial instrument for practicing and developing critical thinking skills. In fact, a recent study conducted in Australia found a positive correlation between the lengths of time students spent learning in a technology-enriched environment and sophistication of critical thinking skills.[50] Interestingly, it is important to note that in this study, students were not explicitly taught critical thinking skills, but rather taught and encouraged to use technology throughout their studies.

One of the most useful applications of mobile is developing skills associated with gathering evidence, evaluating source credibility, and applying the results. Millions of terabytes of information are at your immediate disposal when equipped with a mobile device. However, Diane Halpern argues the implications surrounding the abundance of information in today's society mandate the necessity of critical thinking skills.[51] She says, "Relevant, credible information has to be selected, interpreted, digested, evaluated, learned and applied or it is of no more use on a computer screen than it is on a distant library shelf. If we cannot think intelligently about the myriad of issues that confront us, then we are in danger of having all of the answers, but still not knowing what they mean." Teaching students to intelligently harness the advantages mobile affords can not only foster cognitive growth through the acquisition of critical thinking skills, but also yields one of the most sought after twenty-first century skills: media literacy.[52]

Aside from being a seemingly unlimited source of information, mobile devices can also serve as critical thinking assistants. Like with problem solving and creativity, mobile can be a wonderful tool for gathering, organizing, prioritizing, and synthesizing information. Just as we encounter information everywhere, the portability of mobile devices allows us to gather and offload information anywhere, anytime. Thinking critically is not reserved for the classroom, and, with the opportunities of mobile, students are better equipped to realize this firsthand and practice these skills in a variety of contexts.

Critical Thinking is Imperative in the Mobile-Enabled Classroom

- Instead of protecting students from the unknown of the Internet, leverage this variance by teaching students' how to critically analyze the credibility of sources.
- Make connections across disciplines.
- Access background knowledge.

CLASSROOMS FOR HIGHER-ORDER THINKING

Throughout our discussion of higher-order thinking skills, a common theme arises: complex cognition is just as much a mindset as it is a skill. Motivation and appropriate beliefs about knowledge are as important as awareness of the strategies and skills associated with complex cognition. Therefore, a space that encourages problem solving, critical thinking, creativity, communication, and collaboration is one that empowers students to dig deeper by bestowing to them the responsibility of learning and fostering feelings of responsibility and worth. Such environments do so in a nurturing way by providing practical resources and modeling effective use, allowing for failure, and allotting appropriate time for learning. Consequently, students have the chance to engage in meaningful learning, which has been positively associated with mastery and transfer, two concepts related to higher-order thinking.

However, constructivist environments are hardly the norm. Furthermore, research on students' epistemological beliefs, or beliefs about knowledge, indicates as students grow older, their beliefs become more sophisticated as they begin to realize learning is an ongoing process, bits of information are not necessarily isolated units, and knowledge can be subject to change.[53] Nonetheless, the majority of students are taught in a passive, lecture-style manner,[54] and instructional techniques that ignore the role of the student diminish the very mindset we hope for. Therefore, as students begin to acquire more sophisticated epistemological beliefs, instructional methods tend to remain the same, yielding a problem known as the epistemological gap.[55]

A recent report put out by Adobe extends this depiction of the classroom.[56] With respect specifically to creativity, teachers and parents surveyed in the report claim insufficient time, undervaluing creativity, a lack of tools and resources, testing, and state mandates that hinder the development of creative minds at school. Parents and teachers both encourage schools to create classroom environments that foster and value creativity by providing resources to students and allotting sufficient time to creative thought.

Revamping lessons from lectures to breeding grounds for higher-order thinking is not a simple task, but we believe it has been made easier through the mobile technologies discussed at length in the previous sections. However, it is important to note, we recommend the integration of mobile technologies to be only one factor of the classroom rewiring, not the cornerstone. Assuming that sitting students down in front of a computer or tablet will revolutionize their higher-order thinking skills is a fallacy. In fact, the LEAD commission found that over $60 billion has been spent on computers in the past two decades, and "most schools that use technology do so in a peripheral way, not a transformative manner."[57] In other words, there is no app for higher-order thinking. Instead, students must first realize that the most meaningful instruction occurs when they take responsibility and guide their own learning. Through this process, educators can then introduce students to the power of mobile for fluently and purposefully engaging in higher-order thinking. After all, utilizing the power of mobile is in itself a marketable and vital skill in today's society.

However, we are aware of the challenges surrounding the use of mobile in the classroom. Many schools' acceptable use policies severely limit or prohibit mobile use altogether, illustrating the deep distrust of devices and a perceived lack of educational value. However, restricting students undermines their role in the classroom, drastically limits access to powerful tools, and teaches students mobile devices are *not* a valuable educational resource. Since 71 percent of teens admit to texting in class,[58] some schools are instead teaching and implementing responsible use policies so students are exposed to the educational and practical advantages provided by mobile devices, and they are explicitly taught how, why, and when to utilize them. Moreover, apps such as *Remind, Poll Everywhere, Celly,* and *StudyBoost* have all leveraged the dreaded text message for on-task, educational purposes.[59] By approximating the technology use of today's workforce, students enter the real world prepared to use technology productively as opposed to being vulnerable and untrained. A discussion about digital citizenship is offered in Chapter 15.

CONCLUSION

There are limitless opportunities for leveraging the power of mobile for developing higher-order thinking skills, and, equally important, the effective use of mobile relies on complex cognition. As discussed in this chapter, complex processes such as problem solving, creativity, critical thinking, collaboration, and communication entail great prerequisites—background knowledge, motivation, and awareness of strategies, just to name a few. For this reason, affordances such as ubiquitous access to information and beneficial apps make mobile technologies the ideal higher-order thinking assistant. Consequently, separating the wheat from the chaff when it comes to using mobile effectively in itself requires critical reasoning and decision making.

Although 44 percent of high school students own a smartphone, today's employers continually complain that recent graduates simply are not prepared for the workforce, often citing higher-order thinking skills as a severe shortcoming.[60] Given the pervasiveness and bidi-rectional influence between mobile and complex cognition, teaching without mobile seems to be a significant disservice to students.

While texting and off-task social networking in class pose a threat to classroom time, mobile usage data suggests children are using their smartphones whether we like it or not;[61] therefore, instead of ignoring this resource because of the notable threats it entails, why not teach students to harness this tool effectively before they enter the workforce? Fortunately, promising findings from the Software & Information Industry Association's Vision K–20 Survey indicate about 46 percent of K–12 districts allow mobile devices now, a percentage they predict will grow significantly in the next five years.[62] From problem solving to creativity to effective communication, mobile technologies offer great educational value.

NOTES

1. Partnership for 21st Century Skills, "Are They Really Ready to Work? Employers' Perspectives on the Basic Knowledge and Applied Skills of New Entrants to the 21st Century US Workforce," *P21* (2006), www.p21.org/storage/documents/FINAL _REPORT_PDF09-29-06.pdf.

2. Microsoft, "21st Century Skills and the Workplace: A Microsoft Partners in Learning and Pearson Foundation Study," 2013, www.ferris.edu/HTMLS/ administration/academicaffairs/extendedinternational/ccleadership/alliance/ documents/21stCenturySkills.pdf

3. Anna R. Saavedra and V. Darleen Opfer, "Teaching and Learning 21st Century Skills: Lessons from the Learning Sciences," *Asia Society* (2012), Asiasociety.org/files/ rand-0512report.pdf.

4. Reuven Gorsht. "Are You Ready? Here Are the Top 10 Skills for the Future," *Forbes*, May 5, 2014, www.forbes.com/sites/sap/2014/05/12/are-you-ready-here-are-the -top-10-skills-for-the-future/.

5. ACT, "The Condition of College & Career Readiness 2012," www.act.org/research/ policymakers/cccr12/readiness1.html.

6. Claudia Dreifus, "Ideas for Improving Science Education in the U.S.," *New York Times*, September 2, 2013, www.nytimes.com/2013/09/03/science/ideas-for-improving -science-education-in-the-us.html?pagewanted=all&_r=0.

7. Ibid.

8. Rachel Monahan and Ben Chapman, "Mayor Bloomberg Insists on School Cell-phone Bans While Parents Demand Ban Lift for Communication," *New York Daily News*, July 16, 2011, www.nydailynews.com/new-york/mayor-bloomberg-insists-school-cell-phone-bans-parents-demand-ban-lift-communication-article-1.161049.

9. Liquid Paper, "About Us," 2014, www.liquidpaper.com/about_us.html.

10. As cited by Ariel Roguin, MD, PhD, "Rene Tehophie Hyacinthe Laennec (1781–1826): The Man Behind the Stethoscope," *Clinical Medicine and Research* (September 2006), www.ncbi.nlm.nih.gov/pmc/articles/PMC1570491/.

11. Ibid.

12. Z. Chen, L. Mo, and R. Honomichl, "Having the Memory of an Elephant: Long-Term Retrieval and the Use of Analogues in Problem Solving," *Journal of Experimental Psychology: General* 133 (2004): 415–433.

13. Daniel Willingham, "Critical Thinking: Why Is It So Hard to Teach?," *American Educator* (Summer 2007), www.aft.org/pdfs/americaneducator/summer2007/Crit_Thinking.pdf.

14. Ibid.

15. Roger H. Bruning, Gregory J. Schraw, Monica M. Norby, and Royce R. Ronning, eds., "Problem Solving and Critical Thinking," in *Cognitive Psychology and Instruction*, 4th ed. (Upper Saddle River, NJ: Pearson, 2004).

16. Familiarity with the problem-solving model is good.

17. H. G. Birch and H.S. Rabinowitz, "The Negative Effect of Previous Experience of Productive Thinking," *Journal of Experimental Psychology* 41 (1951): 121–125.

18. Richard E. Mayer and M. Wittrock, "Problem-Solving Transfer," in *Handbook on Educational Psychology*, eds. D. C. Berliner and R. C. Calfee (New York: Macmillan, 1996), 47–62.

19. David Jonassen, "Using Cognitive Tools to Represent Problems," *Journal of Research on Technology in Education* 35, no. 3 (2003): 362–382.

20. K. Duncker, "On Problem Solving," trans. L. S. Lees, *Psychological Monographs* 58 (1945): 270.

21. http://ecomobile.gse.harvard.edu/.

22. Amy M. Azzam, "Why Creativity Now? A Conversation with Sir Ken Robinson," 2009, www.ascd.org/publications/educational-leadership/sept09/vol67/num01/Why-Creativity-Now%C2%A2-A-Conversation-with-Sir-Ken-Robinson.aspx.

23. "Einstein Alive" website, edited by Arden Bercovitz, PhD, www.einsteinalive.com/quotes/.

24. Jeanne E. Ormrod, *Educational Psychology: Developing Learners*, 6th ed. (Upper Saddle River, NJ: Pearson Education, 2008).

25. Azzam, "Why Creativity Now?"

26. Ormrod, *Educational Psychology*.

27. D. Saunders, and P. Thagard, "Creativity and Computer Science," in *Creativity Across Domains: Faces of the Muse* eds. J. C. Kaufman and J. Baer (Mahwah, NJ: Lawrence Erlbaum Associates).

28. D. Shasha, *Out of Their Minds: The Lives and Discoveries of 15 Great Computer Scientists* (New York: Copernicus, 1995), 5–20.

29. Ormrod, *Educational Psychology*.

30. Ibid.

31. Azzam, "Why Creativity Now?"

32. T. M. Amabile, *Creativity in Context* (Boulder, CO: Westview Press, 1996).

33. David Jonassen, "Using Cognitive Tools to Represent Problems," *Journal of Research on Technology in Education* 35, no. 3 (2003): 362–382.

34. Partnership for 21st Century Skills, "P21 Framework Definitions," www.p21.org/storage/documents/P21_Framework_Definitions.pdf, accessed May 23, 2014.

35. Kidshealth.org, Kidshealth.org/parent/general/body_basics/heart.html.

36. Joseph Castro, "How Does the Cardiovascular System Work?," *Scienceline*, http://scienceline.org/2011/03/how-does-the-cardiovascular-system-work/.

37. National Governors Association Center for Best Practices, *Common Core State Standards*, www.nga.org/cms/home/nga-center-for-best-practices/center-divisions/page-edu-division/col2-content/list---edu-right/content-reference-1@/common-core-state-standards.html.

38. Partnership for 21st Century Skills, "P21 Framework Definitions."

39. Ormrod, *Educational Psychology*.

40. Partnership for 21st Century Skills, "P21 Framework Definitions."

41. Robert E. Slavin, *Cooperative Learning: Theory, Research, and Practice*, 2nd ed. (Boston: Allyn & Bacon, 1994).

42. Elliot Aronson and Shelley Patone, *Cooperation in the Classroom: The Jigsaw Method*, 3rd ed. (London: Pinter & Martin, Ltd., 2011).

43. Project Tomorrow, "Making Learning Mobile 1.0: Leveraging Mobile Devices to Transform Teaching and Learning in 8th Grade Classes at Stone Middle School: Results from the Project Evaluation Study," 2013, www.kajeet.com/4u/education/MLM-report/contentTop/0/text_files/file1/document/Kajeet%20Stone%20External%20Report%20Dec2013.pdf.

44. Jenna Levy and Preety Sidhu, "In the U.S., 21st Century Skills Linked to Work Success: Real-World Problem-Solving Most Strongly Tied to Work Quality," 2013, www.gallup.com/poll/162818/21st-century-skills-linked-work-success.aspx.

45. Diane Halpern, *Thought and Knowledge: An Introduction to Critical Thinking* (Mahwah, NJ: Erlbaum, 2003), 6.

46. Roger H. Bruning, Gregory J. Schraw, Monica M. Norby, and Royce R. Ronning, eds., "Problem Solving and Critical Thinking," in *Cognitive Psychology and Instruction*, 4th ed. (Upper Saddle River, NJ: Pearson, 2004).

47. Roger Bohn and James Short, "How Much Information? 2009 Report on American Consumers," University of California, San Diego, http://hmi.ucsd.edu/pdf/HMI_2009_ConsumerReport_Dec9_2009.pdf.

48. D. R. Krathwohl, "A Revision of Bloom's Taxonomy: An Overview," *Theory into Practice* 41, no. 4 (2002): 212–218.

49. Ormrod, *Educational Psychology*.

50. G. McMahon, "Critical Thinking and ICT Integration in a Western Australian Secondary School," *Educational Technology & Society* 12, no 4 (2009): 269–281.

51. Halpern, *Thought and Knowledge*.

52. Devin Leonard, "The iPad Goes to School," *BusinessWeek*, October 24, 2013, www.businessweek.com/articles/2013-10-24/the-ipad-goes-to-school-the-rise-of-educational-tablets.

53. M. Schommer, "Epistemological Development and Academic Performance Among Secondary Students," *Journal of Educational Psychology* 85, no. 3 (1993): 406.

54. R. C. Pianta, Jay Belsky, Renate Houts, and Fred Morrison, "Opportunities to Learn in America's Elementary Classrooms," *Science* 315, no. 5820 (2007): 1795.

55. C. C. Tsai, "Taiwanese Science Students' and Teachers' Perceptions of the Laboratory Learning Environments: Exploring Epistemological Gaps," *International Journal of Science Education* 25, no. 7 (2003): 847–860.

56. David Nagel, "Education System Stifles Creativity, Survey Finds," April 23, 2012, http://thejournal.com/articles/2012/04/23/education-system-stifles-creativity -survey-finds.aspx.

57. LEAD commission, "How Can We Help Administrators and Educators Find and Adapt Best Practices from Other Schools, When Most of These Programs Are New?," www.leadcommission.org/challenge/how-can-we-help-administrators-and -educators-find-and-adapt-best-practices-other-schools. Accessed September 22, 2014.

58. Amanda Lenhart, Rich Ling, Scott Campbell, and Kristen Purcell, "Teens and Mobile Phones," Pew Research, April 20, 2010, www.pewinternet.org/2010/04/20/teens -and-mobile-phones/.

59. Audrey Watters, "Texting in the Classroom: Not Just a Distraction," *Edutopia* (September 21, 2010), www.edutopia.org/blog/texting-classroom-audrey-watters.

60. Susan Adams, "The College Degrees and Skills Employers Most Want," *Forbes*, April 16, 2014, www.forbes.com/sites/susanadams/2014/04/16/the-college-degrees-and -skills-employers-most-want/.

61. Common Sense Media, "Zero to Eight: Children's Media Use in American 2013," www.commonsensemedia.org/research/zero-to-eight-childrens-media-use-in -america-2013.

62. MMS Education, "2014 Results from the SIIA Vision K-20 Survey," http://siia.net/ visionk20/2014_VK20.pdf.

CHAPTER **6**

Instructional Management and Levels of Technology Access

A ccording to a 2014 Pew poll, almost every American school today can technically be defined as a bring your own device (BYOD) school, whether that is the official policy or not. Approximately 77 percent of students of all ages admit to carrying cell phones to school.[1] However, since more than 80 percent of students cannot use their devices in the classroom,[2] the infiltration of mobile devices has become a behavior-management nuisance. Easily accessible distractions such as texting and social media often win in the battle for students' attention, which raises the question: If they're using their mobile devices anyway, why not encourage and teach productivity and responsible use? In essence, that question has fueled the recent mobile learning movement. Instead of fighting against the current mobile movement and trying to hold back the wave with a policy banning mobile devices, mobile learning programs suggest proctoring and

Figure 6.1 Bringing Mobile Devices above the Desk

monitoring the use of mobile devices, bringing them out of the back-pack, and more importantly, above the desk (as seen in Figure 6.1).

Approximately one-third of students nationwide have school-issued mobile devices, and mobile adoption is increasing rapidly.[3] Relying on best practices, anecdotal words of wisdom, and a careful implementation plan, a mobile learning plan can enhance student learning and improve student outcomes. Mobile learning is not only exciting for kids, but an important component for developing college and career readiness in today's society. And, with more affordable devices and a surge in federal funding for high-speed broadband access in schools across the country,[4] mobile learning is increasingly becoming a norm.

In our interviews with teachers and administrators, we've seen a large variety of implementations of mobile devices in schools—from just the teacher having an iPad to 1:1, bring your own device (BYOD) to device carts shared by several classes. We'll discuss each of these implementation models in the sections that follow. There are many ways to get mobile devices in the hands of students effectively, and ways to do it within almost any budget. There are also many questions and logistical concerns about different technology set ups. We address those issues in this chapter, as well as provide a roadmap for operating different levels of technology access in schools. This chapter is divided by level of access, with specific concerns and suggestions that are associated with each. As the mobile learning landscape continues to shift rapidly, we feel it's important for developers, educators, and administrators to be abreast on the latest trends, varieties of implementations, and the best ways to create an environment where technology is a valued, integral part of the classroom.

MOBILE LEARNING PROGRAMS

Regardless of technology access, any mobile integration paradigm can benefit from acceptable use policies, digital citizenship curricula, and professional development.[5,6] A strong, forward-thinking leadership team is also obligatory for the success of mobile.[7] Given the expense and infancy of mobile learning, leaders must be prepared to deal with existing as well as unforeseen challenges that range from theoretical to practical, petty to detrimental, technical to pedagogical. Therefore, before choosing to dive into mobile learning, experts are almost unanimous in the opinion that mobile begins with thorough planning with a diverse team comprised of all relevant stakeholders.[8]

Acceptable Use Policies and Digital Citizenship

Even if instructors are deliberately teaching students to be digital citizens as described in Chapter 15, misbehavior is inevitable. A key tenet of digital citizenship is teaching students to work with the resources available to them, rather than blocking them from potentially subversive material. For instance, a school can block YouTube because there is inappropriate content on the site. There are also, of course, volumes of useful, educational content on that site. Teaching children how to be their own filter is important, a life skill.[9] The acceptable use policy (AUP) will dictate what is okay and what is an infraction, and students will be expected to comply with it as they do any other rule in the school. Of course, school officials should consider general student characteristics when drafting an AUP. For example, implications of student age and behavioral tendencies could impact how an AUP in one grade or school compares to another. Nonetheless, in a classroom with high access to mobile devices, digital citizenship can be a concept immersed in every lesson.

Also, many students likely have their own or access to mobile devices outside of school, and the boundaries established by parents for using a family's personal device differ from those for school-owned technologies. Therefore, in order to prevent misconduct, whether accidental or intentional, schools must establish clear and concise terms of use with direct consequences for misuse.

Device Management

Physical

Laptops, tablets, and cellphones have been around long enough that we all understand their fragility. Seeing an iPhone with a cracked screen, for instance, is not uncommon. It is important for schools to encourage protective cases on mobile learning devices, as they can cut down overall cost. One teacher noted a good way to protect the devices and curb off-task device use is to have the students hug the iPads while walking in between classes.[10] Getting insurance through the device company (such as Apple's Applecare) is another good option, as some device breakdown is inevitable. The *Find my iPhone* app is a huge help in locating lost or missing devices connected to a Wi-Fi network. It is worth mentioning, however, that in our discussions with teachers, this issue wasn't nearly as big of a deal as we assumed it would be. Few administrators and teachers mentioned high levels of devices breaking or malfunctioning.

Logistics

Many districts also invest in device-management systems to gain greater control over students' interactions and permissions. With features such as web filtering, app blocking, and wireless synching, device-management systems mitigate several of the concerns stakeholders have with widespread mobile deployments. To eliminate cheating, instructors from Franklin Academy in North Carolina report using their device management system to put students into guided access, a mode available on iOS devices that locks users into a particular app, when administering tests via the iPad.[11] Getting high volumes of devices set up quickly is another logistical issue for schools; tools like *Apple Configurator* can address the launch of major mobile initiatives easily.

Another key to making effective use of mobile technology is to make it easy for teachers to test and install apps. You may recall the teacher from Chapter, 1, who, according to her school's policy, was required to jump through many hoops to simply test an app. When she found an app that she might want to use in a lesson, she had to email the device cart managers to get it approved, and the app was then downloaded on all three device carts before she could even access and try out the app. So, simply to test an app, all the devices now must have the app.[12] Of course, not all apps are a good fit for the lesson, and sometimes determining that is difficult simply based on online resources and app store summaries. This process is overly difficult and discourages the kinds of innovative app use mobile implementations should encourage.

Student Actions

Another aspect of device management is monitoring student actions on the devices. Fortunately, just as academically appropriate actions are tracked (lessons accessed, answers provided, etc.), off-task behavior can be tracked on mobile devices. For iOS devices, instructors can ask students to close all open programs prior to class, then spot check to see what apps are currently open. For lessons that do not integrate students' devices, it is advised to remove the distraction. One elementary teacher found that having students leave the devices facedown when not in use for schoolwork was an effective way to monitor off-task use.[13] More serious infractions, such as cyber-bullying and other misuse, have also raised issues for 1:1 environments. For example, Title IX requires schools to protect students from bullying, and victims could more easily bring charges against a school when the bullying occurs on a school-owned device.[14] While device management systems can head some misuse, this is not a failsafe solution. Recently, Los Angeles Unified School District, the largest implementation of mobile devices for education to date, reneged students' permission to take their school-issued devices home. The decision came after several students found ways to circumvent the device-management software to gain free reign over the device.[15]

Mobile learning specialists often stress that when technology is used to complement pedagogy, device management becomes less of a concern.[16] Therefore, for minor infractions, taking the device away from students and hindering their ability to engage in classroom activities is counterproductive. "Definitely don't take away their device as a consequence if they're off task. Don't take it away for abuse. You can lock down an app or restrict their use," Rebecca Goddard, a former classroom teacher currently serving as a school technology specialist, says.[17] It is important to view the mobile learning device just as we would a textbook or a pencil: an invaluable tool. When students doodle, do we take away their pencils? In sum, preparing for misuse can be more viable than relying solely on preventative measures; thus, developing comprehensive AUPs appears to be the norm for delineating clear lines regarding who is responsible in the event of accidental or intentional misuse.

Teaching With Mobile Technology

Since students today seem to be born with a device in their hand, it is easy to assume learning with technology would be instinctive; however, knowing how to use a device by no means implies knowing how to use a device productively. Many students simply use mobile technology for personal and social purposes and have little regard for how these tools extend to their own learning.[18] For example, 83 percent of classroom teachers surveyed in a recent Pew survey agree that "the amount of information available online today is overwhelming for most students." Similar to the process of flipping the classroom detailed in Chapter 4, the beginnings of a 1:1 learning environment should be spent modeling and scaffolding productive uses of mobile devices.

Deploying a lesson with mobile devices requires unique strategies for classroom management; while still grounded in good pedagogy, teaching with devices is different. Aside from managing off-task behavior (described in the previous section), instructors must remember engagement when learning with devices does not necessarily mean eyes on the teacher. Students should often be looking down, working independently or collaboratively in groups. Instead of leading the class, instructors more frequently take on a facilitative role, walking around monitoring progress and interjecting as needed. Mobile-enhanced lessons are expected to go at a slower pace. Time is obligatory for deep engagement—teachers should allocate greater amounts of time for mobile-enhanced lessons.

While student autonomy is often a goal of mobile learning, close and constant scaffolding by modeling to students how to use their devices in novel ways is recommended in order to maintain focus and on-task behavior. Give clear directions and teach kids how to use it before implementing it. For Amy Wilkinson, who uses mobile devices to facilitate various centers in her kindergarten class, this means "not just setting up an iPad and saying 'use this app.' Instead, you have to model how to use it first to ensure they're using it how you want them to use it."[19] Having a clear backup plan is a best practice in any mobile classroom, as you just never know when the Internet will go out, or a device will not be charged. As much as we all love technology, having a backup lesson plan that does not rely on technology is a best practice.[20]

Being creative is an essential component of the mobile classroom. Rebecca Goddard, formerly a classroom teacher and currently a technology specialist, notes that in teaching a math lesson using complex equations she really wanted to incorporate technology, but couldn't find an app or website that did what she wanted to do. She ended up using slides in *Keynote* that enabled students to manipulate the numbers.[21] Being forced to find her own solution, one she engineered by creatively using existing resources, is the essence of what it means to teach in the mobile classroom. And, conversely, it's also important to remember that the mobile devices aren't for everything; it's okay (and advisable) to use other materials for some lessons. For further discussion, see Chapter 4 about pedagogy.

When approaching how to incorporate a device or app into a lesson plan, think about tool-oriented apps, not just content. Goddard, who helps teachers at her school to effectively use mobile technology in their classes, says she tries to steer teachers away from drill and practice apps. "The iPads aren't just for games; apps should focus on collaboration and workflow, giving them skills they need for other aspects of their life."[22] App stacking, or app smashing, the practice of using multiple apps to accomplish a classroom goal, can often be the best alternative, allowing for maximum flexibility in the absence of the perfect app. For instance, in a middle school English class, students might be asked to create puppet shows depicting scenes from a book they've read. They use the browser *Safari* to get images, the *Brushes* app to crop and edit the images, and the *Puppet Pals* app to animate and record audio for the performance. Choosing good apps can also seamlessly enable sharing of class material. *Dropbox, GoogleDocs, Showbie,* and *Groupboard* are all ways to share documents and files that can be accommodated using apps and mobile devices. In Goddard's school (which uses iOS devices exclusively), an Apple TV is used to display screens and share work, serving the function an overhead projector did in years past.

Since this is such a new field, and one many teachers weren't trained in while they were in college, it's important to find a professional learning network to stay in touch with what is new and useful in the field. Find someone who inspires you to use the technology in ways that enhance your teaching, advises Goddard.[23] Word of mouth among colleagues is a huge resource. Tricia Hudacek, a reading specialist noted that one teacher at her school discovered and piloted a program using *ClassDojo* to manage her classroom. After having success with it, she offered a training session for her coworkers.[24] Julie Stern suggests social media as a resource for finding apps. Finding resources and thought leaders on Twitter or Edmodo has been useful for her, as well as following hashtags for educational technology conferences and chats.[25]

The most salient advice we received from experienced teachers in mobile classrooms was to make gradual changes.[26] Take one or two mobile modules and do them well, and branch out from there. Mobile lessons hold the promise to be more effective and engaging, but they are also new to everyone and can fall flat. Go slow, and learn together.

LEVELS OF ACCESS IN THE MOBILE CLASSROOM

When a school has mobile technology access, there are many ways that access can be distributed. How many devices does the school have per student, and how are they shared or parceled out? In this section we'll

1: Teacher

1:1

1: Many

BYOD

Figure 6.2 Levels of Mobile Device Access

discuss the four most prominent access models: 1:Teacher, 1:Many, 1:1, and bring your own device (BYOD) (see Figure 6.2). For each, we discuss concerns relating to professional development, strategies for implementation, and methods for making it successful in practice. There is, of course, substantial overlap in these environments, so each section may include anecdotes and discussions that are of interest to other models.

1:TEACHER

Even without a classroom set, a single, personal mobile device is a powerful tool for educators. Many implementations entail a tablet or laptop being given to the teacher to be used in classroom management and assessment. There are many useful apps to make the classroom run efficiently, even if it doesn't entail having a device in every student's hand.

Tony Vincent, an advocate and thought leader in the educational technology field, notes seven functions for tablets as a "teacher's pet." Tablets offer the ability to show classroom materials and lessons on a big screen, manage the classroom, assess student work, interact with students, manage teacher files, create instructional media, and the teacher can learn new things.[27] The perks for teachers who have mobile devices clearly go beyond using them for one purpose; there are many ways to utilize their functionality to engage and enrich the entire class.

The app most often mentioned in association with classroom management is *ClassDojo*. It promotes tracking positive and negative behaviors, and allows teachers to share the information with parents and students easily, motivating better behavior. It is free and popular among the teachers we talked to in our research. One teacher noted that the app makes a little ping sound when a good or bad behavior is assigned, and he typically sees all the students sit up a little taller when that ping is heard; it reminds students the teacher is watching and provides students with awareness of peer models for behavior.[28] Tools like *ClassDojo* allow teachers to track information they wouldn't otherwise have, and have concrete data to share easily. Positive behavior is hard to note and reward.

Along those lines, there are many apps to support the other functions Vincent notes. (His infographic, *iPad as the Teacher's Pet v2.0*, cited previously, also provides ample resources on apps for each function. While we won't summarize each here, we recommend exploring this resource online.) Finding the right blend of mobile support and traditional methods in the classroom is a challenge each teacher will have to address individually. For instance, not all schools (or districts, or states' board of education) allow certain tasks, like online grade books, to be done on mobile devices. Like any mobile-learning deployment, using a device for classroom management is a gradual process and requires balance.

Professional Development

Just as we can't expect students to automatically understand how to use mobile devices for educational purposes, we should not assume teachers will receive an iPad and think of the many ways it could improve or change their classroom. It is, therefore, essential to provide ample professional development to garner these skills. This involves group training as well as giving additional time to explore the devices and their capabilities. One really beneficial professional development session for kindergarten teacher, Amy Wilkinson, had the teachers playing the role of students. This simple twist allowed them to interpret the devices as children and better evaluate their potential.[29] Additionally, redefining what a technologically integrated lesson is to teachers may be necessary. Goddard mentions that the professional development session she administered to teachers at her school began with her teachers believing researching online and having students create an outline and slide show presentation was a fully integrated lesson. "Now," she says, "they're Skyping with classes across the country and collaborating outside the classroom."[30] Educating teachers about what is possible and how to incorporate that into their classrooms is a key function of professional development.

1:MANY

1:many initiatives often manifest as tablet carts and/or classroom sets. In essence, schools invest in enough devices to support a single classroom, and devices are restricted to in-school use only. Alternatively, districts might allocate funds to provide individual classrooms with a particular number of devices that can be shared among the students. From a financial standpoint, a 1:many implementation is far more feasible while still exposing students to a mobile-enhanced learning experience; however, the level of integration is compromised. Nonetheless, with the proliferation of personal devices among students today, exposing students to appropriate and effective use of mobile devices in the classroom is a great tool for transferring such skills to use on their own devices. In other words, a 1:many-based curriculum can easily transform into a 1:1 movement by utilizing free and platform-general apps that students can use on any device outside of the classroom.

Implementation Strategies

Device Protection and Accountability

When devices are shared, it can be difficult to hold students accountable for misuse. When distributing devices to students, use a number system to maintain order. If a device is damaged, stolen, or used inappropriately, instructors can simply match the device number to the student to whom it was assigned. For easy access to the assigned number, Tony Vincent recommends displaying the device's number in a large font on the wallpaper of the device.[31] Furthermore, Vincent suggests disabling certain personalization features since the devices are being shared. Specifically, do not allow students access to app store passwords and prevent the device from synching with other computers.

Classroom Access

The most common paradigm for 1:many implementations is the device cart—a mobile unit with a classroom set of devices that travels around a school. However, many experts argue sharing devices significantly undermines benefits of mobile learning—specifically anytime, anywhere access to all one's personal data, resources, and tools. Also, findings from researchers at Project RED found maximum benefits are only realized when technology is integrated into daily teaching.[32] Stern notes that the iPad carts available to her classes must be reserved a week or two in advance, requiring a lot of planning. Signing devices in and out also carves into instruction time and makes the cart more of an inconvenience. Having a subset of devices in the classroom at all times, however, allows teachers to take advantage of teachable moments. For example, Stern explained that when a question from a student is posed, the moment is prime for getting out devices and searching together for an answer. These teachable moments would give students a simulation of the real world, as well as greater opportunities to learn practical, educational uses for mobile technology.[33] Without the elements of portability and ubiquity, mobile devices do not provide much advantage over other technologies such as laptop or desktop computers.

Instead, schools are encouraged to distribute devices such that they can be integrated into daily instruction. iPad professional development expert Jamie Hall suggests dividing carts up so that each classroom has access to a number of devices at all times.[34] For early elementary (K–3), sharing the classroom's devices might be more feasible when center-based learning is more prevalent and activities that rely on personal data are less frequent. For older grades (4+), schools could choose to pilot a classroom set of devices in order to gather data for making the decision to invest in a 1:1 initiative. At a minimum, devices should be allowed to remain in a single classroom for the length of a particular lesson. For example, students should be allowed to interact with the same device during a single project-based learning lesson, lessons that generally span multiple days. This way, students can pick up where they left off, work at their own pace, and are not wasting class time transferring and loading work from the previous day.

Professional Development

Device Management. A particular advantage of maintaining control of the devices is personally setting up the device to eliminate wasted class time. Before the students access the device, teachers can ensure all the apps and software are updated (a process that can be expedited by using a device-management system), the device is connected to the network, and the device is charged. Also, some instructors find it useful to group apps into folders, particularly for younger students learning individually or in center-based activities. As a result, lessons that require more than one app do not fall victim to wasting time searching for each app on the home screen.

Also, a number system is not only beneficial for accountability, but also for more closely realizing the personalization and ubiquity of mobile devices. Since devices were not originally designed to be shared, many apps utilize local storage as opposed to storing user-created data in a cloud database. Therefore, when the same device is checked out each time, students can build projects, portfolios, and so on, using a single device without having to worry about losing data. Note, however, that data privacy should be a concern when storing data locally and among other students at the school. Constantly clearing data at the end of each lesson can prevent unintentional privacy violations.

Lesson Planning. A classroom set of mobile devices is a great resource, even if access is subject to the constraints of sharing among the school. As presented in Chapter 5, facilities for promoting creativity, problem solving, collaboration, and critical thinking afforded by mobile technologies have the potential to bring certain lessons to life and deeply engage students with content. Wilkinson, a kindergarten teacher, notes one lesson that produced particularly high levels of engagement and critical thinking from her students. Using the app *SlideStory*, her students write their own books, record their voices, and share them with the class. "They spend more time on their stories, and sharing makes it more evident to them if their story doesn't make sense," she says.[35] Problem- or project-based learning activities and lessons that benefit from virtually taking students outside of the walls of the classroom through simulation apps are wonderful examples. Since such projects often span multiple days, 1:many deployments that allocate a small number of devices per classroom align well with supporting a one device per group set up. Creating groups and defining specific roles for schools with shared classroom sets, instructors should ensure extended availability so students do not have to shift to another tool mid-project. Moreover, the reliability of Internet access must be considered. Apps that can be used offline or those that do not require significant bandwidth can help to preserve the vision of the lesson.

Conversely, 1:many best practices suggest avoiding tools for daily use, such as note taking and time management tools, or those that rely on personal data. Study skills are best learned when instruction is integrated into their daily activities.[36]

In other words, teaching a student to take organized notes on a device using *Evernote* will be more beneficial if that student is allowed to continuously practice and receive feedback. Thus, since mobile devices are often shared in 1:many scenarios, utility-based tools should be limited to other materials that will be consistently available.

1:1

The 1:1 movement, wherein schools aim to provide one laptop or mobile device to each student to facilitate truly integrated technology-based learning, is increasingly becoming a reality as schools look beyond the initial financial investment and see the promise of a mobile-enhanced education. With 1:1, the mobile device becomes an essential component of students' education that takes full advantage of the many affordances discussed throughout this book. The Franklin Academy in Wake Forest, North Carolina, has a 1:1 model and shares their experiences for other schools' benefit. They've noted that with the use of iPads, the "submission of hard copy homework in the classroom" is reduced, as well as "the number of separate notebooks maintained and carried around by students on a given day." They also note that there is a "general decrease in the need for face-to-face meeting when students are completing group projects, thus increasing student interaction with the material as a group outside the normal classroom times."[37]

Implementation Strategies

1:1 initiatives must not be deployed hastily; they should be implemented only after careful and thorough analysis and planning. Such planning includes establishing when and how the roll out will occur, revamping existing curriculum so mobile is integrated as opposed to retrofitted, developing policies for logistical management of devices, scheduling ongoing professional development around mobile learning, and devising long-term plans for continual support and refinement overtime. For instance, Franklin Academy's 1:1 deployment involved several years of using devices in a 1:many setup before the transition occurred.[38]

Devise a Deployment Strategy

Moving to 1:1 affects all educational stakeholders including teachers, administrators, parents, students, specialists, and IT personnel; therefore, all parties should be represented when going 1:1. Deploying a 1:1 implementation has many implications—from technical infrastructure to pedagogy—so developing a clear plan is critical for success, while rushing into deployment leaves great room for error. Many technology specialists warn that mobile devices are not appropriate in all situations; therefore, investment should never precede an assessment of needs. If it becomes clear that mobile devices can serve a pivotal role, piloting is strongly encouraged: identify teachers willing to participate in the program and gather appropriate data by documenting successes as well as roadblocks and challenges.

Finally, decisions should be made for what the fully deployed integration will look like in both the short- and long-term. Will students take their devices home or leave them at school? What precautions will be taken to prevent misuse? Who will be responsible for damaged or destroyed devices? What defines acceptable use in school? How does acceptable use differ outside of school? How will the content on the devices be managed? What privileges will students have in terms of personalization and customization? What professional development will be provided for teachers? These questions only scratch the surface of things to consider.

Once a set of best practices has been established and details of the implementation have been decided, leaders should begin to share their experiences and gather buy-in from other teachers, students, administrators, specialists, and parents. Goddard, a technical specialist, notes that parents in her district got enthusiastic and invested in the technology program. She notes that you "have to work with the parents and ease into it," by bringing them along as you build the technology program. It takes a level of getting used to, but after they see the benefits, many parents are on board. She notes, as did all of the teachers we interviewed, there haven't been any major complaints from parents.[39]

Assess Technology Requirements and Update Infrastructure

Relevant to stakeholder buy-in, Tim Clark, chief technology and information officer for Forsyth County Schools in Georgia, states, "If you don't have the infrastructure to back it up when you need it, you're going to lose teachers and you're going to lose students because they don't see it as reliable."[40] Unfortunately, although 92 percent of teachers agree access to the Internet affects "their ability to access important teaching materials,"[41] only about 30 percent of public schools have the broadband speed necessary to reliably access the Internet. Currently, the federal government is pushing to provide connections at no less than 100Mbps in all classrooms across the country; however, connections in successful 1:1 schools often surpass that minimum with connection speeds exceeding 1Gbps.[42] Aside from improving broadband capabilities, information technology professionals at 1:1 schools also suggest investigating features such as private clouds, network connections, and teacher/student and private/public networks. Thus, purchasing devices is only a piece of the 1:1 investment—care should be taken prior to deployment to ensure the infrastructure is in place to support widespread, concurrent use.

Ensure Access Outside of School

For 1:1 initiatives that allow students to take their devices home, it is important to ensure students can access their materials both in and outside of school. However, this falls flat if there is variance in students' access to broadband. To ensure equality, some districts, such as Wisconsin's Green Bay Area Public School District, provide students with mobile hotspots (e.g., Kajeet[43]) along with their mobile device that connect their device to wireless service from a cellular network provider.[44]

Professional Development

Lesson Planning. Lesson planning in a 1:1 classroom parallels the process explained in the 1:many discussion above with the distinctive advantage of ubiquity. As opposed to 1:many installments, 1:1 classrooms are not limited to particular days, times, or lessons. Instead, mobile devices can more deeply be integrated into daily instruction allowing instructors to also demonstrate and teach strategies for utilizing productivity-style and tool-based apps like digital note taking, content sharing, and identifying credible sources for on-demand, online information. Constant access to a mobile device also provides great opportunity for developing self-regulated learners. Data tracking apps, such as *SAS Data Notebook*, allow students to set their own goals, collect and analyze performance data in order to monitor their progress, communicate with teachers and parents, reflect on their work, and make data-driven decisions accordingly.

Instructors should be cautious not to fall into the common assumption that devices are a silver bullet or all-encompassing solution to quality education.[45] According to iPad-for-education advocate, Jamie Hall, the most successful 1:1 classrooms are those that use a variety of resources in daily instruction. "There are many situations when [mobile devices] are not the optimal solutions for a particular lesson … Technology should follow pedagogy," Hall explains.[46] Furthermore, since approximately three out of four teachers strongly agree that "search engines have conditioned students to expect to be able to find information quickly and easily" and 7 out of 10 find "today's digital technologies discourage students from finding and using a wide range of sources for their research," teaching students to look beyond their devices is a viable endeavor for producing lifelong learners.[47]

BRING YOUR OWN DEVICE (BYOD)

BYOD programs explicitly blur the lines between school-based activities and real-world experience by seamlessly embedding educational tools within students' everyday lives. It is no secret that students, especially teens, seem to be tethered to their mobile devices, but the breadth of usage is limited. A recent study conducted with university-age students revealed the majority of respondents were "largely unaware of their potential to support learning." [48] But, this should not come as a shock. Without moving cellphones above the desk at school, students will continue to conceptualize mobile devices purely as means for entertainment and socializing. BYOD programs, however, open students' eyes to the opportunities afforded by mobile devices for learning and equip students with skills necessary for college and career success. In fact, in the same investigation noted above, researchers found that by briefly explaining a few applications of mobile devices for learning, "the students quickly began to understand and consider the opportunity." Led by their instructor, BYOD allows students to explore and practice effective use of their own mobile devices for productive and educational purposes. Consequently, these resources live on their devices and become readily available beyond the classroom.

Also, although the educational benefits of a BYOD program might look similar to those afforded by 1:1 initiatives, there is a strong case to be made for allowing students to use a *familiar* device. The mobile-device market is ever-expanding, and individual devices offer distinct differences, such as the underlying operating system, size, durability, customization and personalization options, available apps, and accessibility tools. After developing certain preferences, it can be difficult and even uncomfortable to transition to using a new device.

By capitalizing on the device familiarity established outside of school, class time that might have been otherwise used to teach students how to use provided technologies can instead be allocated to more productive activities.

Lastly, BYOD implementations also have the potential to bridge the gap between schools' desired access to technology and tight budgetary allocations. Many schools simply cannot afford a significant mobile implementation. Also, as of 2013, 37 percent of all teens have their own smartphone,[49] and more than 60 percent of parents indicated they would purchase a mobile device for their students if the device could be used for schoolwork.[50]

Nonetheless, BYOD implementations are by no means simple. Concerns regarding classroom management, safety, theft, privacy, and technology infrastructure often complicate BYOD programs. However, the proliferation of successful BYOD initiatives has yielded helpful lessons learned from wireless network considerations to professional development.

Implementation Strategies

Many concerns raised in the discussion of 1:1 implementations are also issues for BYOD programs. This section will further develop those mentioned previously.

Technology Requirements and Terms of Use

A unique challenge of BYOD is the property debate. Although the devices are being used in school, it is important to draw hard lines between who is responsible for the device. For example, who is responsible for keeping the device charged? What if it is stolen at school? What about virus and malware attacks when students are connected to the school network? On an even more serious note, rules also need to be put in place for what jurisdiction the school has when it comes to seizing and searching students' personal devices. Under the Fourth Amendment of the U.S. Constitution, it is illegal in most cases for school faculty members to search and seize student- and parent-owned devices—a right that has been upheld in BYOD-related court decisions.[51] Thus, it is important to establish similar policies to those regarding other student property such as backpacks before deploying a BYOD program.

Also, similar to the technical requirements for deploying a 1:1 environment discussed in the previous section, allowing students to connect their personal devices to a school network introduces additional complications from connectivity issues to inappropriately using apps for activities such as streaming videos and music. For BYOD implementations that allow for generous use and student autonomy, it is difficult to control what students are doing on their personal devices. In this case, exceptions should likely be made for cases when students are engaging in activities that affect the productivity of others (e.g., needlessly consuming bandwidth for off-task activities).

Ensure Equity

Equitable access to mobile devices poses a significant threat to BYOD implementations in many districts. Setting minimum technical specifications (e.g., Internet access, battery life) for devices can promise all students can participate in all mobile-based activities while also putting great financial burden on some families. In order to level the playing field, some schools have adopted a hybrid BYOD-1:1 platform where students without adequate devices are issued a school-owned device. Therefore, the school is only responsible for buying a handful of devices as opposed to an entire school set. Moreover, from large, charitable organizations to local PTAs, there are several options for low-income schools to acquire supplemental devices for little to no cost. Finally, as mentioned in the 1:1 discussion above, out-of-school access to broadband can ruin the potential for mobile integration; therefore, pointing students toward free Wi-Fi locations in the community or providing students with mobile hotspots are great ways to support equal access.

Professional Development

Device Management. As previously mentioned, a significant concern with allowing personal devices in the classroom is the lack of control over content and apps with personal devices. At the classroom level, this concern manifests as a threat to behavior management given student access to various off-task activities and distractions.

Surprisingly, many BYOD veterans attest that allowing students to use their own device actually *decreases* the instances of off-task behavior. For example, leaders from Forsyth County Schools in Georgia note, "We have noticed that disciplinary issues regarding technology have [gone] down since the implantation of (BYOD). It is surprising in some ways how normal it seems with the devices in the school."[52] Similarly, teachers at Oak Hill Local School District find, "students text less in class when they have the opportunity to text their friends in the hall."[53] When it does occur, off-task and inappropriate use provides a great opportunity to teach students the differences between the use of mobile in professional and casual settings. Regardless, best practices suggest that instructors be upfront and consistent with their terms for acceptable use by clearly stating the consequences for misuse, as well as stating a policy for notifying students when it is okay to use their devices and when they should put them down and focus elsewhere.

Also, ensuring teachers are proficient on a wide variety of devices is important for minor troubleshooting in the classroom. Proficiency across platforms can save both time and resources; but keeping up with the constant availability of new devices and operating systems can be quite difficult. Training staff to provide technical support for all mobile devices would turn teachers into IT support staff or system administrations and take away from the time they could spend teaching. There are two ways to avoid this. First, instructors should not forget the expertise of their resident digital natives—the students in the classroom. Students often already have exposure and are sometimes already experts at using their own device. Second, key teaching personnel can play a larger support role by serving as device experts armed with troubleshooting techniques and knowledge of the latest features for particular families of devices.

Lesson Planning. Like 1:1, BYOD programs afford great opportunity to deeply engage students with the content by utilizing techniques for encouraging higher-order thinking, as discussed in Chapter 5. Therefore, instructors are charged with identifying and creating lessons that leverage the advantages of mobile devices, such as access to rich content, interactive tools and simulations, collaboration and communication tools, and taking advantage of device use outside of the classroom.

Also, the challenges present in all 1:1-style classrooms should also be considered, such as choosing apps and designing activities that do not clog the network's bandwidth, and always being prepared for offline use. Unique to BYOD, lessons must be normalized to accommodate a classroom of different devices. The Oak Hills Local School District in Ohio uses the following example:

> A history teacher would like his students to turn in a history paper on George Washington. Looking around the room, he notices the following:
>
> - Five students have Windows laptops with MS-Office.
> - Twelve students are using smartphones—Androids and iPhones.
> - Three students have MacBooks.
> - Four have iPads.
> - One has a Kindle.
> - One student has a Linux netbook.
> - Twelve students have nothing at all, which means they'll use the Media Center computers [that do not have MS-Office on them].
>
> The question is how to collect the history paper in a standardized format that won't drive the history teacher crazy and be easy for the students.[54]

Given the variables of this scenario, finding resources that run on all platforms can be difficult. Therefore, in a BYOD classroom it is important to identify mobile and web apps that are available across platforms. For student-led activities that do not necessarily require public sharing, allowing students to choose their own tool from a list of apps not only alleviates the challenge of finding cross-platform tools but also allows students to accommodate their own needs and preferences. Lastly, constraining the range of devices acceptable for a BYOD program is another method for mitigating this issue. We suggest putting minimum requirements on the devices students bring. Schools could stick with one operating system or require a certain size screen and memory for BYOD devices.

CONCLUSION

There are many ways to implement a mobile plan, and each school should determine which is the best fit. A mobile learning plan brings many variables into the school, but it also brings many new and exciting ways to reach students and engage them in the learning process. In schools with mobile learning plans, more than half of the parents and teachers agreed that mobile learning "provides a way for students to review materials anytime, extends learning beyond the school day, personalizes learning, increases student engagement, and improves school to home communications."[55] School, and education, should be engaging. The goal of education is to create a generation of curious, competent learners who know how to function in a society. As mobile devices become a pervasive tool in our society, our classrooms must adopt these technologies if we are to help students achieve that goal.

NOTES

1. Amanda Lehnhart, Rich Ling, Scott Campbell, and Kristen Purcell, "Chapter Four: How Parents and Schools Regulate Teen's Mobile Phones" in *Teens and Mobile Phones* report, www.pewinternet.org/2010/04/20/chapter-four-how-parents-and-schools -regulate-teens-mobile-phones/.

2. Joshua Bolkan, "Report: Middle School Students Using Smartphones More Interested in STEM," *The Journal*, http://thejournal.com/articles/2012/11/29/ report-middle-school-students-using-smartphones-more-interested-in-stem.aspx. 11/29/12.

3. National Release of Speak Up 2013 National Findings, Congressional Briefing, April 8, 2014, www.tomorrow.org/speakup/2013StudentFindings_CB_recording.html.

4. White House, ConnectED Initiative, www.whitehouse.gov/issues/education/k-12/ connected.

5. Unesco, "Turning On Mobile Learning in North America," *Unesco*, 2012, http:// unesdoc.unesco.org/images/0021/002160/216083E.pdf.

6. Elliot Soloway, Cathie Norris, "Realizing Increased Student Achievement with Mobile Technologies: Here's the Plan," *The Journal*, January 9, 2013, http:// thejournal.com/articles/2013/01/09/realizing-increased-student-achievement-with -mobile-technologies.aspx.

7. Project RED, "Findings," www.projectred.org/about/research-overview/findings .html.

8. Unesco, "Turning On Mobile Learning."

9. Katrina Schwartz, "Teach Kids to Be Their Own Internet Filters," *MindShift*, October 4, 2013, http://blogs.kqed.org/mindshift/2013/10/teach-kids-to-be-their-own -filter/.

10. Linnea Czerney, Brentwood Elementary School, Raleigh, NC, interview with authors, August 22, 2013.

11. Franklin Academy High School iPad Initiative Wiki, "Changes for 2013–2014," ipadfa.wikispaces.com/Changes+for+2013-2014.

12. Anonymous, Cary, NC, teacher interview, May 2014.

13. Brentwood interview.

14. Jackie Wernz, "Legal Issues for BYOD and 1:1 Programs in Schools," *Edlawinsights*, February 12, 2013, http://edlawinsights.com/2013/02/12/byodprograms/.

15. Howard Blume, "LAUSD Halts Home Use of Ipads for Students after Devices Hacked," *Los Angeles Times*, September 25, 2013, articles.latimes.com/2013/sep/25/local/la-me-ln-lausd-ipad-hack-20130925.

16. Forsyth County Schools, "BYOT Frequently Asked Questions," August 4, 2013, www.forsyth.k12.ga.us/Page/34766.

17. Rebecca Goddard, technology facilitator, Rowan–Salisbury Schools (North Carolina) interview with authors, May 5, 2014.

18. Forsyth County, "BYOT."

19. Amy Wilkinson, kindergarten teacher, Washington GT Elementary, Raleigh, NC, interview with authors, April 9, 2014.

20. Julie Stern, sixth-grade language arts teacher at East Cary Middle School, Cary, NC, interview with authors, April 22, 2014.

21. Rebecca Goddard, interview.

22. Ibid.

23. Ibid.

24. Tricia Hudacek, reading specialist, email correspondence, April 17, 2014.

25. Julie Stern, interview.

26. Brentwood interview.

27. Tony Vincent, "iPad as the Teacher's Pet," Infographic, April 2014, http://learninginhand.com/blog/2014/4/9/ipad-as-the-teachers-pet-version-20.

28. Brentwood, interview.

29. Wilkinson, interview.

30. Goddard, interview.

31. Tony Vincent, "Classroom iPod touches and iPads: Do's and Don'ts," http://learninginhand.com/blog/classroom-ipod-touches-ipads-dos-and-donts.html.

32. Project Red, "The Research," www.projectred.org/about/research-overview.html.

33. Stern, interview.

34. Jamie Hall, interview with authors, May 2, 2014

35. Wilkinson, interview.

36. J. Hattie, J. Biggs, and N. Purdie, "Effects of Learning Skills Interventions on Student Learning: A Meta-Analysis," *Review of Educational Research* 66, no. 2 (1996): 99–136.

37. Franklin Academy High School iPad Initiative Wiki, ipadfa.wikispaces.com/Data+%26+Observations.

38. Franklin Academy High School iPad Initiative Wiki, Deployment Model, http://ipadfa.wikispaces.com/Deployment+Model.

39. Goddard, interview.

40. Tim Clark, www.centerdigitaled.com/classtech/BYOD-Forsyth-Infrastructure.html.

41. Pew Research Center, "How Teachers Are Using Technology at Home and in Their Classrooms," *Pew Research*, 2013, www.pewinternet.org/2013/02/28/how-teachers-are-using-technology-at-home-and-in-their-classrooms-2/.

42. Tonya Roscorla, "Bring Your Own Device Prompts School Infrastructure Investments," Center for Digital Education, March 13, 2012, www.centerdigitaled.com/classtech/BYOD-Forsyth-Infrastructure.html.

43. Kajeet, www.kajeet.com/4u/education/index.html.

44. David Nagel, "Green Bay District Supports Chromebook Deployment with 4G LTE for Access On and Off Campus," *The Journal*, January 30, 2014, http://thejournal.com/articles/2014/01/30/green-bay-district-supports-chromebook-deployment-with-4g-lte-for-access-on-and-off-campus.aspx.

45. Bryan Goodwin, "Research Says … One-to-One Laptop Programs Are No Silver Bullet," *ASCD* 68, no. 5 (2011): 78–79, www.ascd.org/publications/educational_leadership/feb11/vol68/num05/One-to-One_Laptop_Programs_Are_No_Silver_Bullet.aspx.

46. Jamie Hall, interview with authors, May 2, 2014

47. Kristen Purcell, Lee Rainie, Alan Heaps, Judy Buchanan, Linda Friedrich, Amanda Jacklin, Clara Chen, and Kathryn Zickuhr, "How Teens Do Research in the Digital World," *Pew Research*, November 1, 2012, www.pewinternet.org/2012/11/01/how-teens-do-research-in-the-digital-world/.

48. Ben Woodcock, Andrew Middleton, and Anne Nortcliffe, "Considering the Smartphone Learner: an Investigation into Student Interest in the Use of Personal Technology to Enhance Their Learning," *Student Engagement and Experience Journal* 1, no. 1 (2012): *2047–9476*, http://research.shu.ac.uk/SEEJ/index.php/seej/article/download/38/8.

49. Pew Research Center, "Teens and Technology 2013," *Pew Research*, www.pewinternet.org/2013/03/13/teens-and-technology-2013-2/.

50. Project Tomorrow, "Creating Our Future: Students Speak Up about their Vision for 21st Century Learning," www.tomorrow.org/speakup/pdfs/SU09NationalFindingsStudents&Parents.pdf.

51. Justin Bathon, "Your iPad Rollout Could Get You Sued," *The Journal*, http://thejournal.com/articles/2013/09/02/your-ipad-rollout-could-get-you-sued.aspx?admgarea=Features1.

52. Forsyth County, "BYOT."

53. Oak Hills Local School District, http://ohlsd.org/portfolio/byod-questions-and-answers, accessed September 22, 2014.

54. Oak Hills Local School District, http://ohlsd.org/portfolio/byod-developing-the-tools/, accessed September 22, 2014.

55. Speak Up, "The New Digital Learning Playbook: Understanding the Spectrum of Students' Activities and Aspirations," 2013 National Findings K–12 Student, April 2014, www.tomorrow.org/speakup/SU13DigitalLearningPlaybook_StudentReport.html.

SECTION **2**

Creating the Mobile Learning Experience

Creating educational apps presents a unique opportunity to developers, but also comes with many hurdles and challenges. Section 1 presents developers with a thorough picture of the underpinnings of educational theory, as well as the realities of using technology in the classroom. It is essential for developers to understand what educators are looking for and what their students need in an app to be able to create an innovative and appropriate product.

Building upon that understanding, this section aims to present a discussion of the features and methodologies that are best suited for developing mobile apps. We present key design principles that set educational apps apart from their competitors, and enable a more intuitive and usable experience. We also outline the key features of the app development cycle and team, urging interdisciplinary support and frequent communication with teachers and students.

An area of constant debate and discussion as it pertains to students is data privacy and learning analytics, and mobile learning puts an even finer point on this issue. We discuss the obligations developers have to their users' data, privacy policies, and the ethical ways data can be collected and analyzed to provide a more personalized experience within the app. Use of mobile features, bandwidth, and student data all center on one concept we offer in this section: the good app citizen. We offer advice on how to make responsible use of the technology with respect to schools' Wi-Fi, technology capabilities, and data privacy by discussing what good app citizenship means.

Mobile learning is an exciting opportunity for today's students, and developing apps to enhance their educational experience can be rewarding. This section is designed to provide the background that developers need to create a better mobile learning experience and succeed in the field.

CHAPTER 7

Mobile Technology's Defining Features

Mobile devices offer many exciting and distinct features in educational settings. When educators and school districts embark on a mobile learning initiative, they're aiming to tap into the 10 key differentiating factors (as discussed in Chapter 3) that enhance students' learning experience. These factors set mobile devices apart from their predecessors and make them appealing to students, teachers, and administrators: connectivity, awareness, multimodal experience, familiarity, personalization, comprehensiveness, consolidation, portability, relevancy, and security. But in this chapter we will focus on specific aspects of the devices: hardware options, operating systems, and other features that, through sound app development and thoughtful pedagogy, maximize the learning experience. In this chapter, we provide a developer-focused discussion about the key features of mobile learning—that is, how to tap into mobile devices' educational potential by making the best use of its hardware, software, and accessories, as shown in Figure 7.1.

A key component of this discussion, and a theme of this section on developing educational apps, centers on how apps can be good app citizens. This term, though nebulous, relates to how apps work with the

Figure 7.1 Mobile Technology's Defining Features

user and the device in a fair and neighborly way. This can mean many different things as it relates to mobile technology features. Responsible use of bandwidth and Internet connection, reasonable app size (so as to prevent using too much device memory and precluding other apps), working well with other apps, and not collecting more personal data than is required are all examples of what makes an app a good citizen. It also encompasses the judicious use of technological features that mobile devices offer. For instance, just because tablets have a gyroscope doesn't mean every app should take advantage of the feature; it is clearly unnecessary in, say, an app that involves learning to read. Making apps that are good app citizens should be a guiding principle in app development for education, and it will guide our discussion of mobile technology features.

HARDWARE

Current tablets and smartphones offer a wide range of hardware capabilities—a high-quality camera, GPS and location services, and easy access to the Internet through Wi-Fi and 3G—all on one device. Here, we list and describe the most notable hardware components, including hardware add-ons, and some examples of excellent use of these hardware capabilities into educational apps. One major item to consider is not only the incorporation of a feature but the integration of the feature. Making an app that seamlessly lets users add a photo or track their location is not considered a bonus anymore—it is expected. And a caveat: though all of these functions are novel and cool, bear in mind the distrust consumers have for an app with access to too much personal data. An app that is a good app citizen will make sure that the information it is requesting to access is useful to the functioning of the app. Think carefully about what is useful and what is just cool.

GPS

The Global Positioning System, commonly known as GPS, is primarily used to offer locational services, making navigation personalized and accurate. GPS was one of the first features of mobile devices, and has improved and been used in different ways ever since. GPS's earliest and most common use is for navigation—using apps like *Google Maps* and Apple's *Maps* to detect the user's location and provide turn by turn directions to a desired destination. Besides uprooting the after-market automobile navigation system, GPS introduced a wide range of features in apps that aren't dedicated solely to maps, such as allowing users to check in at locations and share it with friends (*FourSquare*), finding reviews of restaurants nearby (*UrbanSpoon*), and adding geotags to shared photographs (e.g., *Instagram* and *Facebook*.) As it relates to education, GPS can add innovation with exciting uses in geolocation. *Firefly Counter* is an app affiliated with the Vanishing Firefly Project at Clemson University to track and monitor the population of these insects. Eventually, they aim to identify the cause of growth or decreases in population, but they rely on users counting and submitting data from all over the country. This crowdsourcing approach relies on use of a free app and uses GPS functionality to track the location of the data.[1] This sort of activity gives students an active role in academic research while cultivating an interest in nature, and simultaneously gives researchers data they need.

Enabling geotagging for user-generated content offers more possibilities for an educational app. At DePaul University, Dr. Jane Baxter teaches an anthropology course where students create a guide of historic cemeteries in Chicago using *Evernote*. The app's geotagging feature is huge, as it allows the automatic input of the location of the sites they wish to catalog. Making manual notes of precise locations can be difficult anyway, as cemeteries aren't usually well marked and orderly. "I think it really helped the students document their experience in diverse places in a much more effective way than I've seen before in mobile learning," says Baxter, of *Evernote* and the geotagging feature.[2] This function can be useful for general use of *Evernote* as well, allowing users to review notes by location. Students who change classrooms or buildings for specialized courses might want to browse notes by location. Geocoded notes could also help students determine where homework was done, or where an interview or research was conducted.

Indoor positioning is another valuable manifestation of GPS technology, and while it is in its early stages, it seems poised for big growth and contributions to the mobile-learning market.[3] This will be particularly useful for informal learning environments, such as museums, by allowing learners to be guided directly to exhibits or works of interest. We are only at the cusp of what can be imagined for education with the addition of indoor positioning and geofencing (the location service that notifies users when they enter a defined geographic area). This technology will be greatly enabled by new location technologies such as iBeacons, which are discussed in this chapter as well.

In terms of app citizenship, one major caveat for the use of GPS in apps is to only use this functionality if there is a reason. As we've shown, having location information and geotags can enhance the value of the data. However, if it isn't vital, don't track it. With the uptick in concern over data security and privacy, users will quickly turn away from an app they feel is unnecessarily tracking personal information, and current location is especially intrusive. Fear of how this information will be used is a big influencer of user actions in the app space.

For example, in our development of the *SAS Flash Cards* app, we initially offered a geotagging function that would enable users to see where else in the world other students were working on the app, and showing where in the world the last 100 decks were played and what those decks were. We thought it would be fun for users to see usage in this way. We thought students might feel a sense of community with their neighbors or even other students across the globe. But, given that many of our users are children, there is a risk of this locational information being used by other users for less positive purposes. Initially, we obscured the data so that the pins were not in the exact location of the user, however by that point, we later reevaluated whether or not this functionality was truly necessary. It was not; we eliminated it.

Camera and Video

Tablets and smartphones come with increasingly excellent cameras. While having a camera on a mobile device isn't necessarily novel, the ability to easily integrate photographs into apps offers many possibilities in the educational setting. Broadly, taking photographs of the world around us is seen as a way to offload our memory. Whether it's a picture of a white-board brainstorm or a bird that we saw outside, it is a quick and handy way to remember (and make digital) more details than we could without a mobile device. It further allows for notations and metadata to accompany those photographs. Knowing the exact date and time a photo was taken, for instance, is helpful information that attaches itself to any photograph without the user having to do anything. Figuring out how to surface this information in a useful, enhancing way to the user is the challenge presented to developers.

Besides simple point-and-shoot capability, cameras on mobile devices also facilitate easy sharing of information. QR codes allow for simple sharing of URLs that use the camera, so the whole class can visit the same website quickly. Some teachers tout the screenshot functionality, using as a method for students to turn in work seamlessly via email.[4]

An app that is a good citizen, as with any of the robust hardware features that can be incorporated, will evaluate whether it is necessary to access a user's photos or enable users to take photos from within the app. Apps will need to ask the user for access to their photos on the device, which comes in the form of a pop up. Developers should think about how the app will be used, and consider whether or not there's an advantage to incorporating photos or the ability to take pictures. Like any feature, adding it can enhance the app, but if it doesn't, don't add in camera and video functionally.

Gyroscope and Accelerometer

These two hardware features enable some engaging and unique functionality for games, simulations, and science experimentation. Games and game-based learning hold the most promise as it relates to the gyroscope. Users can tilt the device to simulate motion and measure pitch, roll, and yaw, creating a three-dimensional controller. This can be particularly helpful in creating enhanced user experiences through immersive learning environments. Another dimension for virtual control of the immersive learning experience includes input from a manipulated accelerometer. Accelerometers are tools for understanding vectors of force. *Sensor Kinetics* is an app that gives the user visualizations of the gyroscope, allowing them to measure the effect of gravity and see graphical representations of their motion. This enables students to conceptualize physics and motion laws, as well as grasp concepts in a new way. *StarWalk* also uses the gyroscope to estimate the angle at which you are holding the device. It also relies on GPS locational information to identify the stars, constellations, and planets in real time. While these two hardware additions differentiate mobile devices from most computers, there is still a vast opportunity for integration into educational apps.

While the gyroscope and accelerometer offer interesting functionality, many times tilting the device for actions can make it more difficult to use, and this is especially true for special populations and young children.[5] It is an advanced control, and understanding your users' abilities before adding gyroscope functionality is important.

Wi-Fi and 3G Connectivity

A major advance of tablets and smartphones as it relates to education is the instant on, instant access. In terms of hardware, this means 3G, 4G, and Wi-Fi connectivity that enables apps to be connected anywhere, not just in the classroom. *Leafsnap* is an excellent example of enabling learning outside of the brick and mortar classroom using 3G and wireless connectivity, providing an electronic field guide to help the user identify different species of trees and plants by photographing their leaves. The connectivity also enables apps to be updated more frequently and provide the most current, relevant information.

One thing for developers to think about as it relates to being a good app citizen is how it handles usage of the Internet. It is easy to accidently create an app that hogs the Wi-Fi by constantly requesting and sending data. Through good testing and research, developers should determine which content can be baked into the app versus which content should exist outside the app, accessible via the Internet. With bandwidth issues and limited data plans, getting a reasonable model for an app is essential for use in an educational setting. This provides a backup plan in case of an Internet outage, or if the connection is too slow to facilitate a whole class doing the same task simultaneously.

SOFTWARE

The software capabilities and perks are largely determined by the operating system the app will run on, as iOS and Android present very different requirements and overall experiences for users and developers. We will attempt to discuss software in an agnostic sense here and point out differences as needed.

One benefit of mobile app creation is the ease of updating. While updating desktop and laptop computers can be cumbersome and easily put off by users (resulting in many users running old versions of the software), updating on mobile systems is much easier and painless; iOS now allows users to perform updates automatically, and users often don't even know it is happening. For developers, it is important to understand what version of the operating system your users have access to. At the very least, a good rule of thumb is to select a minimum version of the OS that was available at the start of the summer months, when most tablets in schools return to IT departments for updates. Simple web searches can yield the latest upgrade statistics for both iOS and Android users. With auto-updates and less fragmentation of devices Apple tends to have very high conversion rates to the latest operating system. Android, with a larger user base and larger fragmentation of devices and capabilities, has historically experienced smaller percentages on the most recent operating system, and fairly even distribution across the latest two or three major releases. As of July 2014, Apple was touting 90 percent of devices accessing the app store were running the latest major release, iOS 7, with 9 percent on iOS 6.[6] At the same time Android found 17.9 percent on the latest OS, KitKat, 56.5 percent on the previous version, Jellybean, and 11.4 percent and 13.5 percent on the previous two releases before that, respectively.[7,8]

Of course the major consideration for all of this data is to consider which application programming interfaces (APIs) (new features and functions available in the OS) developers can take advantage of.

Mobile OSs are stacked full of new features with each new release, some of which will only be available to upgrading users. It is very important for developers to be in tune with which OS their users are using, as this influences the user experience and which features and functions are able to be accessed.

Creation

When the iPad was released, one big criticism was that it didn't appear to be ideal for user-generated content; early impressions of the device often centered on user consumption but not creation. In 2010, Lev Grossman opined in *Time* magazine, that while the iPad was a "lovely device for consuming content, it doesn't do much to facilitate its creation … the iPad shifts the emphasis from creating content to merely absorbing and manipulating it. It mutes you, turns you back into a passive consumer of other people's masterpieces."[9] This quote only serves to underscore the significant changes that have occurred for the iPad's, and other tablets', abilities and reputations since entering the market. In fact, many of the most popular and highly rated educational apps are oriented toward student and teacher creation and inclusion of multimedia sources. Creation apps are growing in popularity in the app market in general, too. Apple's *GarageBand*, for instance, allows users to create songs and music (which could accompany a presentation or other work). The trend toward user-created content is far reaching, and developers could take a cue from Apple itself to dabble in this field. This amounts to creating a tool that can be used in multiple ways, rather than a content-specific app with a very targeted focus.

ThingLink is an app that enables users to make an image interactive, by adding links to videos, music, notes, and outside links. This basic concept presents limitless educational options, since it isn't restricted in any way to one subject or targeted age range. It is used in lesson plans that span subjects, whether it's a history report using an image in Creative Commons, or creating maps showing events and attractions.[10] *SAS Data Notebook* is another example of a basic tool that enables inclusion of multimedia resources seamlessly to let students curate their learning experiences in a way that is useful to them. Apps like these, tools that provide basic structure and functionality, allow the user to add meaning to information as well as facilitate unique creations, often things that developers would never have imagined. This capability is important to keep in mind when developing, as facilitating multimedia, adding voice, music, photographs, notation, and searching are all things that give the user freedom to customize the experience to suit their needs.

Good citizen apps work well with other apps and features on the device. When developing an app, think about how to allow access to all of the hardware features that mobile devices have. Mobile devices come with all of this great content and hardware right on the device: a camera, music, authoring tools, to name a few. These are valuable resources for the user, and the ability to pull that content into an app is part of what makes the mobile experience special. This ability to create using multiple sources on the device is often expected, as well.

Accessibility

Mobile devices have been a breakthrough technology for those with special needs, and especially so in the educational setting. iPads and Apple's iOS stand out as the most accessible in the field. Their operating system and accompanying developing guidelines offer a high level of accessibility automatically. To submit an app to the App Store and win approval means that the app would generally score well for users with special needs. There are additional measures to take when developing and coding your app to ensure full accessibility, however. And if you're developing in Android, while there isn't the rigor of an approval process requiring a certain level of accessibility, there are many resources on how to develop in a way that provides maximum access to special populations. In Chapter 14, we discuss the innovative things mobile devices can do for users with autism and visual impairment.

Security

Data privacy and security are important issues with mobile learning, even more so as most users are young children. There are very specific and rigorous laws in place to safeguard users (the Children's Online Privacy Protection Act and Family Educational Rights and Privacy Act are detailed in Chapter 15 with other data privacy discussions). There are many innate software security features that mobile devices offer, so it is an easy feature for developers to implement.

Touch ID is a new feature in Apple's iOS, enabling users to connect the fingerprint unlock feature to passwords and access, a feature educational apps can tap into to make access secure and simple. Apps that require parental consent will need the parent's thumbprint, not just a password (which a child could certainly access). Single sign on uses other sites, like the handshake agreements many apps for adults have with *Facebook* that permit sharing of information and log in access. Parental notifications are another area of concern for educational app development. Apple's Family Share program offers unprecedented levels of control over children's usage. Security is an area that is experiencing a lot of attention and change as we write this book, and it is very important to stay on top of this topic as best practices continue to evolve.

The good app citizen takeaway from security is to be up front about what data you are collecting and offer an easy-to-read privacy statement. Parental notifications and approval are often required for school-age users, as well. Further, if you are collecting and storing data about users, be sure the data is secure and that you're maintaining and destroying it per the user agreement. And—we've mentioned it above but it bears repeating in a discussion about security—if the data is not necessary, don't collect it.

Updated, Compatible Software

Being a good app citizen requires that apps be up to date. Developers should be sure to perform updates as they become available, or even create new apps that take advantage of the latest features offered by the OS. Even more important than the latest and greatest features from the OS is integration into the OS in ways that users want to use the app or move their content around.

Avoid big changes to your app updates that might break certain functionality, and reserve them for only when they are truly needed. If you are updating your app, be sure to prepare and test data migration for previous versions of your app. Analytics, as we will discuss in Chapter 10, will help you understand the distribution of app versions and identify which migration paths will be most common. Some schools don't update immediately when a new version becomes available. While you want to take advantage of the latest and greatest functionality, be sure you are not making the app unusable for users without the latest upgrade. A good rule a thumb we follow is to take the OS available at the end of the previous school year as the new minimum OS for future apps and updates. Of course, this is only necessary when entertaining new OS features and functions for incorporation. The assumption this rule makes is that the IT department is likely to have access to devices over the summer and BYOD students are prepping devices for the start of new school year.

Migration is an important step to provide a seamless user experience from one version to the next. If you are changing the data model, take special care during migration. If you are making changes server side that impact older versions, consider options for creating new services, as opposed to modifying existing ones, so that users who may not upgrade are not shut out of use of the app altogether. Rely on analytics to understand the user community that is being left behind if breaking changes are not avoidable. Finally, we recommend that developers find ways to communicate these forthcoming changes with users, perhaps—even through a feature of the app—and explain why the upgrade will improve the app experience.

Compatibility with other apps and operating systems is another factor to consider. App smashing has become a regular, often discussed phenomena in mobile-learning implementations. App smashing is made effective when apps are able to communicate with one another. This can be accomplished via the cloud, but more often through the operating system. For example, apps can now display a dialog to users that contains apps that can handle particular file types. The app developers don't really need to know anything about the other apps, other than it's possible for a particular file types to pass to the OS and the OS will hand it off to the other app on the user's behalf. The resulting behavior for users is successful app smashing. Multitasking is another feature that has proved useful in app smashing. Android and Windows mobile operating systems both allow split-screen behaviors so multiple apps can be viewed and interacted with simultaneously. Actions like transferring content from one app to another can occur seamlessly through the OS.

The Cloud

In many school settings, mobile devices aren't for only one student. Sharing devices among classes or even among the whole school is sometimes the only way schools can get devices in the hands of their students. So, if the work one student does on the device is to be saved and useful after the class period ends, that student's work must be saved somewhere common to allow access at a later time. The cloud offers the ability to save work on a remote server by requiring authenticated access to differentiate users from one another. It also opens the door to a more personalized app experience, should developers choose to use that data. Google Chromebooks are the foremost example of success using the cloud, with nearly all data being stored on the web, requiring web-based authentication to access the device. Today an individual user's cloud experience is comprised of numerous servers owned and operated by many parties. Mobile providers are offering clouds with the OS for storing app data, backups, and other information. Developers can even gain access to these clouds through APIs. Other developers, especially those offering cross-platform experiences, are maintaining their own clouds to support their own apps. While this infrastructure is often invisible to the user, it is very valuable to users to have access to this content from multiple devices or the Internet. A good app considers the user's experience, and if it makes sense for users to have access to their work across devices, it should provide cloud service to facilitate that.

Push Notification

A major service offered by mobile providers is push notification. Push notification allows developers to trigger messages to users outside of the main app interface. Providers have maintained some oversight of such notifications, so developers that want to send a notification to a user must do so through the services of the mobile provider. For example, if the state of data for a particular app has changed (e.g., a teacher has posted a grade for a student, or all students have submitted their homework), an app developer may decide to notify users of such an event. The developer will then construct a notification, usually through their own services, and automatically send it to the mobile provider to be placed in a queue for the user and distributed appropriately. Push notification does require some maintenance responsibilities for the developer to ensure clean push-notification data is sustained to mobile providers and good user experiences are delivered. As with many of the software features we note, to be a good app citizen means to only use push notifications if they are appropriate; users tire quickly of having push alerts for things they do not think are important enough to justify interrupting other tasks.

Integrated Packages: Health Kit and Google Fitness

As personalized user experiences expand, the information students can maintain in their mobile devices grows. In 2014, both iOS and Android announced plans for their latest operating systems to integrate health and fitness data from apps in a single location, including more apps in the package, and all of this at the discretion of the user. So, one app can track how many steps a student took while another app displays the data and shares it with the physical fitness instructors. Principals might be interested to see if there's a correlation between physical activity on a certain day and behavioral interventions. This sort of connection and synergistic sharing of data can make the user experience even richer, giving a less segmented experience. We expect the trend toward app integration will continue, and developers will need to consider how and when to allow it with their own app(s).

ACCESSORIES

One of the more exciting areas that set mobile devices significantly apart from other technologies, in our view, is the plethora of accessories that are available. Each offers a relatively simple, seamless add-on that improves the overall experience, sometimes even transforming the device into something else altogether. There are many, many accessories to change and personalize the user experience on a device, ranging from highly specialized to more universal: keyboards, Bluetooth headsets, refreshable Braille displays, thermometers for science experiments, and so on. This trend toward making mobile devices more than just phones or web browsers is exciting, and presents developers with even more features and options to work with. While there are many noteworthy accessories, we will discuss three—Apple TV, iBeacons, and wearable technologies—as they present the biggest opportunities to the mobile learning world. While developing an app with a necessary accessory in mind isn't always a great idea, because it presents extra financial hurdles for many users, accessories are worth considering as means to improve the user experience and unlock more functionality in certain situations.

Apple TV

For classrooms that have iPads or iPod Touches, an Apple TV is an affordable and robust accessory that enables sharing and projection. Using the AirPlay function, Apple's "proprietary protocol stack for wireless streaming of media,"[11] Apple TV acts as an instant projector, enabling the teacher or any user in the room who is connected to the network to share their screen. This has become very popular among teachers, as the number of devices in classrooms continues to rise. In developing an app for education, plan on users wanting to use AirPlay, and consider how the experience of using an app changes when they do. For instance, you can allow screen mirroring (projecting the display on the device and on the Apple TV simultaneously), which aids in usability. Using a "touch indicator" is another way to make the viewing experience meaningful for the larger group, showing on the projector what is being touched on the device screen. Developers can enable a circle to display on the projector view where the screen is touched, so the audience can see what button is being selected or which areas are being discussed.

For classrooms that don't have an Apple TV, but do have access to an Apple laptop or desktop, the latest versions of Apple OS X support AirPlay as well. With a projector connected to the computer, an iPad can be mirrored and thus displayed to the entire class. Other operating systems are offering similar devices (most notably, the Google Chromecast); however, we note the Apple TV here because it is the most mature and popular device.

iBeacons

Low-energy Bluetooth devices are more commonly and memorably known as iBeacons. Though they're little more than a Bluetooth chip that can be placed in a static location with a powerful battery, iBeacons offer many exciting possibilities for education when paired with mobile devices. iBeacons come with a major field and minor field that can contain identifier information for the applications to which they connect. This allows an app to display contextual information about the users' whereabouts after the mobile device is detected in a defined range. Such devices are being rolled out in massive numbers at retail locations to both track shopping habits and offer just-in-time information and discounts to consumers traveling through the store. One exciting educational application for iBeacons relates to museums, where iBeacons can be deployed at exhibits to alert applications to display relevant information to users, such as video, pictures, and audio guides. This sort of information will improve the overall learning experience of the museum and even guide the learner to the most relevant information. While the GPS handles how to get there, iBeacons can contextualize the experience for the user. In the classroom, iBeacons could be set up as stations, pushing information to students as they arrive in the center with the day's assignment. With an enabled app, teachers can trigger an iBeacon to inform an app to load the desired warm up exercise as students enter the classroom. At the time of writing this book, iBeacons are new and present many possibilities; we believe we are only at the beginning of what will be possible with this technology in the future.

Wearable Technologies

Wearable technologies integrated with mobile devices are emerging now and offer broad implications for education. Various wearables are readily available today and in mass production, such as pedometers like Fitbit[12] and Nike+.[13] Other wearables, like smart watches, are just beginning to emerge. Still others are being explored for practical application and production, such as Google Glass.[14] Many of today's consumer wearables focus on health sensors, like counting steps, monitoring pulse, and respiration. For education, they offer many possibilities for student health and fitness, such as providing athletic coaches and physical education instructors with their students' and athletes' daily information. Such tools could provide the diagnostics to educators to create individual training plans. Physical education teachers can ensure students are working hard and staying in safe zones. Smart watches have only begun to emerge as consumer products in 2014 with many rumored future enhancements anticipated in the near future. We can expect that smart watches will work well with mobile devices and may contain many sensors, including health-related sensors, but also GPS, gyroscopes, and accelerometers. Such sensors will enable a range of applications yet to be thought of, and developers will play a large role in finding ways to use these technologies in original ways. Much innovative thought around smart watches in education revolves around teacher usage to receive timely information during class without the need for a phone or tablet nearby.[15,16] Lastly, Google Glass has been one of this decade's largest, most widespread experiments to date. As numerous practical applications are pursued, Glass presents some interesting and innovative opportunities in education. For instance, teachers can assess student attention through monitoring of gaze or even assess their own attention, perhaps highlighting areas of the class or particular students that receive the most glances. As wearable technologies continue to emerge from labs to consumer shelves we expect to see innovation that will be worthy of educational use.

There are so many accessories being developed for mobile devices that can turn a mobile device into an amp for musical instruments,[17] a microscope for science class,[18] a virtual science lab,[19] a wind meter,[20] a water meter,[21] and so much more. We highlighted just a few of the accessories that seem ripe to impact classrooms now or in the not-so-distant future. AirPlay and Apple TV are great for sharing device screens with the whole class quickly and easily. iBeacons are emerging to provide contextual information to apps based on microlocation. And wearable technologies move students and teachers closer to ubiquitous computing with promises of innovative applications. These accessories underscore the exciting and growing world of mobile technology, with a huge potential impact for education.

CONCLUSION

The technological features that differentiate mobile devices from computers and other technologies are groundbreaking. In a few short years, the iPad has created a whole new market, and introduced more possibilities for education than we can possibly enumerate in this book. Developers seeking to make apps for education should tread carefully when deciding which features to incorporate, always thinking about the distinct needs of the educational user and what a good app citizen would do.

As we write this chapter, these technology features and accessories are the state of the art, and we've tried to outline the innovative and exciting things developers can do to incorporate them and bring users an optimized mobile learning experience. However, hardware and software capabilities are changing all the time. To be truly up to date with mobile technology requires developers to stay in tune with each device's updates and capabilities. Many of the principles we discuss, including how to make efficient use of the right tools, will hold true.

NOTES

1. Vanishing Firefly Project, Clemson University, www.clemson.edu/public/rec/baruch/firefly_project/, accessed August 5, 2014.
2. DePaul Magazine, "Cellphone Anthropology," February 28, 2014, http://depaulmagazine.com/2014/02/28/cellphone-anthropology/.
3. Google, "Indoor Maps," https://support.google.com/gmm/topic/3517937?hl=en&ref_topic=3495909. Accessed 8/5/14.
4. Rebecca Goddard, technology facilitator, Rowan-Salisbury schools, interview with authors, May 5, 2014.
5. Sesame Workshop, "Best Practices: Designing Touch Tablet Experiences for Preschoolers," www.sesameworkshop.org/assets/1191/src/Best percent20Practices percent20Document percent2011-26-12.pdf.
6. Apple, Developer Support, https://developer.apple.com/support/appstore/. Accessed August 5, 2014.
7. Android Developers Dashboards, https://developer.android.com/about/dashboards/index.html, accessed August 5, 2014.
8. You can always find the latest appstore info here: on the iOS, https://developer.apple.com/support/appstore/, and Android, https://developer.android.com/about/dashboards/index.html developer pages.
9. Walter Isaacson, *Steve Jobs* (New York: Simon & Schuster, 2011).
10. Thinglink, "73+ Interesting Ways to Use ThingLink in the Classroom," www.web2teachingtools.com/support-files/thinglink_73pluswaystousethinglinkintheclassroom.pdf.
11. Seth Goldenberg, "Creating a Dual-Screen AirPlay Experience for iOS and Apple TV," Redfin Dev Blog, May 7, 2012, http://blog.redfin.com/devblog/2012/05/creating_a_dual-screen_airplay_experience_for_ios_and_apple_tv.html#.U860wvldUeF.
12. Fitbit, http://www.fitbit.com/.
13. NikePlus, https://secure-nikeplus.nike.com/plus/.
14. Google Glass, www.google.com/glass/start/.
15. Katie Lepi, "The Teacher's Guide to Wearable Tech in the Classroom," *Edudemic*, May 29, 2014, www.edudemic.com/wearable-tech-in-the-classroom/.
16. NMC.org Wiki, "Wearable Technology," http://horizon.wiki.nmc.org/Wearable+Technology.
17. iRig, www.ikmultimedia.com/products/irighd/.
18. Olloclip, www.olloclip.com/4-in-1-iphone-lens/.
19. Pasco, www.pasco.com/ipad/#widget_1_slider_2.
20. Vaavud windmeter, http://vaavud.com/.
21. Sensorex, http://smartaquameter.com/.

CHAPTER **8**

The Educational
App Development
Process

A great educational app meets the needs of educators, parents, school districts, and most importantly, learners. It is engaging, easy to use, and effective, something that students look forward to using and teachers look forward to incorporating. But how do developers create such an app? The process, as pictured in Figure 8.1 and detailed in this chapter, involves several key steps. First, a strong basis in educational research and pedagogy is vital, as well as starting out with the right mix of individuals and expertise on the development team, including educators, designers, and developers. The development cycle for educational apps, like most other software products, involves a continuous cycle of development, testing, release, evaluation, and user feedback that influences the next iteration of the product. Developing educational apps is an exciting opportunity, and in this chapter we lay out the key differentiators of the market. Special development considerations apply to school settings and young audiences that are not true of other genres of apps or software. We explore each of these issues as we describe how the right development team and process can ensure the production of quality educational apps.

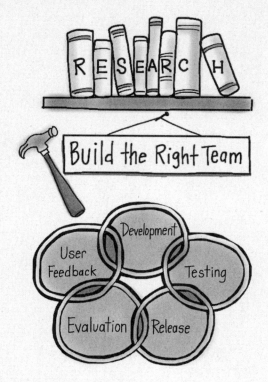

Figure 8.1 The Educational App Development Process

RESEARCH STAGE: IS IT A GOOD IDEA?

App ideas come from all kinds of sources, whether it is an idea contributed by a teacher, a developer responding to specific feedback about an existing app, or even turning existing content or software into an educational app. There are certainly many avenues that lead to the creation of educational apps, and the important point is this: make sure it is a good idea. The first step in the development process is to do some further investigation to see if the app is feasible, marketable, and useful. Along these lines, there are several important questions app creators must ask at the beginning of the development cycle.

What Type of App Is It?

This will determine many decisions and questions throughout the development process. Maybe the app is a tool, meant to be used repeatedly in various settings. If so, in what settings and how often? Or perhaps the app is content driven, focusing on a particular era of history or a literary movement. Then, it is important to identify the exact scope of the content and how it will be delivered. Will it be an encyclopedia of content, a directed tutorial, drill, and practice exercises, or maybe a game? These questions will help to identify what your app will contain and how it will be used. A full discussion of the types of educational apps is given in Chapter 3 (see Table 3.1).

What Else Is Out There?

Development teams should first see if other apps and tools do the same thing the app intends to do. If an existing app has the exact same features, it may not be worth the effort unless the app can outshine the competition. Looking through the reviews of existing apps can help developers identify what features users like and dislike and identify opportunities for new development. Nonmobile media should not be ignored either. In many cases books, physical tools, websites, or traditional software packages may meet the same needs. We recommend that developers explore everything that might be competition or inspiration.

What Do Educators Already Do?

It is important to see what educators are currently doing to know how any potential app fits into the curriculum and lesson plans. Will the app improve an existing process? Will it supplement existing curriculum? Can it be used to meet multiple needs? Will it be used in the classroom, for homework, or both? This is one opportunity to involve educator feedback early on to understand how the app would actually be used.

Is There a Need?

After considering all of the questions above, development teams can determine if there is a need for a particular app in the market. New products should offer something that similar apps don't, be useful for educators, and provide unique educational opportunities. Hard-to-teach topics and subjects are always a good place to start. Another angle is to focus on the techniques teachers use that are inefficient or could benefit from technology. Developers who keep in mind the exact need the app meets during its creation will be better prepared to deliver a high-quality app and market it appropriately.

Will Students Like It?

For an app to be engaging and accomplish its goal (teaching the student what it aims to do), it needs to appeal to students. "My philosophy for developing high-quality content for children," says Dr. Alice Wilder, the researcher behind great apps like *Super Why!* and *Blue's Clues*, "is that the only way to know what kids like, what they understand, what challenges them and what they learn from is to ask them."[1] Involving the target audience in each step is a best practice, but especially in the early development and research stages, it can lead the product in new directions. "The insights they give us along the way, while often tweaky, make a huge difference in the end product," says Wilder.[2]

BUILDING THE RIGHT TEAM: CAPTURING A VARIETY OF EXPERTISE

Educational mobile technology sits at the intersection of many different disciplines. It involves an understanding of how students learn, effective classroom practices, intuitive design, and innovative technologies. Apps that incorporate expertise from all of these areas stand a better chance of being successful and useful. Such success requires a diverse, interdisciplinary team made up of educators, researchers, designers, and developers, as shown in Figure 8.2.

Interdisciplinary Expertise

Educators

While educators may not be the primary target audience of your mobile app, they often dictate what apps are used by students and how often. Teachers and parents typically serve as gatekeepers, selecting the educational apps they want their students to use and encouraging fellow teachers and parents to do the same. School districts and administrators

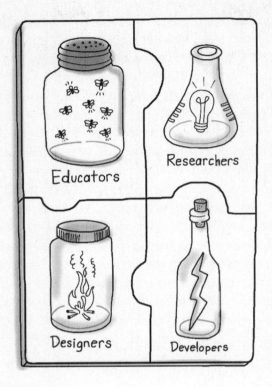

Figure 8.2 The Right Team

also commonly identify software to invest in and recommend it to (or require its use by) teachers. Consequently, it is critical for a successful app to have buy-in from educators, administrators, and parents. Educators, specifically, have important knowledge about classroom practices and limitations. They know what areas of learning are difficult for students and what types of activities are effective and engaging. They know the capabilities of their students and the limitations of their technology infrastructure. And, educators also bring a strong understanding of the learning process and pedagogy, a key tenet of any educational app.

Educators have historically been involved in the development of educational software in two distinct ways.[3] In the first, the educator is the *designer*, proposing new ideas for tools and apps that suit a specific need. The educator thus assumes creative responsibility, designing an app for a specific need. However, because educators often lack the technical knowledge, translating an educational need into an app design is often difficult and time consuming, and the results may leave much to be desired.

In the second approach, the educator is a *consultant*. In this scenario, app developers have an idea or even a prototype and seek educator input. Educators are able to identify important errors early on and make recommendations to improve ease of use. Educators may also serve as evaluators at the end of a release cycle, providing feedback to inform the next iteration of development. This approach is highly effective, though it requires the developers to have a well thought out, specific idea before involving the educators. We believe both approaches have merit, and selecting an approach depends largely on the individuals and applications involved. Having educators as integral parts of the team also allows them to serve a mixture of both roles, from designing the initial idea to refining and evaluating throughout the process. Regardless of the approach, it is important to involve the educator as early and often as possible to ensure the app meets the needs of those who will be most responsible for how it is used.

Educational Researchers

It is important for teams to include both educators and educational researchers when possible. Educational researchers have in-depth knowledge about the psychology and theory behind how students learn. They have knowledge of how best to account for and support different stages of cognitive development, an understanding about how students acquire knowledge, and the implications cognitive processing and constructs, such as motivation, have on instructional design. This awareness can help developers create apps that follow the recommended best practices informed by state-of-the-field research on how people learn. Furthermore, educational researchers can help in evaluating the effectiveness of apps. They have expertise in designing rigorous research methods and ways to measure learning and engagement. Evaluation can be used iteratively throughout the design process or after the release of the app, providing public evidence of the app's effectiveness. Involving educational researchers will help ensure the efficacy and success of the app.

Designers

While designers are already involved in the development of most mobile apps, their expertise is crucial to the development of educational apps, especially given the needs of the users involved. For example, time-strained teachers need an app that is easy to navigate and has a low learning curve. They do not want to spend a large amount of their classroom time guiding students through a difficult app. Another audience to consider is young learners, who typically have different interactional needs from adults, and require clean and simple user experiences. For example, preschool-aged children have very predictable needs and abilities. With this demographic in particular, visual design is critical. In an app for learning to read, the commands must be primarily visual, since the user does not have the ability to read (yet). Visual design must highlight actionable items and provide intuitive interaction without relying on major textual cues. Young children are also more likely to be frustrated by unresponsive buttons or unclear instructions. They may make more mistakes, so actions should be easily reversible.[4] Preschoolers are more susceptible to distractions or may be overwhelmed by too much content and complexity. Furthermore, they may lack the skills necessary for understanding complex instructions or methods of interaction.[5] A full discussion of creating apps for preschoolers is given in Chapter 13. Designers capable of balancing these needs while making an attractive, engaging app are a valuable asset to the development team.

Software Developers

And finally, the team should include talented software developers responsible for creating the app and implementing all the recommendations of the educators, researchers, and designers. These individuals should be good communicators, capable of interpreting the needs and recommendations of others, and integrating them into the final product. Developers apprise the team of technical capabilities and constraints. They may be able to suggest innovative ways that the newest features of mobile devices improve ease of use and effectiveness. They also must be capable of developing apps that can meet the technical limitations of classrooms such as low bandwidth and older devices.

We believe that beyond simply having developers on the team, it is important to have the right developers, individuals who are flexible, interested in the educational market, good communicators, and who are up to date in the latest technology trends and capabilities.

Communication

The most important part of having a diverse team is integrating each unique area of expertise. It is only by incorporating all of this knowledge that the app will be successful and effective. Therefore, communication among team members is critical. Everybody's work is informed by the other experts on the team. For example, user experience design should be informed by research findings on how individuals process information and respond to visual stimuli. New technologies presented by developers may spark the creativity of an educator to imagine an amazing new feature that will revolutionize her teaching. These innovations and collaborations can only occur if team members have open communication and respect for the expertise of the other team members. One way to support these inspired interactions is to encourage team members to observe others at work. For example, have developers visit classrooms and watch a lesson unfold. Educators can also learn a lot and provide valuable insight if they watch a designer in the process of creating a new educational interface.

It is also important to recognize that team members will have their own views concerning objectives and limitations. In many cases, these may conflict. Educators may have ideas beyond the technical capabilities of the devices or the developer. User experience may be dictated by limitations of the classroom setting. It is important to discuss these limitations in a respectful way recognizing each team member's opinions and reasoning. Assume that everyone wants the app to be the best it can, but that may mean different things from different perspectives. With mutual respect and communication, the most important objectives of each member can be met resulting in a balanced and carefully designed app. Frequent and open communication ensures that all elements of the app are developed to the satisfaction of each member of the interdisciplinary group, preventing the need to discard work that isn't in line with the group vision.

Other Stakeholders

Beyond the specific team members, other individuals can contribute to the development process. Legal consultants are important, especially when dealing with apps that disseminate content or collect data. Legal specialists help ensure that the app's content is not bound by copyright or other restrictions. There may also be legal limitations regarding what countries can use the app based on its content. Enlisting legal help will help avoid serious issues later in the development cycle. Policymakers and other high-level school officials are potential collaborators. They can often influence how mobile devices are adopted and deployed throughout school systems. They may be able to suggest apps that would help motivate legislation or use an app to demonstrate the power of mobile technologies for education. Finally, the team should identify any other stakeholders that may have interest in the app. Are there employers interested in the skills the app teaches? Are there educational organizations in related areas? These individuals may be sources of valuable information.

BUILDING THE APP

With the right ideas in mind and a well assembled team, it is time to start creating a new educational app. There are plenty of ideas about which development methods are best—Agile, Waterfall, a hybrid of the two, or something else entirely. Whatever method is used, the same basic steps apply: development, testing, refinement, and release. While we do not describe general best practices for these, we do highlight some particular areas of consideration when working on educational apps.

Development

Most development starts by crafting lists of requirements and stories of user-interaction patterns. This is no different from the development of any other application, though there are a few additional considerations for educational apps. First, what is the target age group? This will dictate content, presentation, and interaction style.

Second, what are the technical specifications of the settings being targeted? Apps developed for 1:1 classrooms may differ from those for classrooms with a shared-device cart. How will information be stored and saved? Perhaps the classroom has just one device controlled by the teacher. On the other hand, supporting BYOD programs requires implementing the same app on a variety of platforms. Whichever interaction is targeted, the team should be mindful of the implications for interaction styles and data persistence. It is not always possible to count on the same student using the same device. Finally, developers should consider what mobile affords that goes above and beyond other media. Some educational applications may benefit from being on a lightweight, portable device. Others could take advantage of hardware features such as built-in cameras, microphones, or GPS. Keeping these in mind will help to create apps that take full advantage of all mobile offers and may simultaneously help narrow the field of specific devices that need to be considered for development. There are many more considerations to keep in mind when developing a good educational app, such as the platforms available and privacy concerns, as well as cost.

Being a good app citizen (see Figure 8.3) is a primary consideration when developing an educational app. In Chapter 7, we discussed this concept as it relates to the incorporation of unique mobile features, but there are other important ways throughout the development process that apps can distinguish themselves as good app citizens. When developing an app, it is especially important for the development team to understand how their app fits into the device as a whole, ensuring it won't use too much bandwidth or storage, and will perform as expected if a classroom full of users wants to access the app. Professional development expert, Jamie Hall, says he pays special attention to features like these when selecting apps.[6] Although the students and teachers might use the same terms as developers in describing what is wrong with an app, if an app doesn't perform as expected, it will quickly be tossed aside for a more efficient app. Make no mistake; if an app doesn't practice good app citizenship, it won't be recommended by teachers to others and won't be used as often.

Figure 8.3 A Good App Citizen

Testing

As the app is being developed, it is important to continually test and check back against the original specifications. The requirements may change after development begins, but it is important to keep the original objectives and restrictions in mind. Specifically, this is the time to consider the setting in which an app will be used, especially if it's a classroom setting. Some classrooms have very poor Internet connectivity, which must be considered if an app will have high bandwidth needs. It is also necessary to test the app on older devices and older operating system versions, since many schools will not have the latest and greatest technology available. Reports come out regularly that detail the age and type of devices being used in classrooms, and it is important to stay up to date with this information. Development teams should also consider what happens when 30 or more devices use the same feature, at the same time, on the same network, as this is a common classroom scenario. Furthermore, educational settings, especially those with BYOD programs, need apps that can support multiple devices with different hardware capabilities. Screen size and resolution, camera availability, and processing speed are some examples of features that may vary widely and should be taken into account. Finally, during testing, we recommend paying particular attention to the behaviors and skills of the intended audience, especially if the app is for younger children. Testing by touching everywhere and deliberately trying to misuse the app will help make sure that it responds well and ensure that an app is accessible to young students.

Release

An app release may look very different depending on a developer or company's philosophies. Some app creators prefer to focus on rapid releases with incrementally increasing feature sets while others prefer to release a fully featured app on a delayed time frame. Some apps may require all the features that have been specified in order to be functional, in which case a full release is needed. We recommend considering the minimal set of features required for an app to be useable for the first release. Afterwards, it's best to focus on rapid releases with necessary improvements and added features. This approach allows early user feedback that can inform the next set of features and may inspire ideas that hadn't initially been imagined.

Other considerations for release timing are related to the educational market. For example, with typical school years beginning in the fall, this may be an important release milestone to consider. Other considerations could include education technology conferences or expos where creators would benefit from demoing or promoting their app.

Additionally, app creators should focus on marketing and support strategies that align with how educators and parents navigate the app market. Developers should think about the materials educators may need in conjunction with the app, such as sample lesson plans. Companies that offer professional development or lesson support for educational apps may be more accessible to busy educators. We also recommend providing clear demonstrations and videos that show how the app is used so educators and students can get up and running quickly without wasting precious school time.

One strategy for helping to guide educators toward the right app out of the many available is to focus on the specific functionality and features that are needed. We propose a set of criteria for evaluating apps in Appendix B. It helps if educators can find the details needed to evaluate an app quickly, perhaps even without downloading the app. We recommend that app creators include details about how the app may be aligned to standards or used by varied populations in the details before downloading the app. For example, if an app supports students with visual impairments, it is best to make this clear in the list of app features, rather than hoping an educator discovers this feature after downloading the app. In a similar vein, any information related to research foundations or efficacy studies should be easy to access and read. This helps educators be sure that the app they are choosing has been well thought out and studied for effectiveness.

Another important consideration is cost. Free apps are great for educators and school systems where there is often a limited budget. However, even paid apps can benefit from having a freemium plan where users can at least explore an app for free before purchasing. However, there are often many more factors to consider. A detailed discussion of different pricing strategies can be found in Chapter 11.

Finally, development teams must keep in mind that educators often find apps through word of mouth among colleagues or online blogs or review sites. Using social media properly can help promote adoption. We recommend that you make information about your app easy to share and digest in social media platforms and keep in touch with what users and reviewers are saying. Responding to social media referrals shows app developers care and are active participants with the community of users.

Evaluation and User Feedback

The final component of the development cycle is evaluation and feedback. This can happen throughout the cycle or after the app has been released to market. During development, the focus is typically on verification tests: Does the app meet the requirements? Beyond this, app creators should make sure their project meets the specific needs as described by educators and other consultants. Once the app is completed, or at least a beta version is ready, it's common to do more validation testing: Does the app do what it is supposed to? At this point, it is beneficial to involve students who may be the actual users of the app. Developers should test the app for usability, engagement, and, of course, learning.[7] Once again, this testing is especially critical for apps targeted to younger audiences, who use apps very differently from adults. While designers, researchers, and educators can provide insight into best practices for the design and function of the app, it is important to evaluate the final product. We agree with Juan Hourcade's sentiment that "Knowing about children's development and being aware of potential risks does not provide enough information to design technologies. Children need to be involved in some way as well."[8] Studies that measure the efficacy of an app can help inform future iterations and improve traction in the market as educators look for apps proven to be beneficial. We provide more tips on how to evaluate your app in Chapter 10.

Once an app is released, app developers can begin thinking about future development by asking questions: What did we learn from educator feedback or during your evaluation studies? How can that inform future versions? Another important consideration is feedback from the community at large once the app is available. Reviews can come in through app stores and other social media. In many cases, it's possible to single out reviewers and sources for more information. If a reviewer provide comments on features she thinks would improve the app, follow up with the reviewer and ask more questions. This individual clearly cares about the success of technology and wants to use it and see it improved. Such feedback could be highly beneficial in improving the app. Moreover, it's important to reply to every email that comes in, and fix problems that arise in a timely fashion. Brian Bennett, a former teacher, recalls a program he used where he emailed the developers when the program was misbehaving. He got a response back from the support team within hours and "it made me more loyal to the program, and more willing to work through problems rather than cut and run."[9]

Again, it is important to consider the role of social media. App creators can solicit user input on other social media channels like Facebook or Twitter. These are great opportunities to make the public aware of an app and seek feedback from users. Users like to see that developers care about their feedback and will be happy to provide it. Finally, we recommend that app creators make every effort to incorporate feedback into future versions of their apps and to let it be known. Showing that good ideas will be implemented helps to encourage more feedback.

CASE STUDY: APP DEVELOPMENT AT SAS CURRICULUM PATHWAYS

The strategies and tips for developing educational apps have been heavily based on our experience developing apps as part of SAS Curriculum Pathways. Throughout the development of each app, we have learned a great deal about how to manage interdisciplinary teams and involve educators, users, and consultants. To help illustrate our points, we will briefly describe the lifecycle of some of our apps and how these strategies came into play.

SAS Flash Cards is a tool-based app featuring user-created and uploaded content. Users can create, share, and practice their own flashcard decks while accessing decks created by users around the world. It was first released on the same day as the iPad in 2010, making it one of the first educational apps on the market. Since its initial release, this app has seen the introduction of many new features and revisions.

This project's development cycle demonstrates how user feedback can be effectively incorporated into future versions of an app. For example, many added features, such as audio uploads, auto-play features, and a scratchpad for showing work were all added based on user feedback. Users provided this feedback through an in-app contact us feature, as well as through reviews in the app store. Through these channels, we came in contact with J.E. Ober (JEO) elementary school in Garrett, Indiana, which had been using *SAS Flash Cards* for a variety of purposes. Establishing contact with this group of users allowed frequent conversations and opportunities for feedback and opened the doorway for future collaborations with their school district, such as *SAS Data Notebook*.

SAS Data Notebook is a data-management tool that allows students to track their own educational goals and progress, as well as take and organize class notes. All of this can be shared among classmates or with the teacher. It is modeled after paper-based notebooks that have been used in schools to promote self-regulatory behaviors.[10] It was developed through significant collaboration with JEO.

This project demonstrates the role that educators can play in informing and guiding the development of an app. Educators at JEO, a 1:1 iPad school, described the desire for an app to replace the large, unwieldy paper-based binders that had been used in the classroom. They provided guidance in the types of data that should be represented, how it should be organized, and how students and teachers would likely interact with such an app. Since its release, they have continued to collaborate with us by providing feedback on what features and aspects of the app have been the most beneficial as well as areas that the app could continue to improve to meet their needs. Because the team collaborated with educators and administrators, the app has successfully been implemented not only in the JEO school district but also in other schools worldwide.

SAS Read Aloud is an app for early literacy education. Its development was motivated by national statistics claiming that proficient reading is a critical factor in academic and lifelong success[11] and that high numbers of students are not reading at a proficient level.[12] Using these findings as a guide, we delved into related research on the phases of learning and how students acquire important skills, like print knowledge and phonological awareness. This research was incorporated into the design of the app so that the interface conforms to research standards and best practices on introducing young children to reading. For instance, research shows that drawing students' attention to salient text features during shared reading experiences is critical for developing early reading,[13] so these features are highlighted in *SAS Read Aloud*.

This project, in particular, highlighted the need for a diverse team. Developers worked closely with designers to ensure that the special interaction needs of young students were being met. Legal consultants were critical in identifying content that could be included in the app that was offered free of charge. Educational researchers guided leveling the selection of pedagogical approaches while market researchers identified features, such as parent recording, that were novel in the market. Together, the team helped to create a research-based app tailored to the target audience and unique to the market.

CONCLUSION

The introduction of mobile devices has changed the way people interact with technology and has also changed the way it is produced. Users now expect frequent releases and updates, easy-to-use interfaces, and communication with the technology creators. This is true for the educational app market as well, where apps are being used to meet specific needs in very specific settings. App creators must keep these needs and constraints in mind when developing and marketing their educational apps. We recommend taking advantage of the shifts in social media in education to open up communication with users and other experts to ensure that the apps being created will meet the needs of the target audiences. Communication, collaboration, and awareness are key to developing apps that can have a real impact in education.

NOTES

1. U.S. Department of Education, *EdTech Developer's Handbook* (DRAFT), March 2014.
2. Ibid.
3. Enrique Hinostroza, Lucio E. Rehbein, Harvey Mellar, and Christina Preston, "Developing Educational Software: A Professional Tool Perspective," *Education and Information Technologies* 5, no. 2 (2000): 103–117.
4. Juan Pablo Hourcade, "Interaction Design and Children," *Foundations and Trends in Human–Computer Interaction* 1, no. 4 (2007): 277–392.
5. Allison Druin, "The Role of Children in the Design of New Technology," *CiteSeerX*, 2002, http://citeseerx.ist.psu.edu/viewdoc/summary?doi=10.1.1.134.4492.
6. Jamie Hall, interview with authors, May 2, 2014.
7. Gavin Sim, Stuart MacFarlane, and Janet Read, "All Work and No Play: Measuring Fun, Usability, and Learning in Software for Children," *Computers & Education* 46, no. 3 (April 2006): 235–248.
8. Hourcade, "Interaction Design."
9. U.S. Department of Education, *EdTech Developer's Handbook*.
10. Sandra Byrne and Christine Schaefer, "The Baldridge Program: Self-Assessment for Continuous Improvement," *Principal*, March/April 2006, www.google.com/url?sa=t&rct=j&q=&esrc=s&source=web&cd=1&cad=rja&uact=8&ved=0CCsQFjAA&url=http%3A%2F%2Fwww.nist.gov%2Fbaldrige%2Fpublications%2Fupload%2FPrincipalMarApr06Baldrige.pdf&ei=ec90U76mB4qPqAbI-IK4DA&usg

=AFQjCNGPQsekSWJuaNH9QwUX2noZq0DoeA&sig2=efDMH4UmbweB9OR8J
26zhA&bvm=bv.66699033,d.b2k

11. Annie E. Casey Foundation, *Early Warning! Why Reading by the End of Third Grade Matters*, Baltimore, MD, 2010, www.aecf.org/resources/early-warning-why-reading-by
-the-end-of-third-grade-matters/.

12. National Center for Educational Statistics, "The Nation's Report Card: Reading 2009: National Assessment of Educational Progress at Grades 4 and 8," Washington DC., 2009, http://nces.ed.gov/nationsreportcard/pdf/main2009/2010458.pdf.

13. Shayne B. Piasta, Laura M. Justice, Anita S. McGinty, and Joan N. Kaderavek, "Increasing Young Children's Contact with Print During Shared Reading: Longitudinal Effects on Literacy Achievement," *Child Development* 83, no. 3 (2012): 810–820.

CHAPTER **9**

Design and User Experience

Though an app might be developed with attention to the best research and educational practice, if the user interface and design aren't engaging and satisfying, the app will likely fall flat. Design encompasses the look and feel of the app and the elements within it, the navigation and layout of information, the ways functions and features are communicated, and the ease with which users can accomplish tasks they need to. Good design is crucial to the overall user experience, setting up the user to seamlessly engage with the app and learn, rather than get frustrated and lost within complicated systems.

DESIGNING A GREAT APP: MAKE IT EASY

In our research and development of educational apps at SAS Curriculum Pathways, we have developed guidelines for how to design apps that are optimal for education and accessibility. The following principles, shown in Figure 9.1, are ways in which apps are judged by users (with or without their explicit use of the terms or concepts detailed here) and guidance for developers on how to make design choices.

In writing this book we interviewed dozens of educators and administrators, and in response to the question, "What makes a

Design Principles

1. Keep It Simple

2. Smart Location of Items on Screen

3. Immediate Feedback

4. Colocation of Feature and Function

5. Smart Icon Use & Conventional Navigation

6. Segmentation

7. User Age and Experience

8. Direct Manipulation

9. User Interface Metaphors

Figure 9.1 Design Principles

good app?" the most common answer was "It's easy to use." But, what does that really mean? We think for most users, being able to pinpoint what exactly makes an app easy to use is difficult. Being able to open an app and have it do what they think it will, and do it successfully and intuitively is all encapsulated in this response. For developers, creating an easy-to-use app means thoughtful consideration of their users' habits, needs, and abilities, and presenting their app in adherence with good design principles. The educational benefit of an app's content is contingent upon the way in which it is delivered.

First and foremost, the guiding principle we offer is to make the app easy—easy to use and easy to process. From there, each of the principles detailed in this chapter are truly a means to this end. The multimodal nature of mobile devices has introduced several new techniques for producing simple, well-designed user experiences that align with the way we cognitively process information. By providing a multimodal experience for users, that is, offering different platforms of interaction in a mutually supportive way (like audio and visual cues), developers can create an app that is easier to process, overall.

The argument for multimodal experiences complements the theoretical limitations of working memory discussed in Chapter 2. To optimize instruction, it is vital to account for students' current cognitive load—the amount of information the student is actively processing at any given time. If students become overloaded, they quickly become confused and frustrated; but, when too little load is being introduced, the learning experience is not being optimized. However, as proposed by cognitive psychologist Allan Paivio's dual-coding theory[1] and Alan Baddeley's model of working memory,[2] humans rely on separate subsystems to process verbal (auditory) and nonverbal (visuospatial) information. Thus, when information is presented as complementary verbal and nonverbal components, students theoretically process the same information in two separate forms thereby "additively [contributing] to memory performance."[3] Along the same line, information associated with visual imagery is often more easily remembered. For example, texts presented with corresponding images that support storing concrete, mental imagery in memory are often found to be more interesting and more deeply comprehended.[4] However, it is important to note, redundant information is not necessarily beneficial; thus, verbal and nonverbal information should be unique components working together to convey a single meaning.[5] (We wouldn't recommend providing, for instance, a written and audio cue that gives the exact same information, verbatim, as that would be redundant and provide no extra meaning.)

Keep It Simple

Keeping it simple is a basic, yet difficult principle to adhere to. For designers and developers, the desire to dress it up, add features, and enhance the app can be strong, but we urge you to check these reflexes and consider the app from the users' perspective. Users of all ages are more successful at using interfaces with simple designs, and this is amplified among younger users who exhibit less literacy and more impulsive behavior when performing actions on the app.[6]

For the design of an app, what does it mean to keep it simple? Good apps don't have extraneous graphics, icons, and themes; everything on the screen has a purpose and is contextualized. Think about users of various ages and abilities—would it confuse someone that a picture is in a square box that sort of looks like a button, but isn't a button? Does that large character illustration draw the attention away from the functionality of the app? Is the most important information displayed in adherence to the way most users scan similar interfaces?[7] Understanding the workflow of the app and thinking through where the users will expect buttons and next steps to be, as well as what items are useful or just decorative, requires testing and strong planning (usually using storyboards). This keeps the theme and workflow coherent, with a compatible look and feel throughout. And, while multimedia effects can enhance the functionality at times, using multimedia in a supportive rather than a decorative way is very important.

Additionally, don't be afraid of negative space. Cluttered interfaces can confuse the user, obscuring the intended next steps. Moreover, smaller devices like smartphones and iPod Touches, have smaller screens, making reading text inherently more difficult. For these users, less is definitely more. Just like good art and graphic design, apps with simple interfaces that utilize negative space are seen as easier to use for everyone.

Smart Location of Items on Screen

When laying out the screens of an app, think about the locations that would optimize understanding. Also, the actions that are the most common should be easy to find and reach. This principle implies working within the users' typical actions to facilitate their path through the app. For instance, if you want a user to read a paragraph then click a button to go to the next page, it makes sense to put the Next button at the bottom right of the screen rather than, say, the top left, because English speakers read from left to right and top to bottom. Providing global navigation throughout the app, ideally, navigation that mirrors app standards, is another best practice when adhering to this principle.

The "rule of thumb" applies here, which considers what areas of the screen the user can comfortably reach when holding a device.

For example, think about how a user holds a mobile device, and taps icons with his thumb. The thumb has a certain reach on each hand, and the most important actions should be within that area. The tray along the bottom with the phone, email, and Internet apps are the most widely useful apps, and placed there for that reason.[8] By watching users try an app, developers can understand what their most important features are (such as a Home icon) and place them in a central and logical location. Think about different ways users might hold the app, as well as how the location would affect the accessibility of the app.

Immediate Feedback

When users take an action (for example, click a button), they want to know that the action was completed. How do apps do this? On mobile devices, as on computers, providing visual or aural feedback for the users that corresponds to action being taken on the application behind the scenes is the best way to let the user know their action is being executed.[9] If a user pushes a button, provide animation to make the button get smaller and larger when released, simulating the pushing of an actual button. Also, if the task will take several seconds to execute, provide a loading status so the user doesn't continue pushing the button or feel it has failed. Feedback, in the form of audio or animation, can also be used if a user is having trouble (or the developer can assume they're having trouble based on length of time since the last action was executed) by providing guidance using bouncing or a color change of next-step buttons. Glow hints are a good way to reengage users that might be confused or stalled out in the app sequence. Audio cues to indicate actions or prompts to action are other ways to provide feedback, though make sure the app is coded to allow the user to mute the cues by muting their device. Some teachers note that a classroom full of students working on the same app can become overwhelming if they all have audio cues on,[10] so enabling this action is important to some users.

Colocation of Feature and Function

A major idea behind all of these principles is to eliminate unnecessary mental processes for users, so the workflow of the app aligns with the user's natural cognitive processes, which means properly colocating features and functions. For example, if the app offers an audio prompt to accompany a visual or written object (feature), the audio controls (function) should be near the object, not in another area of the app. Or, if there is text that accompanies an illustration, it should be close enough that the user can see both simultaneously, without scrolling, to have the desired impact.[11] Similarly, consider the following scenario:

> A bill-paying app presents users with their current balance on the home screen and provides the option to make a payment. The user clicks the make a payment option taking him to a new screen. Here, the user is asked to enter the payment amount without providing information about the current balance of the account.

This example illustrates a violation of the colocation of feature and function principal. The interface requires the user to memorize his current balance in order to input the payment information on the next screen. Instead, the feature and function should be colocated: the payment box and amount due should be presented in the same view. Placing supportive multimedia in logical locations improves the overall user experience.

Smart Icon Use and Conventional Navigation

Icons, when used well, lighten the cognitive load of users when they navigate an app. Rather than reading the word Help, using a picture of a question mark on a button seamlessly communicates that that button will take the user to a help center. When using icons to make app design and navigation simpler, it is important to work within the conventions of the industry. For instance, a user is accustomed to a button with a house on it indicating Home. A button with an *H*, for instance, wouldn't mean anything to a user. Creating new buttons and norms for an app presents many hurdles for users. While we understand the desire to set your app apart and create a unique look and feel, sticking to industry standards for icons and buttons is a very important element of usability.

"People tend to be unaware of the navigation experience in an app unless it doesn't meet their expectations," says Apple in their developer library.[12] While there are many standards and ways to accommodate users in the navigational setup of an app, the primary tenet is to provide consistency. Offering a logical and predictable way to navigate to certain screens, always having the option to go back or Home, so users don't get lost within the app or have to remember awkward symbols that are unique to the app. This means that there is a proper way to do something: Consistent navigation that allows users to successfully get where they intend to go is a basic concern of good design.

Segmentation

As discussed in Chapter 2, our ability to process information is limited. Adding 7 and 12 in our head is far easier than dividing 4,598 by 257. Why? The division problem creates far more cognitive load (for more information, see Chapter 2). The limitations of working memory can inhibit the density of our thinking. Users should not be obliged to hold extraneous information in their working memory while interacting with an app. Segmenting, or chunking, the content—that is, aggregating the information into meaningful units—will make the app more usable. If you are presenting children with a series of math problems, consider breaking each problem into its own screen. This segmentation of content is advantageous because young users don't scroll often, and it is generally less overwhelming to tackle one problem at a time. This helps kids to focus on the task at hand rather than get ahead of themselves. This sort of segmentation is seen in children's books as well. Consider *Where the Wild Things Are* and *Madeline*, classic children's books that offer relatively few sentences, and often just a phrase on each page that matches the illustration. This construction, though it might appear awkward to adult readers at first glance, offers children the opportunity to process the content and accompanying pictures in bite-sized chunks.

User Age and Experience

The design should be adapted and targeted toward the user. A 4-year-old will have different interests and abilities from a 14-year-old, and a 40-year-old. For example, as reading skills transition into more automatized processes, the cognitive demand of processing texts decreases; therefore, while young readers can easily become cognitively overloaded when presented with large amounts of text or long sentences, fluent readers will not because the process of reading is likely automated. Similarly, apps designed for young children should consider the fact that many of these users will not be able to read directions or navigational cues; thus, these interfaces should rely more on icons and images.

In terms of interface elements, one study surveyed users of different age groups, noting that certain tasks that adults disliked or found difficult, such as "hunting for things to click" and "animation and sound effects," were things that young users enjoyed and found useful in their navigation. Similarly, things kids found difficult to use, like scrolling, search, and tabbed browsing were popular among older age groups.[13] This is an important finding, as age and ability have a huge impact on the way information is organized. Take these demographic details into account when designing a supportive reward structure that will entice and motivate these groups. Also, bear in mind that younger users process information holistically; older users are better at ignoring unnecessary information. Younger users tend to have a harder time distinguishing between actual content and advertisements.[14] For the look and feel of an app, user age can also have implications. Children are very in tune with elements of design that they see as being for kids younger than they are, and this can cause them to write off the app as boring or insulting.[15] Understanding your demographic and their perceptions of design is a key consideration.

Direct Manipulation

With the many technological advances of mobile devices, offering more opportunities for direct manipulation to control functions is a key differentiator. Think about interacting with a map: using pinch to zoom and swiping to move the center are much more intuitive and logical maneuvers than using the + or − buttons and arrows in the corner of the screen to do the same functions. Further, in educational settings, direct manipulation increases engagement and understanding for students.[16] It's been shown that interacting with content using pinching to zoom results in kids having a better understanding of the scale of the universe (such as the size of the sun compared to the Earth, and the size of a planet compared to a particle) than they did by traditional methods of teaching.[17] Taking advantage of the functionality that allows users to directly manipulate objects on screen gives them a deeper learning experience, and should be employed wherever possible within an app. It also offers an opportunity to provide feedback while executing a command, like dragging and dropping a file to its storage location, that the command is successful.[18]

User Interface Metaphors

Metaphors are a way of "understanding and experiencing one kind of thing in terms of another."[19] On a mobile device, this means if a user reads several pages of text by simulating a book and swiping to turn the page, rather than scrolling to see more text, it is a metaphor used to enhance the user experience. Likewise, using sliders to change states in settings or wheel pickers to select values are also considered metaphors. Use of these symbols can ground functionality and icons in terms of the familiar, if used appropriately. As we discussed in the principle above in relation to icons, using the outline of a house to denote a way to get to the home screen of an app is very common, and good use of metaphor (even more so as the home screen is not where a user actually lives). It is important to keep metaphors clear and simple: for instance, using a phone book graphic to indicate a directory is okay, but using a coffee mug to indicate a discussion forum (because people chat in coffee shops), involves too many mental leaps and will confuse users unnecessarily.[20]

PUTTING GREAT DESIGN TO WORK

The design principles we enumerate above are a good starting point for discussions about practical app functionality and navigation issues. While we can all agree in theory that simple design and logical icons are great, in reality, how does this apply to creating and using apps? Sure, you don't want to burden users with long paragraphs to read, but what if you have a lot of information to convey? Below are discussions of some usability challenges informed by strong design principles, tasks that most apps will need to accomplish, or issues apps encounter.

First Launch

The user's first launch of an app is inherently different from what the typical day-to-day launches will be. The first launch is full of questions; the user knows only what you've told him in the App Store and nothing of the navigation, look, feel, and capabilities of your app. But, paradoxically, users are notoriously unwilling to read instructions; so guiding them through the functionality and features of the app is even more precarious.[21] If the initial experience fails to hook the user, it's entirely possible that the app won't get a second launch. Our discussion of what makes a good first launch and how to help users through screen tips necessarily relies on the design principles we've itemized above.

It is a best practice to provide a welcome prompt, with a brief introductory tour of the app. This could be in the form of an overlay that provides quick descriptions of the functionality that might not be obvious (i.e., "swipe here to see more news"[22]), or a short tutorial, if a step–by-step description is more appropriate. In keeping with our warning about users' cognitive load limits, it is important to keep introductory tips brief and focused; no need to provide a full user guide detailing the full functionality and quirks of the app. The initial launch is designed to provide a quick overview, and since users can't use the app and see the tips at the same time, whatever the user gleans from the first launch screen will need to be held in the working memory. So, while a welcome prompt or overlay is a great idea, keep it as simple and focused as possible. Finally, the welcome guide should be constructed to activate upon the user's first launch, but not on subsequent launches.

Tips and Help

A well-designed and constructed app should be intuitive and require little need for help. It is, of course, the goal of all developers (or should be!) to make an app any user can pick up and figure out without reading any help documentation or tips.

In reality, however, sometimes help is necessary to answer questions that arise, so it's important for apps to address these needs with appropriate and easy-to-find tips. Two levels of help are suggested: tips (either pushed on the user or appearing when certain areas are active or touched), and a help book.

As people use an app, offer helpful tips at various intervals, pointing them to functionality they might not have tried yet. While this is a great way to increase user engagement with the app (if the tips are targeted to be useful to the user), it is a key consideration that the help is offered in a way that users can dismiss it and not have to see it again. Tips should be scannable and simple.[23]

Ultimately, a good rule of thumb for tips that might be pushed on users is: less is more. The shorter the text and the greater the reliance on images, the more likely it is that users will attend to them. Similarly, avoid long lists of tips, as they will likely overwhelm the user.[24] Using visual elements to communicate the information is a good idea, as users might be able to glean the meaning without actually reading. If the app will offer tips to users throughout their use of the app, the tip format should not be easily confused with the actual interactive elements of the screen.[25] Well-written, targeted tips can eliminate user frustration and the need to read the full help documentation (which users generally think is a hassle).

Apps should offer a Help menu within the app, offering answers and guidance on standard questions and interactions with the app. Remember that Help documentation is a living space—use log data as discussed in Chapter 10 to inform updates based on user experiences. Having help documentation offered in a succinct, searchable manner is essential to pass muster on usability. Understand that the user is likely frustrated if he is visiting the help section, so make every effort to make this section easy to navigate and within the same design paradigm as the rest of the app.[26]

Logical Navigation and Finding Content

How the information in the app is presented, or how the user navigates from screen to screen or resource to resource, are important concerns when designing an app. While we discuss conventional icons and navigation in the principles above, it's also important to consider a few other factors when laying out content within an app.

Consider the concept of direct access versus sequential access. An example of sequential access is reading a book: users must read page one, then page two, and so on. So, if the information the user is searching for is on page 10, she must read nine pages of information to get what she's looking for. Many apps offer similar construction, funneling users through screens in a predetermined sequence and making it more difficult for the user to get where she ultimately wants to go. This is, obviously, a usability headache at best and a hurdle that could send users packing at worst. Allow for direct access whenever possible.[27]

Further, it is vital that an app provide a logical and global navigation scheme: a consistent way to get home. Always have necessary buttons in the same place on the screen and accessible on all screens, (usually including Home, Help, and Back) to accommodate the user's most frequent actions. If a user stumbles upon something buried deep within the app, offer a path back, showing how he got there (i.e., breadcrumbs). Users should always know where they are within an app, and know how to get to other useful resources.[28]

Login Walls

There are many advantages to getting users to create a unique profile and login credentials to access an app. Among other things, for the user it means the ability to better access past work and have a more customized experience within the app. For the developer, it means having user data in a more usable format, as well as contact information. It can, however, be seen as a hassle to users, especially for websites and apps that only provide basic information. It requires that they fill out a form, remember a password, and potentially share personal information. Oftentimes, apps are constructed to compel users to create login credentials before seeing any or all of the resources contained within. The dilemma for developers is just how much information to include behind the login wall. That is, how much can the user navigate and sample the content before the app demands that the user create an account to interact further?

Indeed, the login wall concept is similar to the first launch discussion: after users create an account, they'll be automatically logged in next time and the conversation is irrelevant. However, like the first launch, if the login wall is mishandled, the user may choose not to return.

Our recommendation is to include enough information for users to get a taste of what the app offers. Creating an account, entering a password, and filling out a form is tedious for users, and even more so on a mobile device, and this process is a considerable deterrent. Offering them the information to confirm that creating an account is worth their time and effort is necessary.[29]

Forgiveness

While it might sound silly to say, your users are human. Being such, they are prone to mistakes—double taps when a single tap was required, deleting data accidently, hitting back or next too soon, and so on. Apps must provide affordances for this type of accidental behavior. Students and younger users are even more prone to these errors, given their impulsive clicking habits and limited experience with navigation. Apps can do this by providing confirmation screens (e.g., "Are you sure you want to exit without saving your work?") to prevent unintentional navigational errors. This could also impact design through the study of where users are prone to accidentally touch the screen, as that might not be an ideal area for an important button. Beyond the accidental, users might also want to explore the app, which is something that developers should encourage. Offering safety nets (like an Undo or Revert to Saved button) makes users feel comfortable trying new things within the app.[30]

Ultimately, when designing an app and its navigation, it is important not just to think about the ideal test case, but to also consider the potential and probable pitfalls that can occur.

CONCLUSION

Apps that succeed in the educational market are apps that pass the easy-to-use test. In order to pass this test, it is essential that developers stick with the tried and true principles of good design to ensure a positive user experience. Good design might sound like something that's nice to have, and in the grand scheme of things, it's easier to focus on other aspects of the app and let design come last. This all too common approach to app design is a mistake, as design and usability are a huge determining factor on if an app gets downloaded, and if it even gets a second launch. By designing the layout, content, and navigation with the user in mind, and according to popular conventions, developers can take advantage of the success of apps that have gone before them to offer mobile education in a usable and accessible format.

NOTES

1. A. Pavio, *Mental Representations: A Dual Coding Approach* (New York: Oxford University Press, 1986).
2. A. D. Baddeley and G. J. Hitch, "Working Memory," in *The Psychology of Learning and Motivation: Advances in Research and Theory*, ed. G. H. Bower (New York: Academic Press, 1974): 47–89.
3. A. Paivio, *Mental Representations*, 226.
4. Mark Sardoski and Allan Paivio, *Imagery and Text: A Dual Coding Theory of Reading and Writing* (New York: Routledge 2013).
5. Richard Mayer, *The Cambridge Handbook of Multimedia Learning*, 2nd ed. (New York: Cambridge University Press, 2005).
6. A. Bruckman and A. Bandlow, "Human–Computer Interaction for Kids," in *The Human–Computer Interaction Handbook* eds. A. Sears and J. A. Jacko (Mahway, NJ: Lawrence Erlbaum Associates, 2003), 428–440.
7. Center for Parent Information and Resources, "How People Read on the Web," Nichcy.org/dissemination/tools/webwriting/reading.
8. Josh Clark, *Tapworthy: Designing Great iPhone Apps* (Sebastapol, CA: O'Reilly Media, 2010).
9. Alan Dix, Janet Finlay, Gregory Abowd, and Russell Beale, *Human-Computer Interaction*, 2nd ed. (Essex, England: Pearson Education, 1998).
10. Brentwood Elementary teachers, interview, August 2013.
11. Mayer, *Multimedia Learning*.
12. Apple Developer Library, Navigation, https://developer.apple.com/library/iOS/documentation/userexperience/conceptual/mobilehig/Navigation.html#//apple_ref/doc/uid/TP40006556-CH53-SW1.
13. Hoa Loranger and Jakob Niellsen, "Teenage Usability: Designing Teen-Targeted Websites," *Nielsen Norman Group*, February 4, 2013, www.nngroup.com/articles/usability-of-websites-for-teenagers/.
14. Bruckman and Bandlow, "Human–Computer Interaction for Kids," 428–440.

15. Shannon Halgren, Tony Fernandes, and Deanna Thomas, "Amazing Animation: Movie Making for Kids Design Briefing," Proceedings of the SIGCHI Conference on Human Factors in Computing Systems, Denver, CO, 1995, 519–525.

16. Dan Saffer, *Designing Gestural Interfaces: Touchscreens and Interactive Devices* (Sebastopol, CA: O'Reilly Media, 2008).

17. Matthew H. Schneps, Jonathan Ruel, Gerhard Sonnert, Mary Dussault, Michael Griffin, and Philip M. Sadler, "Conceptualizing Astronomical Scale: Virtual Simulations on Handheld Tablet Computers Reverse Misconceptions," *Computers & Education* 70 (January 2014): 269–280.

18. Apple, "OSX Human Interface Guidelines: Feedback and Assistance," https://developer.apple.com/library/mac/documentation/UserExperience/Conceptual/OSXHIGuidelines/Feedback.html#//apple_ref/doc/uid/20000957-CH9-SW1.

19. G. Lakoff, and M. Johnson, *Metaphors We Live By* (Chicago: University of Chicago Press, 2008).

20. Jesse James Garrett, *The Elements of User Experience: User-Centered Design for the Web and Beyond* (Berkeley, CA: New Riders, 2010).

21. Jakob Nielsen, "How Little Do Users Read?," Nielsen Norman Group, May 6, 2008, www.nngroup.com/articles/how-little-do-users-read/.

22. Aurora Bedford, "Instructional Overlays and Coach Marks for Mobile Apps," Nielsen Norman Group, February 16, 2014, www.nngroup.com/articles/mobile-instructional-overlay/.

23. Ibid.

24. Ibid.

25. Ibid.

26. Apple, "OSX Human Interface Guidelines."

27. Raluca Budiu, "Direct Access vs. Sequential Access: Definition," Nielsen Norman Group, July 13, 2014, www.nngroup.com/articles/direct-vs-sequential-access/.

28. Apple Developer Library, "Navigation."

29. Raluca Budiu, "Login Walls Stop Users in Their Tracks," Nielsen Norman Group, March 2, 2014, www.nngroup.com/articles/login-walls/.

30. Apple, "OSX Human Interface Guidelines."

CHAPTER **10**

Data, Evaluation, and Learning Analytics

Data drives the modern world. As we continue to monitor and store it, the amount of data available is growing at a rapid pace. In fact, in 2013 it was noted that 90 percent of the world's data was generated between 2012 and 2013.[1] The growth in data has been powered both by new technologies that make it easier to collect, store, and analyze, as well as a growing demand for data. Data has proven to be, if properly analyzed, an incredibly powerful tool for providing insights about how the world operates and how its people act. This is true both in the business world and for education. Data on how students use educational technologies help tech companies improve the usability and effectiveness of their apps. It can also inform changes to pedagogy and be used to create more sophisticated learning systems. Developing mobile learning apps is an ongoing process, and simply creating the app and distributing it is not enough; an ongoing evaluation and improvement process is necessary. Here we discuss the important steps for evaluating an educational app. They involve first identifying the questions to answer, then collecting the necessary data, then using data analytics to gain actionable insight for improving the app.

ASKING THE QUESTIONS

To evaluate an app, keep in mind which aspects are being evaluating and why. Is it primarily for product improvement? Is it to enable evidence-based claims about an app's effectiveness? In Table 10.1, we

Table 10.1 Areas for Evaluating Apps

Adoption (calculated metrics)

Conversion	What proportion of potential users eventually purchase/download an app after viewing it?	$\dfrac{\text{Downloads}}{\text{App Store views}}$
Retention	How long do users continue using the app over time?	$\dfrac{\text{Number of users who launched app n days after download}}{\text{Total number of downloads}}$
Growth	How does app usage change over time?	App downloads or launches by date.

Usability (calculated metrics)

Completion Rate	Are users able to successfully complete a task?	$\dfrac{\text{Successfully completed}}{\text{Task attempts}}$
Completion Time	How long does it take a user to successfully complete a task?	Time on task
Error Rate	How many errors does a user make when attempting to complete a task?	$\dfrac{\text{Number of errors}}{\text{Task attempts}}$

Purpose/Alignment (consultations)

Standards Alignment	Does the app align to state or common standards?	Consult official standards documentation
Instructional Impact	How does the app facilitate, build upon, or replace existing classroom practices?	SAMR rubric[a]
Efficacy	Does use of the app affect student performance?	Classroom assessments and teacher feedback

Pedagogical Soundness (validated surveys)

Motivation	Do users experience enjoyment and/or attribute value to interacting with the app?	Intrinsic motivation inventory[b]
Cognitive Demand	How difficult and demanding are the tasks in the app?	NASA Task Load Index[c]
Interest	Are users interested by the materials or activities in the app?	Perceived Interest Questionnaire[d]

[a]Miguel Guhlin, "Classroom Learning Activity Rubric," October 31, 2012, www.mguhlin.org/2012/10/classroom-learning-activity-rubric.html.
[b]Edward Deci and Richard Ryan, "Self Determination Theory," www.selfdeterminationtheory.org.
[c]Kim Chrestenson, Phil So, and Brian Gore, "NASA TLX: Task Load Index," http://humansystems.arc.nasa.gov/groups/tlx/paperpencil.html.
[d]Gregory Schraw, Roger Bruning, and Carla Svaboda, "Sources of Situational Interest," *Journal of Literary Research* (June 24, 1994), http://jlr.sagepub.com/content/27/1/1.short.

highlight some of the key areas on which evaluation should focus. Many of these overlap with the areas for evaluation we offer in the Great App Checklist (Appendix B.) That is because we believe tech companies should be evaluating their apps on the same set of criteria as educators, to make sure the apps meet the needs of those who use them. We also include examples from the development process involved in our own app, *SAS Flash Cards*.

Adoption

Measures of adoption help developers understand how regularly their app is being used and by whom. Many of these metrics relate to app downloads and launches. For example:

- How many new users are downloading the app per day?
- How many users launch the app once, but never again?
- Do English-speaking countries have higher download rates than other countries?
- Did the latest marketing campaign increase app use?

Answers to these questions help developers understand if their app is actually reaching the intended audience and allow them to see the impact of their actions on downloads and use. For example, it can be expected that app downloads will increase after a marketing campaign or release of an update. Or, for educational apps, there are predictable spikes in downloads three times a year—early September, early June, and December (in accordance with the traditional school calendar)—and developers can and should plan for these.[2] Exploring usage patterns around these times can help differentiate campaigns or feature sets that were particularly successful from those that did not have the desired impact. Identifying these can also point the way to future investigations to understand why these impacts did or did not occur. In our own experience, adoption analysis of *SAS Flash Cards* showed that downloads commonly occurred in geographic pockets associated with school districts. This let the development team know that the app was more commonly being downloaded and distributed by school systems rather than individual users, which highlighted the need to investigate ways to support in-school usage patterns.

Usability

Usability is often a key feature that separates the most successful apps from those that never grow or sustain a user community. Two apps may support the same function, but if one is easier to use and is more intuitive, it is likely to become adopted and more widely used. Some sample questions to help evaluate usability include:

- Do users interact with features in the order and frequency that is expected?
- How much time is spent accomplishing an action?
- Is there evidence of a lot of backward navigation, suggesting users have gone down the wrong path?
- Is the interface intuitive, or does it require a lot of instruction?

Some of these questions can be answered using data collected from real user interactions. For example, logging the time of each action can allow developers to see how much time it takes a user to complete a task. If it is more than expected, this may indicate a usability flaw, a mistaken assumption on the part of a developer.

Understanding how users perceive an app's design can be difficult, and for this reason, interacting with users directly is essential to understanding how usable the app is. For example, teachers may be able to articulate what exactly makes an interface difficult for second graders, while this may not be clear from the data. In the following sections we'll discuss more about each of these types of investigation and the importance of choosing the correct methods for the questions of interest. In the case of *SAS Flash Cards*, usage data indicated that users were primarily using decks they had created themselves, rather than those that had been downloaded from other users. This prompted a user interface change to bring personal decks to the forefront and make them easier to access. We offer a thorough discussion of app design and usability in Chapter 9.

Purpose and Alignment

Educators typically select an app with a purpose in mind. They may have some routine task that they would like an app to support, or a topic area for which they would like to have additional content. Since the goal of an educational app is to meet the needs of those who use it, it is important for an evaluation to ensure that the app is actually addressing those needs. Some questions that may be asked include:

- Does the app actually accomplish the goals for the educator or for the student?
- Is it aligned to standards or curricula?
- Is it appropriately leveled for the target group?
- Does the app replace existing activities or offer new methods for instruction?

This type of evaluation likely involves direct input from the target users—often educators or students themselves. As mentioned in Chapter 8, getting their feedback on these areas is critical for an app to be successful in the education field and should be part of every stage of evaluation. For example, educators who provided feedback about *SAS Flash Cards* told us that while the app was great for practice, it could also provide formative assessment on how students were learning. They wanted to see the progress in how many cards students were getting correct/incorrect over time. Therefore a feature to email session stats was added so teachers could use it for this purpose.

Pedagogically Sound

In addition to purpose and alignment, developers may also be interested in exploring more sophisticated pedagogical aspects of their app to ensure the app effectively promotes learning. For example:

- Are the problems leveled with appropriate difficulty?
- Does the app put too much cognitive load on the user?
- How does the reward structure support users' motivation?

These questions go beyond meeting a specific educational task and goal, by further investigating if the educational process is being supported in the most beneficial way. Many of these questions stem from a deeper understanding of learning processes (as discussed in Chapter 2), and investigating them often requires the specialized knowledge of educational researchers or other experts. However, addressing these questions can go a long way in supporting the validity of an app, offering opportunities for improvement, and promoting its efficacy to users. Providing leveled content in an app, for instance, is a huge selling point that can set an app apart from competitors.

GATHERING DATA

Once app developers have an idea of the types of questions they may like to answer, they next need to collect the data that allows them to do so. Mobile devices offer an unprecedented data collection opportunity for developers, and, if used correctly, this can facilitate smarter app development, updates, and design. There are two primary methods for gathering mobile data: logging and sampling. Logging provides a snapshot of what is happening as the app is being used in the field. Alternatively, with sampling, developers can collect data from a group of users interacting with the app in a facilitated setting, either a focus group or experimental population. This allows for manipulations designed to answer specific questions or obtain data that goes beyond how the app is used (e.g., surveys). Google, for instance, tested 41 different shades of blue to see which its customers preferred, by offering different versions to different users.[3] When used together, these types of data can paint a robust portrait of how an app is being used and how it can be improved.

Log Data Collection

Even the simplest forms of data offer a wealth of opportunity to software developers and technology providers. However, this data needs to be harnessed in a meaningful, actionable way. Someone who is new to data collection may often wonder where to start. What types of information can be collected? How should it be transmitted and stored? The answers to many of these questions are dependent on the specifics of the app, the insights gained from collecting data, and the expertise of the team.

Basic Usage

Perhaps the simplest and most informative data to collect relates to the broad usage of an app. App stores can report how often an app has been viewed in the store, purchased, and downloaded. The store may even track app purchases for you. For example, Apple's new iTunes Analytics provides this information for apps in their App Store, along with details about location and device type. However, this information is not all that is necessary to measure if an app is successful. In some cases these numbers may be misleading. Download statistics from schools or organizations that use a mobile device management (MDM) system often download apps onto a large number of devices; therefore, download reports may not accurately capture how many students now have access to an app. Repeat downloads and updates may also skew information. Furthermore, these statistics only provide information on the download of an app, and not how frequently it is launched. These statistics are starting to be tracked by app stores, but there are many reasons for developers to track downloads and usage themselves. Specifically, they can collect the data and represent it in a way that is meaningful for their own questions of interest.

Beyond download and store statistics, some basic usage events that can be logged to include when the app is launched and closed. Since many systems allow apps to run in the background even if they are not in focus, it is often helpful to log times when the app is hidden and brought back into view. Logging the time of each of these events allows estimates of how long the app is being actively used at each launch as well.

Another critical piece of information to capture is any event that threatens the successful use of an app. This is especially true if the event results in a crash of the app. Logging this information will allow development teams to understand how stable their app is and identify opportunities for bug fixes. However, if only the crash event itself is being logged, it may not be possible to determine the cause of the error. For example, suppose an impatient user clicks an unresponsive button repeatedly and in rapid succession and causes a crash. This could highlight the need to improve responsiveness, or disable any input during this time in order to prevent a future crash. In sum, logging more detailed user and system actions can support interpretation of the information.

Detailed Action Logging

Beyond logging the most basic events, logging detailed user action information allows developers to get a better sense of how users are interacting with an app. In order to capture the most useful information, it is important to first consider the most basic actions users perform within the app. Are they clicking buttons to accomplish a task? Are they entering information through text fields, check boxes, or other forms? Are they dragging and dropping, or otherwise using touch-based gestures? Some user actions don't have any effect on the app (e.g., clicking in a noninteractive space) and probably aren't worth logging. If, on the other hand, these user actions result in a meaningful change or response in the app, they may be possible candidates for log events.

However, just because the user does something doesn't necessarily mean it's worth logging. It all depends on what the app team would like to know. For example, if a user is scrolling through content, they may or may not wish to capture this action. If the content is dynamically loaded as the user scrolls, then capturing this user action may provide beneficial information to inform how often the app should be prepared to load content. On the other hand, if the content is static, this may not be a concern. However, the team may be interested in knowing how long users spend attending to different components of the content. In this case, logging scrolling events may provide a useful approximation of which areas of content are visible at different points of time. Again, the decision of what to log depends on the types of questions being asked.

The previous example also points to another important component of logging user actions. In most cases, it is very beneficial to log both the start and end times of an action. This allows for an understanding of the duration of activities and can help illuminate areas for improvement. For example, if a user clicks a button to download some content, it would be useful to log that action along with the time it occurred.

Suppose the user's next action is interacting with the content five minutes later. If only the start time of each action is captured, the team may infer that it took approximately five minutes for the content to download. However, if logs also captured the time that the download finished, the developer might be able to see that it took only 20 seconds to download, and the user simply didn't interact with the app during the rest of the five minutes. Capturing the duration of actions allows developers to see how much time users spend engaged in particular tasks, which provides insight into future app development.

One final piece of advice regarding logging is to consider the context of actions. This is especially important if users can take the same action in many different contexts. For example, is there a particular screen on which more people click the Help icon? Context can also include information about a user's state within the app. For example, imagine an app that focuses on learning puzzles. It may be interesting to note how close the user is to completing the puzzle when they take particular actions. Users who ask for hints or help at the very beginning of a puzzle may signal something quite different about the age appropriateness of the activity than when a user reaches out for help at the end of the puzzle. For each individual app, think about which types of contextual information may be useful to paint a complete picture of the users' behaviors.

Rich Mobile Data

Mobile apps also allow for the simplified collection of other forms of data that were once too complex. For example, we can now log the geographic location of the user. This can help developers identify if their app is being used more in certain geographical locations than others. As an example, if an app focuses on a historical event such as the Boston Tea Party, it might be interesting to see if it used more in and around the Boston area. This information, beyond being interesting, can influence marketing activities. Apps also have access to a wide range of multimedia information such as pictures, audio, and video. Synthesis of these types of data is often too complex for everyday purposes, but with powerful automated tools it may be possible to use this data to better understand how users interact with your app.

Transmitting the Data

There are many different strategies for capturing, storing, and transmitting log information. The two most common are plain text log files and structured databases, each with its own advantages and disadvantages (see Figure 10.1). One technique used by many systems is to capture a stream of information in a plain text log file. This approach is popular because it is easy to set up, requiring little advanced planning before implementation. When an action or piece of information to be logged occurs, all the relevant details are recorded (e.g., start time, end time, context), and then written to a persistent file. It is easy to add log events or change the types of information that are being captured. Developers can even make changes across different versions of the app without having significant back-compatibility issues. The major downside to this approach comes when it is time to retrieve information from the log files. Here, heavy post-processing (editing, restructuring, aggregating, linking) is required to extract meaningful information. The ease of this will depend heavily on any standardized formatting that is used. This type of format is often more difficult to analyze, especially when

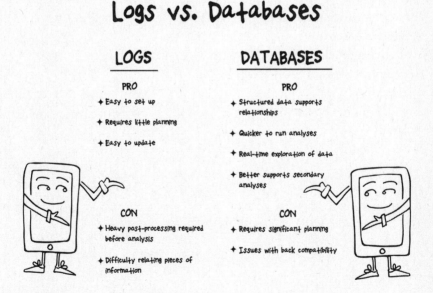

Figure 10.1 Logs versus Databases

attempting to explore questions that were not originally in mind when the data was being collected.[4]

An alternative approach is to log information directly to a database. This requires significant up-front thought in designing the database to ensure that information can be stored in a way that is meaningful and allows for desired analyses. One of the key benefits is that "logging straight to a database supports immediate efficient access"[5] of information. This allows for real-time exploration of analyses. It also better supports secondary analyses beyond what was originally intended. However, depending on design, a database design can also be less flexible, requiring more effort when changes are made to the kinds of data being logged.

One recommendation in either case is that developers should think carefully about the types of questions they may wish to ask and how different pieces of information need to be linked together to answer these questions. The process of figuring out what data to log should start by figuring out the questions the data needs to answer. When thinking of how to log, developers should consider which pieces of information need to be tied together to answer these questions. For example, in order to tie a student's time spent interacting with content features to their performance on a related quiz, it will be necessary to have a way to identify the student, and link the relevant quiz and text reading behaviors. Logging a unique user ID and timestamp with every piece of log information helps with this task. These two data points allow you to identify who is doing an action and when. Without this information, piecing together an understanding of user patterns or sequences of behavior becomes difficult, if not impossible. Unfortunately, identifying a unique user in the context of educational mobile software poses some challenges. Many classroom settings use shared devices so data may not belong to an individual user. If an app involves a user logging in, this can be alleviated. However, if this is not possible, it is important to keep in mind that a device's data may not belong to an individual user, and it may be beneficial to look at data in terms of active sessions rather than across a complete history.

However data is being stored, the information must be sent from the user's individual device and to the developer or analyst.

This requires some consideration of mobile data transactions on the devices. For example, some devices have options for both cellular and wireless Internet data. In these cases, cellular data may be limited or have an associated cost, so it is advised not to transmit logging data in these cases. Another consideration is whether the app is already transmitting data for purposes that are transparent to the user. For example, if a user is already downloading content, then this may be an ideal time to send information back to the server as the user is already expecting to be connected to the Internet and transmitting data. Finally, it is important to consider how often to transmit data. Developers may wish to transmit regularly to keep individual transactions to a minimum size, or batch log data into larger sets in order to make fewer requests to the server. The more often log data is transmitted the better real-time information can be processed. This approach is also less likely to miss large chunks of information, specifically from users who do not use the app regularly. However, there is a tradeoff to consider in the number of times data is transmitted. App providers should carefully consider these tradeoffs to decide the best frequency to transmit log data.

SAMPLE DATA COLLECTION

Beyond collecting usage data, there are many other types of information that may be beneficial, especially in an educational context. Surveys, case studies, focus groups, and controlled studies allow developers to answer more specific questions about their products but also require more time and forethought to set up properly.

Surveys

Surveys are a relatively low-cost way to get specific information about how users are engaging with an app. They can often be easily administered online or even through the app if desired. Surveys can be sent to the entire user base or a targeted subset depending on the goals of the survey. When choosing to use surveys, there are some important things to keep in mind. One of the most important first steps is to determine if the survey seeks to measure variables associated with the student (e.g., intrinsic motivation) or aspects of the interface (e.g., how much users like a feature).

Research-based surveys allow development teams to measure specific constructs. These surveys typically include a specific set of questions and evaluation criteria. In most cases, rigorous research has gone into developing these surveys to ensure that they are reliable and truly measure the construct to which they are aligned. Using these surveys also allows researchers to compare their results across studies.

Informal surveys are better if there are simple or specific questions that the developer is interested in asking. For example, "Rate the usefulness of the Help feature on a scale of 1 to 7" will provide feedback on the feature of interest. Since the researcher develops these questions, it is important to keep in mind how you intend to analyze the data. Ratings, or items using a numeric Likert scale, can support quantitative analyses. Conversely, multiple-choice questions may be more useful if there are a set of options for users to consider, such as "I typically use this app: a. In the classroom; b. At home; c. Both." These results can be used to do categorical analyses. Finally, open-ended questions or structured interviews can provide interesting feedback beyond what the researchers may have imagined. For example, the question "Why do you like this app?" could yield a broad range of results. However, it is more difficult to analyze these data points, as each response typically needs to be read and interpreted by a human to gain any insight, and they aren't easy to quantify.

Case Studies and Focus Groups

Case studies and focus groups are a great way to explore detailed questions about how an app is being used and whether it is meeting users' needs. Focus groups typically involve gathering a group of users or prospective users to get feedback over a short period of time. It is important to have a careful agenda when organizing a focus group. Should there be free-flowing dialog about what works and what doesn't? Should users be asked to propose new features and changes, or should the focus be more on specifically critiquing existing ones. Should the focus be on usability, curriculum alignment, or some other criteria? Our Great App Checklist in Appendix B is a good place to start.

Case studies are an excellent opportunity to get detailed information about how an app is actually used. For example, observing day-to-day classroom use of an app can provide insightful feedback about what features are used most, where students are getting confused about how to use the interface, how students and teachers respond to features, and what types of things may be missing. This can be especially helpful for tool-based apps that can be used in a variety of ways, including things developers may never have considered. Careful observation of real-world use can provide far more insight that even the most detailed usability logs because it provides something logs do not: context.

When selecting individuals for focus groups or case studies, consider how the population you've chosen reflects the target population of users. For example, if an app is intended for use in a 1:1 iPad setting, it is likely only useful to look at schools with this set up. Schools using apps in a 1:many setting will not be able to provide the right kind of feedback because of the constraints of their setup. Similarly, it is often most helpful to consider users who are familiar with the technology and have access to it in the appropriate setting. Getting feedback from teachers who do not have mobile devices in the classroom may not be as useful as interviewing seasoned mobile veterans.

Controlled Studies

As mentioned at the beginning of the chapter, some types of questions can only be answered through controlled experimental studies. This type of setup is best if the goal is to compare two or more conditions on an outcome. It is also great for investigating complex processes like learning gains, or changes in motivation or interest achieved through using the app. However, this type of analysis takes a lot of background knowledge and expertise to set up correctly. If developers are interested in this type of evaluation for their app, they may wish to consider hiring research personnel or partnering with a local university or agency. This type of evaluation can help push an app to the next level and is great for proving efficacy to potential users.

MOBILE DATA ANALYTICS: TURNING DATA INTO INFORMATION

Once the data starts rolling in, the exciting part begins: finding insights and answering questions. While having data is nice, it is only once it has been turned into information that it becomes truly useful. It is important to keep in mind throughout this process what your initial questions were and how you intend to use the insights you gain from the analyses.

App Improvement

One of the most common questions developers want to answer concerns product improvement. How are users interacting with the app, and what can be done to make it better? One of the first steps in exploring this area is to understand whether users are interacting with the app in the intended way. Are they showing expected sequences of behavior? Are there any features that are being over- or underused? Overused features present an opportunity for expansion. Perhaps this feature should become a central component of the app. Underused features suggest a problem. It may be too obscure or hidden in the interface, or maybe too difficult to use. Perhaps it is not as useful a feature as the development team thought it would be. This too presents opportunities for redesign. There are many other problematic behaviors to be explored as well. For example, are there common actions that precede app crashes? This could highlight flaws in the code or memory management. Similarly, are there patterns that precede users quitting the app voluntarily? This is especially important if the users never return, as it could indicate something about your app that is too difficult or frustrating.

Another exciting opportunity presented by mobile-data analytics is the ability to explore more explicit cause and effect questions through experimentation. This is a common approach in the research community but can be used to help improve and understand any type of app. One type of analysis that is growing in popularity centers on the selection and presentation order of educational materials.[6] If an app involves content provided sequentially (such as levels in a game, puzzles, problem sets, etc.), then it may be possible to investigate if presenting them in a particular order can improve the user experience. For example, if in an initial version of the app, information is presented at random, log data may capture how users respond to different orderings. This allows developers to explore which sequences optimize a particular outcome, such as learning, engagement, or time spent using the app. This helps developers better understand the best way to present materials to future learners. Another possibility is to test the addition of a feature on a subset of users before making it widely available to the public. For example, Paul Denny sought to explore how the addition of badges would change students' interactions with the PeerWise learning environment.[7] Through a controlled experiment, he found that adding a badging to the system increased the *quantity* of student interactions but did not have any impact on *quality*. Furthermore, "students enjoyed being rewarded with badges for their contributions and indicated a strong preference for having them in the interface."[8] This experiment allowed Denny to see that adding badging might increase interest and engagement without having a detrimental effect on learning, which is the ultimate goal of the system.

Users and Personalization

Mobile data analytics also allow you to understand more about your users. Just as Amazon collects data about shopping habits and preferences and makes suggestions for future purchases,[9] so too can educational apps collect data and tailor educational experiences towards users.[10] One interesting set of analyses is to identify patterns belonging to users who use the app frequently. These users' patterns could be used to guide the behaviors of less knowledgeable users. For example, imagine you have a note-taking app and you notice that regular users of the app tend to organize their notes in a specific way. You could use this information to provide hints to other users that may help them learn more and better use the app.

App developers can also tailor information to a specific user's interests, abilities, and learning preferences. Suppose an app provides leveled reading materials to young readers on a variety of subjects. If the app can detect that a particular user tends to read books about animals, the app can continue to recommend more books on animals at higher levels of difficulty to allow individual user interests to guide academic growth. Analytics also allow for powerful understandings of student misconceptions and learning needs. Detailed data on student actions, such as correct and incorrect answers, can be used to build robust models of what students know and do not know. For example, cognitive tutor systems have been used to teach a variety of topics and are based on the idea that answering problems correctly involves combining several pieces of individual knowledge or subskills.[11] For example, solving a physics problem involves knowing an equation as well as being able to identify the relevant pieces of the problem (e.g., mass of the object, velocity, etc.). Over time, with lots of different problem-solving activities, these tutors can build up a representation of which subskills students struggle with.[12] These can then be used to guide personalized, targeted instruction in the areas students need it most.

Today's digital technologies, including mobile, have the potential to generate large quantities of data about how students learn in a way that was not possible just a few short years ago. The U.S. Department of Education further highlights the importance of this shift in education and its "potential to make visible data that have heretofore gone unseen, unnoticed, and therefore unactionable."[13] For example, for centuries teachers collected paper-based copies of student writing, annotated it for correctness and clarity, then returned it to the student. The teacher may notice some common patterns in a batch of 30 papers, but this pattern may only occur across a handful of students, and may not be clear in her memory the next year. On the other hand, a digital writing and grading tool could have thousands or millions of student essays, along with teacher grades and insights. This data could be analyzed to provide insight about common mistakes students make, what qualities are tied to good or poor writing, and even how students' writing improves over time. More sophisticated techniques could help to automate grading processes by identifying common weaknesses. They may even point to areas of instruction that need improvement.

Data collection and analytics can also be directly incorporated into the apps themselves to provide insights to teachers and other users. Teacher dashboards are becoming increasingly popular, as they allow educators to see information about individual learning that may be otherwise obscured. For example, the *SAS Reading Records* app, an app that is used to measure reading proficiency in students throughout the year, provides a way for teachers to evaluate recorded student readings, as well as let teachers view detailed information about student fluency and reading behaviors. Teachers can see how student reading improves over time, where entire classes and individual students are performing in relation to their goals, and what areas are particularly difficult for students. Reports that show that a student commonly makes reading mistakes related to errors in sounding out words could signal to the teacher that the student is focusing too heavily on individual sounds and words, and might benefit from additional support in considering the context of the rest of the text.

When designing a dashboard for teachers or users, it is important to consider both what information is most helpful and how it can be displayed clearly. For example, an ineffective dashboard only provides teachers with information they can easily see for themselves, such as how many students are on task. A better dashboard would synthesize this information to show trends in off-task behavior over time and how it correlates with different classroom activities. If a teacher could see that student engagement was consistently lower during group reading activities, she would be able to act on this by changing the activity or finding other improvements. It is also important that the data be displayed to a teacher in a way that is meaningful and not overwhelming. For example, grouping students into color-coded strategies based on how much they are struggling is a simple and convenient way to represent complex data. We recommend using a drill-down approach so that teachers can get a sense of information quickly, but they should be able to look at the nitty-gritty details if they need to.

CONCLUSION

Constant evaluation of an app is a critical component to ensuring that it continues to meet the needs of users. An app that stagnates will likely soon be forgotten. The best way to identify areas of success and areas for improvement of an app is by collecting data for evaluation and then acting upon it. There are many interesting and important questions development teams can ask to get an understanding of their app, and equally many ways to find the answers. Careful consideration and design is needed to do this properly, but with the right approach, it can offer developers incredible insight. The important step is acting upon this knowledge and using it to continually improve apps that result in truly transformative educational technologies.

NOTES

1. "Big Data, for Better or Worse," *Science Daily*, May 22, 2013, www.sciencedaily.com/releases/2013/05/130522085217.htm.

2. WWDC 2014, "Optimizing your Earning Power with iAd," Dave Wilson (presenter), San Francisco, CA, 2014, https://developer.apple.com/videos/wwdc/2014/.

3. Laura M. Holson, "Putting a Bolder Face on Google," *New York Times*, February 28, 2009, www.nytimes.com/2009/03/01/business/01marissa.html?pagewanted=1&_r=0.

4. J. Mostow and J. E. Beck, "Why, What, and How to Log? Lessons from LISTEN," *Proceedings of the Second International Conference on Educational Data Mining* (Córdoba, Spain: Educational Data Mining, 2009): 269–278.

5. Mostow and Beck, "Why, What, and How to Log?," 269–278.

6. Kurt Van Lehn, "The Behavior of Tutoring Systems," *International Journal of Artificial Intelligence in Education* 16, no. 3 (August 2006): 227–265.

7. Paul Denny, "The Effect of Virtual Achievements on Student Engagement," *Proceedings of the SIGCHI Conference on Human Computer Interaction 2013*, dl.acm.org.

8. Ibid.

9. Amazon, "About Recommendations," www.amazon.com/gp/help/customer/display.html/ref=hp_left_v4_sib?ie=UTF8&nodeId=16465251.

10. Ryan Baker and Kalina Yacef, "The State of Educational Data Mining in 2009: A Review and Future Visions," *Journal of Educational Data Mining* 1, no. 1 (2009), www.educationaldatamining.org/JEDM/index.php/JEDM/article/view/8/2.

11. John R. Anderson, Albert T. Corbett, Kenneth R. Koedinger, and Ray Pelletier, "Cognitive Tutors: Lessons Learned," *Journal of the Learning Sciences* 4, no. 2,: 167–207.

12. Albert Corbett and John Anderson, "Knowledge Tracing: Modeling the Acquisition of Procedural Knowledge," *User Modeling and User-Adapted Interaction* 4 (1995): 253–278.

13. U.S. Department of Education, "Enhancing Teaching and Learning through Educational Data Mining and Learning Analytics," October 2012, http://tech.ed.gov/wp-content/uploads/2014/03/edm-la-brief.pdf.

CHAPTER **11**

The Business of Educational Apps

Developing educational apps is an exciting and booming market to enter, once you understand the audience and the unique constraints and affordances it presents. In addition to presenting an opportunity to create a business and a profitable product, there's opportunity to engage students and improve education, which are much loftier goals than most industries can offer. Here we outline the factors that make the educational app market different, detailing some challenges developers face and how to mitigate them, pricing models to guide the creation of a business around an app, and other key discussions necessary for working with the educational app market. The educational app market offers interesting development constraints and opportunities, and with the right background knowledge and navigation, a rewarding developing experience.

THE EDUCATIONAL APP MARKET IS ...

Like any market, the educational app market comes with its fair share of quirks. While there are many important distinguishing characteristics to the educational app market, here are a few key things to know about this market and its audience (see Figure 11.1).

The Educational App Market Is...

... not going anywhere.

... rich in educational standards.

... full of enthusiastic and motivated users.

... varied in resources and policies.

... catching up on connectivity.

... has a lot of privacy concerns.

... competitive, but working toward a common goal.

Figure 11.1 The Educational App Market Is ...

... Not Going Anywhere

More money is being spent every year on technology resources in schools, demonstrating a clear trend. "According to a January 2014 report released by the Software & Information Industry Association based on 2012 sales data, total preK–12 nonhardware expenditures on education software, digital content and resources totaled $7.97 billion."[1,2] Additionally, the sector is expected to grow to $13.4 billion by 2017, more than double in just five years.[3] Some of that growth can be attributed to changes in state laws that allow funds previously allocated to traditional textbooks to be used to buy mobile devices and apps.[4] Therefore, as schools and educators continue to buy-in—literally and figuratively—into the mobile learning movement, there is clearly an opportunity to join the educational app market.

Approximately one-third of students in the United States use a school-issued mobile device in their education, according to a study by Project Tomorrow (2014).[5] Even more students have access to mobile devices at home, with 89 percent of high schoolers and 73 percent of middle schoolers having access to smart phones.[6] As devices continue to rise in ubiquity, interest in using them for education also rises. In a recent survey of teachers and administrators about their interest in a one-to-one solution (either implementing or expanding a current mobile learning program at their school), 82 percent of respondents indicated a high level of interest at their school.[7] As the mobile learning movement continues to grow in popularity, more apps will be purchased, opening new demand in the educational app market. Mobile devices are also increasingly used in homes as well, opening up another area for educational apps outside of classroom. And this growth is very focused in the mobile app arena, since there is less growth being seen in traditional software. The PC isn't exactly dead, but it is a declining market compared to the tablet market.[8,9]

While we must caution the obvious—technological trends come and go—it is widely predicted that mobile devices are the wave of the foreseeable future in educational technology. After several years of consistent growth, tablet sales overall are plateauing (or declining, according to some sources). It is largely attributed to the fact that most people are getting more use out of their tablet and buying another one isn't necessary (yet).[10] Google's Chromebooks are also competing in the mobile computing space, boasting huge growth in 2013 with 20 percent coming of U.S. school purchases of mobile devices.[11] However, the market for adding rich and dynamic educational apps to these popular devices is still very good right now.

... Rich in Educational Standards

Developing an app that is appropriate for certain grade levels, covering skills and lessons that are taught in the classroom might sound difficult for a developer who doesn't have background in education. If a developer wants an app to be used in a certain grade or subject, the standards can be accessed to ensure the app will accommodate the students' requirements. Often these standards are established at the state or national level, but the information is available to anyone who wants it. This is a boon for developers looking to get their app in the hands of students. Aligning to standards is a key consideration in discussions with state and district-level officials as they review an app. Some teachers report that in their schools, only apps the district has approved as fitting in their standards can be downloaded.[12]

...Full of Enthusiastic and Motivated Users

Teachers and students, in general, are very willing to give feedback and tell you about how they use your app. With due diligence from the developer (responding to help requests in a timely manner and reaching out to users for detailed feedback), app users can serve as a valuable and accessible resource. In our development practice, we are constantly surprised at the reactions we get when responding to users—they are often amazed to receive a reply. Through these sorts of communications, we establish relationships with users and get feedback that impacts our development and app updates.

App store reviews are another way of receiving feedback. Since app stores do not currently provide ways for developers to respond to reviews, it leaves few ways to help users overcome the challenge they face if they offer a negative review. Addressing concerns in the product is often the only opportunity to speak directly to the anonymous reviewer and show the problem has been solved. Reviews can also come from other sources, such as independent experts. Moms With Apps, Teachers With Apps, and Graphite all review apps and provide guidance for parents and teachers on their blogs and social media platforms. A positive or negative review from a recognized group like these can definitely affect an app's sales.

Be sure to create a role in your organization and dedicate time in development iterations to respond to and incorporate user feedback. Word of mouth is one of the most powerful sources for finding apps among teachers,[13] and creating advocates is a critical step to be include in such conversations. Responding to user questions leads to good reviews, unsponsored tweets of support, and recommendations to colleagues. Efforts to implement this sort of marketing are worth the investment.

... Varied in Resources and Policies

For all the promise that apps and mobile technology hold for education, there is little control at the classroom level for purchasing. Budgets come from the school or district and can severely restrict the options of a teacher who uses mobile devices in lessons and activities. Many teachers we talked with had absolutely no funds for apps, a factor we discuss in the Pricing Model section that follows.

Many schools are leading the way, offering bring your own device (BYOD) programs, involving students in ubiquitous technological implementations. There are, of course, many schools that are adverse to using technology in education. Many schools ban cellphones altogether. When nearly every child has a device they're prohibited from using in their backpacks, it can be frustrating for teachers who have few opportunities to use mobile devices. Further, the school's mobile devices can be host to any number of restrictive policies. As we mentioned earlier in the book, one teacher noted that to download an app, she had to get it approved by the administrators, and if they approved it, the app was downloaded on all three of the school's device carts. All of this had to happen before the teacher could even see the app for herself![14] Bearing in mind that many policies will restrict use of apps that promote social media tie ins (categorically banned in the school referenced above, as the students are under 13), or even a login, developers should consider if these components can be turned off or if they're completely necessary to include in the first place. While it is certainly not feasible to anticipate or accommodate every possible restrictive policy, the educational market retains many dated policies and a wide variety of resources that shut out certain apps and learning opportunities.

... Catching up on Connectivity

While some schools have huge mobile device implementations and strong wireless support, there are many schools where the bandwidth and technology support staff cannot support the number of devices they must manage. "Even though the nation's tech goals are to get wireless in every school, many schools deal with broken, blocked, and banned technology," says Dawn Casey-Rowe, a high school teacher. "EdTech developers and startups must spend time getting to know the nuances of the schools they intend to serve."[15] In fact, "60 percent of schools in America lack sufficient Wi-Fi capability to provide students with 21st Century educational tools," Tom Wheeler, the FCC chairman notes.[16] The reality for many schools is that the Internet is slow and that Wi-Fi bandwidth is not what it should be in most educational settings, as schools add devices or allow students to connect to the school's network. Developers face a big challenge to make their app functional and successful in a potentially low-connectivity setting. There is a national initiative to close the Wi-Fi gap in schools and libraries, which will address some of this issue in the coming years.[17] And, as mobile devices continue to mature and grow in numbers within the educational setting, even greater bandwidth will be required. For app developers, this means that an app that requires constant connectivity to the Internet or offers online-based animation might not be usable in a classroom full of students. Consider this, and other elements of being a good app citizen (as discussed in Chapters 7 and 8) when designing and coding your app.

... Has a Lot of Privacy Concerns

We dedicate a whole chapter to this issue (Chapter 15), but note here that the privacy requirements for students and children under 13 are substantial. The challenge for developers lies in complying with the relevant laws (COPPA and FERPA) and making proactive and thorough disclosures. Developers should consider carefully what information is necessary to collect, and communicate their policies clearly and prominently with teachers and parents. It is a sensitive issue for many guardians, and apps that are clear about what information is collected and what it is used for stand to gain credibility and support. Secretive and shady data collection can quickly backfire, even if it is technically compliant with the law.

... Competitive, But Working Toward a Common Goal

Educational apps are a huge swath of the overall app market, with more and more being added all the time. There are a few byproducts of this saturation that pose additional challenges to developers.

There is a high standard for educational quality, with many apps that are just for fun, or even drill-and-practice-oriented games being seen as less worthy than more sophisticated tool-based or curriculum-aligned ones. In and out of the classroom, there is an expectation that if a child is playing on an iPad, they're learning something.[18] When teachers have an educational goal in mind while searching for an app, they'll likely have their pick among dozens of good matches. Rising to the top of the pile is a challenge. Realizing that an app will be compared to its competitors, developers will need to raise the bar on quality. This means academic rigor, usability, mobile integration and privacy, among other factors.

Standing out in a saturated market is a challenge. Developers might think they have a great idea, and it might even *be* a great idea, but that alone doesn't mean teachers will use it. Further, with so many apps to choose from for any given purpose or topic, commitment from a user is low. If someone downloads a free app to make an ebook and finds it doesn't suit his needs, he can quickly delete that app and find dozens of other options in the app store.

So much of what is succeeding in mobile learning apps surrounds student creation. The full featured, topic specific, very focused apps are less discussed and shared by educators. Apps that allow students to demonstrate new knowledge, make learning connections, and even cross disciplines are increasingly popular. *Explain Everything* is an app that facilitates presentation building through inclusion of multimedia elements, though it can be used by students and teachers for a variety of purposes. It is a robust tool that allows the users to supply the purpose and the educational content, and has proved very popular in this role.

While the educational app industry is big, and growing, it is a unique industry. It has a very philanthropic spirit, and the feeling of an industry with a common goal. It's a market full of competitors who don't compete, at least not in the traditional, winner-take-all sense. Most who enter this market, while they may be looking to earn a living, are also aiming to improve education and provide an engaging experience for students.

HOW TO SELL YOUR APP: PRICING MODELS

It is important to consider the business model the app will use at the outset, as this will impact other decisions. For instance, if you're planning to have advertisements in a certain area of the screen on the app, incorporate this into the design. "Or, if the plan is to sell units within the app for purchase, it will be developed in a different way," says Bjorn Jeffrey of TocaBoca. "The mistake I have seen done many times is people have a game in the kid space or in the adult space and then they add freemium as an afterthought and then you are just left with basically no business model at all."[19] Figuring out which model is right requires forethought and careful consideration of the market and the product. And especially in the case of educational apps, considering what users are able to pay should be part of this initial process.

It's also worth considering how the pricing model and payment methods feel to the user. Brian Bennett, a former teacher who used mobile technology in his classroom, emphasizes the need for an honest user experience, noting that some apps offer a trial then forbid you to go further until you pay. In this case, it would be better if the app were simply listed as a paid app. Bennett says, "Yes, free is very good because there seems to be less and less money every year," but he adds that sometimes an app that provides value in his classroom might be worth paying for.[20] Free is certainly great, and can lead to more downloads, but users may not mind paying for a quality app that meets their needs. Here we discuss the three most prominent pricing structures for educational apps and their limitations and allowances: free, freemium, and premium (see Figure 11.2).

Free

A 2012 Forrester report noted that more than one-third of respondents said they "haven't paid for any apps they own, and another one-third

Popular Pricing Models for Educational Apps

+ **Free**
+ **Freemium**
+ **Premium**

Figure 11.2 Popular Pricing Models for Educational Apps

have only paid for a quarter of their apps."[21] Even among the general population of mobile device users, the unwillingness to pay for apps when so many free options exist is pervasive. In the education app market, the free bias is strong, often due to lack of funding to purchase apps. Many educators we interviewed for this book noted they had absolutely no funds to use for purchasing apps, so the only apps they considered for class or professional use were free apps. Schools are stretched thin to make technological upgrades; often funds aren't available or aren't prioritized for purchasing apps. Whatever the reasoning may be, many schools and users are in this situation, and developers need to be aware that anything above free may eliminate their app from searches. Hence, a large part of their intended audience may never organically see their product.

But, to state the obvious, many developers are not in the nonprofit business; so, how does one make money by providing a product for free? Advertising within the app is one option, though it is controversial at best, and ineffective at worst. Given that many users are children, marketing is often frowned upon and restricted in many countries. Young kids can accidentally touch the ad, especially if it is flashing to draw attention, launching a link and grinding their app activity to a halt. This is a huge problem, since the whole point is to get children using your app, and have a good experience doing so. Requiring frequent adult intervention to get back to the app will quickly become cumbersome and unsatisfying for the users and teachers. Beyond that, users are sometimes too young to know how to read, making ads for preschool apps very ineffective.[22] These things can also, more importantly, impede the overall user experience of an app.

There are also some restrictions offered up by the operating systems on what is permissible for apps marketing to kids. For iOS, if an app is classified as for Kids in the app store, there are restrictions relating to advertisements that developers need to heed. "Apps in the Kids Category may not include behavioral advertising (e.g., the advertiser may not serve ads based on the user's activity within the App), and any contextual ads presented in the App must be appropriate for kids," Apple says in their Developer Guide. Also, Kids apps must include "parental permission or use a parental gate before allowing the user to link out of the app or engage in commerce."[23] These restrictions aim to limit children's exposure to advertising that could impede the user experience. At the time of this writing, there are no restrictions on ads in apps for children in the Android operating system.

The apps that we develop at SAS Curriculum Pathways are free apps, funded through the ongoing commitment to education and innovation that our software company has made. Though we are certainly unique and lucky in this respect, we continually face this sort of confusion and amazement in our conversations with customers. "Free" is a loaded word these days. For apps like these—those that are truly free (i.e., no ads, no future costs)—there's the constant need to differentiate themselves from apps that aren't truly free. Additionally, free can mean low quality in the minds of consumers. Consumers have grown wary of the word, assuming a free app comes with obtrusive ads or a catch (since so often it does). Differentiating free from freemium can be surprisingly challenging.

Freemium

In most app categories, freemium, as a business model, is surging in popularity, eclipsing paid or free with advertisement models.[24] This essentially means the user is offered a free version of the app, with certain additional functions or content available for a fee. There are different opinions on the appropriateness of this model. Some say it exploits the customers, getting them hooked and then coming in for the credit card, while others see it as an opportunity for consumers to buy only what they'll use and to try the product before purchasing anything at all. As the prevailing moneymaking model for mobile apps, it has implications for the educational app market.

In a survey of top apps in the Apple App Store in 2013, freemium was found to be the clear winner in almost all categories as the most prominent pricing structure. Education, lagging somewhat in the trend, showed 43 percent used freemium and in-app purchases, while 56 percent used one-time fees.[25] "The games which consistently make the most revenue are all freemium."[26] This suggests that although the model is widely popular, there are some specific concerns and issues that the educational app market has that changes the equation a bit.

The economics of the freemium model are basic: to make a profit, an app needs a vast audience. "The typical conversion rate from freemium to paid ranges from 3 to 10 percent, so the prospect pool needs to be deep to sustain your business," says Anthony Smith, CEO of Insightly in a blog post.[27] Working closely with users and experimenting will help developers determine the sweet spot of what functionality to include in the free version and what to tack on as extras for a fee. If the delicate balance is not struck, "the free version can cannibalize the paid offering."[28]

Like all pricing structures we discuss, freemium requires a tremendous amount of forethought when designing the app. Bjorn Jeffrey, founder and CEO of TocaBoca, one of the most prominent children's app companies, notes that "being successful with freemium almost requires that you to design from the freemium model from the beginning. It's not something you can apply later."[29] If using a freemium model in an app is the goal, it needs to be part of the discussion from the beginning.

While we certainly advise creating a high quality and engaging educational app, the freemium model is an additional test to those criteria. Freemium allows—and with profit in mind, requires—the app to show its worth up front. It essentially allows a free trial. Only after the user has spent some time with it, does the app ask for a financial commitment. This is a benefit for a good app; hooking users early makes them feel better about spending money on an app purchase they know they'll value. There's more opportunity for a customized user experience, and the user only pays for what he wants so "spend perfectly matches the derived utility."[30] Bad apps won't survive in the freemium space, which could explain its growing popularity.

As a prominent business model for all apps, freemium certainly is worth consideration for educational apps. Many apps have been deployed using this model, like the *Endless Reader* app, which sells packs of words to budding readers. As they master the level, a new bundle of words is offered. This, of course, requires parental consent and a credit card, the step that can prove the biggest hurdle for educational apps. Most students using apps are unable or prohibited from making app purchases, not to mention that many schools are limited in what apps they can purchase (if they can purchase anything at all). Operating systems are making necessary upgrades constantly to facilitate in-app purchasing while protecting users under 13 (a recent iOS upgrade introduced Family Sharing, enabling an alert to be sent to parents if a child wants to purchase an app, among other features[31]). While there certainly are reasons this model won't work in all educational settings, the user community that would not be welcoming to this model would mostly be schools that do not have funds to purchase any apps at all. If a school can purchase apps, the freemium model would be acceptable, and perhaps even preferred.

Be sure to understand the user experience of in-app purchasing so your app fits in, as well as how the purchasing power can remain with the teacher or guardian. A recent lawsuit illustrates the importance of these measures. The lawsuit demonstrated that Amazon allowed children to make in-app purchases without parental consent. The FTC also recently settled with Apple to the tune of $32.5 million, and requires stricter in-app purchasing consent and password protection.[32] This area is certainly in flux as policies continue to strengthen and create structure in this very new market, but the freemium model and in-app purchasing are at the center of this debate.

Premium

On the opposite side of the freemium model is the premium model in which the user pays a one-time fee for an app. Whereas the freemium experience can be seen by users as a constant reminder of the developer's desire to make money rather than providing a user-centered experience, a one-time fee offers an uninterrupted experience.[33] Especially in an educational setting where students, or even teachers, might not have authorization to make in app purchases, the fewer roadblocks that exist, the better.

Finding the right price point can be a challenge. This is likely a determination each app must make for itself based on the audience and quality of the app. Competitive analysis is a good place to start, as well as advice from potential users. The evaluation of what an app is worth versus what is charged for the app is an imprecise one; users usually don't have a clear picture of what goes into an app or what it's worth to them, but they know when they feel something isn't worth what they've paid. This is a challenging hurdle for developers. While prices are steadily declining on apps,[34] overall, some truisms remain about various price points.

Users expect simple apps to be 99 cents, if not free.[35] To charge $2.99 to $4.99, apps need to offer robust features and a great user interface. Clearly, users can't know if an app is truly worth a higher price tag until they download and start using it. However, if users feel they spent more than they perceive the app provides, they're likely to give negative feedback, which can quickly alienate future customers.[36] Apps can come with very high price tags as well, though if they offer substantial utility, the user may happily purchase it. The costliest we mention in this book is *Proloquo2Go*, the accessibility app that enables nonverbal users to communicate using their device ($219.99 at the time of this writing). This high price tag is justified because it essentially turns a mobile device into an assistive communication device, and while it costs a lot compared to other apps, it costs substantially less than dedicated communication devices. It gives a high amount of functionality and, often, life-changing abilities to users.

Deciding on a price is a big decision, but not a permanent one; prices can vary over time. Experimenting and being flexible with the price is a good idea to stay competitive. Offering promotional pricing, even offering the app for free in the app store for a few hours, is a good way to stimulate sales and gain new users.

HOW USERS BUY YOUR APP

Part of the pricing and business model discussion must involve understanding how states, districts, schools, teachers, and students acquire apps. There are many opportunities for educators to access your app at discounted rates. Developers are increasingly able to bundle apps together at discounted rates as well. Lastly, working directly with hardware vendors that sell into schools to have your app available or as part of a package included upon arrival at the school presents great opportunities to help educators discover your app at discounted rates. In instances where schools dictate to teachers which apps can be used, mass downloads and package deals at the district or school level might make an app more appealing to an administrator hoping for a universal solution.

Volume Purchasing and Education Pricing

Many times, a choice will be made at the district level to use a certain app for teaching a certain skill or at a grade level. If the app needs to be purchased in a high volume, developers can offer discounted pricing to these districts. Typically, these discounts can be up to 50 percent off for 20 or more units.[37] To promote this practice, Apple offers subsidies for educational pricing (in the form of taking a smaller share of the revenue). This program also comes with features that appeal to districts—control of the app through their mobile device management (MDM) system and a streamlined installation and delivery process.[38] Developers should know that this sort of discounted bulk purchasing is the industry norm and an important consideration when trying to work with educational institutions.

Bundling and Promotions

As the consumer purchasing experience in the app store continues to become more sophisticated, iOS has recently started to allow selling apps in bundles. Developers can group several apps together for one price (usually at a discount from what the apps would cost separately), offering a new way to increase adoption of multiple apps. Promotions can also stimulate downloads on an app and help to build a consumer base. Offering a premium app for free for a limited time is a great marketing tool to boost downloads. Another tactic is offering and promoting a free app that ties into a suite of apps, in hopes it would be a gateway app for the user.

Preloaded and Curated Software

There are a few primary ways that schools set up mobile device implementations. In one scenario, the school will purchase and distribute the devices, and individual users can download apps. In another common setup, schools purchase the devices and provision the apps, with an administrator controlling what goes on the devices. Sometimes schools offer a curated purchasing experience, as in Google Play for Education where teachers can purchase apps for their class and distribute them to their students' devices.[39] Schools also use a preloaded option, wherein the devices come with the apps and software that is needed. Amplify tablets have offered large implementations using this approach, offering content directly on the tablet (accessible with or without a Wi-Fi connection).[40] This preloaded experience offers out-of-the-box usability, with minimal device management setup required. It is, understandably, quite appealing for schools, although it comes with a higher price. Developers should be aware that there are many ways that users can come to your app, and to pay attention to the various paths.

Disconnected Purchasing Process

One inherent struggle in producing educational apps is the disconnect between the user and the buyer. Compared to a general market app—say, *Angry Birds*—where the user searches, chooses, buys, downloads, and uses that app, educational apps often have different people performing each of these actions. The user and the adopter are often two different people in the education app market. Depending on the age of the user, parents or teachers could be in control of finding the app and adopting (as children under 13 aren't allowed to make app purchases). In schools, administrators or technology coordinators may be customizing the app for teachers and students. When Apple admits schools to participate in their volume purchasing plan, there are many restrictions on who can purchase apps. Only certain authorized users (program facilitators) can purchase apps at a discounted rate and distribute them to their colleagues.[41] In a perfect world, teachers could search the app store and find the apps they want, download, and use them. This is, unfortunately, not the case for most schools, and it is an important consideration when determining the appropriate marketing message.

MARKETING

In an ideal world, the developer could sit down with a teacher and show them the app they've created, demonstrating its functionality and answering any questions the potential user might have. This is, obviously, not feasible, so the marketing and communications activities discussed here serve the same purpose: to sell users on the app. The marketing and communication activities are, essentially, geared toward creating fans of the app: namely, users who purchase the app and have a good experience with it. These users will recommend the app, blog about it, mention it on Twitter, and tell their colleagues. (They'll also tell you what's weird about it, and offer suggestions on how to change it!) All of the exercises we recommend to bring strong branding and messaging to your app are oriented to that one goal: make users happy. Happy users, especially so in the educational world, are advocates for your app.

Communicate

Knowing your market is essential, as we've said throughout the book. Often, the most successful educational apps are made with teams that include educators (either as consultants or paid members of the team). In our view, it's essential to have at least one teacher, but preferably several, in the field to give feedback on the app as it is being developed. They should ask questions such as "Is this something you'd use in your classroom? What other features would be useful? How much would you pay for this?" After the app is available, these allies can recommend it to their professional networks of colleagues and coworkers, as well as give feedback on what is working in practice and what needs improvement. Having a finger on the pulse of the educational user is vital to developing and selling an app that is useful and does what it needs to do.

To this end, it is extremely important for developers to communicate with their audience. If a user emails about a problem (or even a perceived problem), respond as soon as possible. Follow up with more questions, and do what is necessary to help. Beyond being responsive, having professional collateral material for when you visit with teachers (either at conferences or other events within the professional community) is a great idea. Creating an email list, newsletter, website, Twitter account—all of these things provide more opportunities to engage with the user and increase your overall presence and opportunity to be contacted (and respond).

In-App Marketing

If a developer offers a suite or several apps under the same brand, cross-promotional efforts are important to boost this brand awareness. For instance, when starting any Toca Boca app, a small link to a different Toca Boca app will come up in the bottom corner: a simple, nonintrusive reminder that there are more apps like this that the user can purchase. Other apps place this information in an info box or small advertisement. It need not be flashy and distracting, but it's good to reinforce the brand to a user who has already invested in it.

App Store Experience

What users see when they find your app in the app store is what we call the app store experience. While most of what is allowed in this avenue is imposed by the operating system and its regulations, these allowances are changing often. We suggest developers make use of all the allotted features within the app store listing, as these help users find the app and will be used to compare it to competitors. For instance, the Apple App Store allows for a video preview of the app;[42] Google Play has had this functionality for a while. This preview functionality is an example of a new feature that gives apps an additional avenue to make a positive impression on a potential user. As the app store experience continues to be refined and enhanced, developers need to stay in tune with these updates and increase their own offerings. Once an app preview becomes the norm, as it will, an app that only offers screenshots will quickly be passed over for one that offers a more thorough preview.

Outside Marketing

So, how do teachers hear about apps? How do teachers judge apps? With the limited time and resources teachers have, the most common way for new apps to be discovered is through word of mouth. In our interviews, it seems common for schools to establish a de facto app guru, a peer who is good at finding good apps. This person will recommend apps to other teachers. When one good app is found, it is quickly adopted across the school, as searching and testing apps is seen as a burden. Social media is also very useful for increasing the profile an app. Hashtags (for Twitter chats or industry conferences, for example), infographics, and blogs are good tools to be discovered and shared on social media outlets. Using social media to promote an app and engage with users is a best practice. Be aware of these channels, and create materials to market and use them. There are also entire conferences devoted to educational apps and the use of mobile devices in the classroom, and schools often send their app guru to these events. Teachers share their experience with apps at these conferences, which can drive downloads and buzz around an app. Developers should monitor these events, attending them if possible.

Branding

Another way to create a cohesive user experience is to create distinct apps using a similar name. This aids in discoverability. Parents or teachers may get one app and really like it. The next logical step for them is to see if there are more from that company, assuming all of their apps are of equal quality. It keeps developers on their toes, as one subpar product could reflect poorly on the whole suite.[43] Toca Boca and their apps are a great example of the use of a brand to connect their products.

All of Toca Boca's apps use Toca as the first word, to help users find their apps easily. If developers aim to create more than one app, it is worth considering how the apps relate and ways the names might convey that relationship.

Lesson Plans (or Educational Context)

If an educational app aims to be included in a classroom setting as part of a lesson, it is a great idea to include some suggested lessons where it would fit in. *Hopscotch*, a free app that teaches the basics of computer programming, offers several companion lesson plans to aid teachers in incorporating the app into their classroom activities. *Hopscotch* also has a blog where they post other ideas for inclusion in the classroom. This level of support shows that the developers are in tune with the needs of their users.

CONCLUSION

We hope this chapter illuminates the complex and exciting world of educational apps. While there are certainly challenges that are unique to this market, there are many opportunities to take part in reshaping the education system and make students more engaged and curious. There are many apps to choose from but as the landscape is changing and the number of students and teachers using devices increases, the conventional wisdom, needs, and possibilities for mobile learning will change as well. It is important for developers (or those who wish to be developers) of educational apps to keep abreast of changes in the educational system as well as in technology.

NOTES

1. U.S. Department of Education, *EdTech Developer's Handbook* (Draft), March 2014, http://tech.ed.gov/developers-handbook/.
2. Software and Information Industry Association, "2014 Results from the SIIA Vision K–20 Survey," *SIIA*, June 2014, http://siia.net/visionk20/2014_VK20.pdf.
3. Ibid.
4. Geoffrey Fletcher, "Driving Digital Change," *The Journal*, October 11, 2011, http://thejournal.com/articles/2011/10/04/driving-digital-change.aspx.

5. Project Tomorrow, "The New Digital Learning Playbook: Understanding the Spectrum of Students' Activities and Aspirations," April 2014, http://tomorrow.org/speakup/pdfs/SU13StudentsReport.pdf.

6. Ibid.

7. Interactive Educational Systems Design, Inc., "2014 National Survey on Mobile Technology for K–12 Education," May 2014, www.iesdinc.com/iesdnews.html.

8. Natasha Lomas, "Tablets to Grow 53.4% This Year, Says Gartner, as Traditional PC Declines 11.2%," *TechCrunch*, October 23, 2013, http://techcrunch.com/2013/10/21/tablets-vs-pcs/.

9. Jay Yarow, "The Death of the PC: Tablet Sales Will Beat Notebook Sales This Year," *Business Insider*, www.businessinsider.com/the-death-of-the-pc-tablet-sales-will-beat-notebook-sales-this-year-2013-1.

10. Christian de Looper, "Tablet Sales on the Decline, but Apple Not Feeling Any Pain," *Tech Times*, August 18, 2014, www.techtimes.com/articles/13357/20140818/tablet-sales-decline-apple-feeling-pain.htm.

11. Rolfe Winkler, "Chromebooks Take Other Mobile PCs to School," January 23, 2014, http://online.wsj.com/news/articles/SB10001424052702304856504579338941198812358. Accessed July 16, 2014.

12. Third-grade teacher in North Carolina (anonymous), interview, June 30, 2014.

13. Brentwood teachers, interview with authors, Brentwood Elementary, Raleigh, NC, August 22, 2013.

14. Anonymous, North Carolina Middle School, interview with authors, April 22, 2014.

15. U.S. Department of Education, *EdTech Developer's Handbook*.

16. Tom Wheeler, "Closing the Wi-Fi Gap in America's Schools and Libraries," *FCC Blog*, June 6, 2014, www.fcc.gov/blog/closing-wi-fi-gap-america-s-schools-and-libraries.

17. Federal Communications Commission, "News Release: FCC Releases Report Showing State-By-State Impacts of E-Rate Proposal to Close Wi-Fi Gap in Schools and Libraries," July 1, 2014, www.fcc.gov/document/modernizing-e-rate-providing-21st-century-wi-fi-schools-libraries.

18. "Björn Jeffrey on Why Toca Boca Won't Be Selling to Schools," Games and Learning, March 17, 2014, www.gamesandlearning.org/2014/03/17/bjorn-jeffrey-on-why-toca-boca-wont-be-selling-to-schools/.

19. Ibid.

20. U.S. Department of Education, "EdTech Developer's Handbook."

21. Steve Wadsworth, "How 'Free' Can Pay in Mobile Apps," *Wall Street Journal: The Accelerators*, March 4, 2013, http://blogs.wsj.com/accelerators/2013/03/04/how-free-can-pay-in-mobile-apps/.

22. Ahmed Siddiqui, "App Purchasing (Paid, Lite, and Freemium): What's Working, and What's Appropriate in Apps for Kids?," *MOMs with Apps blog*, July 24, 2011, http://blog.momswithapps.com/2011/07/24/app-purchasing-paid-lite-and-freemium-whats-working-and-whats-appropriate-in-apps-for-kids/.

23. Apple, "App Store Review Guidelines," https://developer.apple.com/appstore/resources/approval/guidelines.html, accessed July 23, 2014.

24. Ben Holmes, "The Economics of Freemium," *Wall Street Journal: The Accelerators*, March 3, 2013, http://blogs.wsj.com/accelerators/2013/03/03/the-economics-of-freemium/.

25. Zoe Fox, "Freemium Is the Most Profitable Pricing Strategy for Apps," *Mashable*, December 19, 2013, http://mashable.com/2013/12/19/paid-vs-free-apps/.

26. Holmes, "The Economics of Freemium."

27. Anthony Smith, "Get Paying Users by Giving Your App Away," *Wall Street Journal: The Accelerators,* March 4, 2013, http://blogs.wsj.com/accelerators/2013/03/04/get -paying-users-by-giving-your-app-away/.

28. David Sacks, "When Freemium Beats Premium," *Wall Street Journal: The Accelerators,* March 1, 2013, http://blogs.wsj.com/accelerators/2013/03/01/when-freemium -beats-premium/.

29. Games and Learning, "Björn Jeffrey."

30. Holmes, "The Economics of Freemium."

31. Apple, "iOS8 Preview: Family Sharing," www.apple.com/ios/ios8/family-sharing/.

32. Brett Molina and Mike Snider, "FTC Sues Amazon over in-App Purchases," *USA Today,* July 11, 2014, www.usatoday.com/story/tech/2014/07/10/ftc-amazon/ 12478459/.

33. Andrew Flachner, "Freemium Limits User Experience," *Wall Street Journal: The Accelerators,* March 4, 2013, http://blogs.wsj.com/accelerators/2013/03/04/freemium -limits-user-experience/.

34. Ryan Matzner, "How To: Determine the Right Price for Your Mobile App," *Mashable,* August 17, 2011, http://mashable.com/2011/08/17/price-mobile-app/.

35. Ibid.

36. Ibid.

37. Apple, "Volume Purchase Program for Education," www.apple.com/education/it/ vpp, accessed July 17, 2014

38. Ibid.

39. Google for Education, www.google.com/edu/tablets/#case-study-carousel. Accessed July 23, 2014

40. Christina Quattrocchi, "Q&A Jake Henry: Lessons from Guilford County's Amplify Tablet Rollout," *EdSurge,* September 23, 2014, www.edsurge.com/n/2014-09-23-q-a -jake-henry-lessons-from-guilford-county-s-amplify-tablet-rollout.

41. Bob Dronski, "Making Sense of the Apple Volume Purchase Program," *Moms With Apps blog,* September 10, 2012, http://blog.momswithapps.com/2012/09/10/making -sense-of-the-apple-volume-purchase-program/.

42. Turner, "Creating Great App Previews."

43. Games and Learning, "Björn Jeffrey."

SECTION 3

Mobile Learning for Everyone

One of the most exciting and appealing qualities of the mobile learning movement is how learning on mobile devices makes learning more accessible and available to everyone. In this section, we explore the many ways mobile devices can be used to reach different groups or environments, as well as mobile learning issues and initiatives intended to protect all users. This section provides useful background and discussions for educators and developers.

We discuss informal learning, and how devices that can go with students create a plethora of new learning opportunities and environments, truly breaking the mold of the classroom. It's no secret that children love mobile devices and in Chapter 13, we explore the special considerations when teaching and developing for the preschool group. Mobile devices also have proven to be groundbreaking in accessibility for special populations; we discuss students with autism and students with visual impairment and the affordances of mobile devices for each. And in Chapter 15 we discuss the challenges and obligations relating to data: data privacy for developers, and digital citizenship for students and educators. As this topic continues to be at the heart of the mobile learning movement, and will surely continue to evolve and become more nuanced, it is a vital concern for educators, developers, and learners to be engaged with.

CHAPTER **12**

Informal Learning

L earning environments can be thought of as a spectrum. At one
end, we have the more traditional notion of learning, known
as formal learning, where instruction is structured, grounded in
curricula, teacher-led, and generally occurs in a school setting.[1,2]
On the other end lies informal learning, learning that often occurs
spontaneously based on our own interests and curiosities.[3,4,5] This
form of learning does not have a corresponding curriculum or hours
of operation; it happens as we drive around town, meet new people,
observe others and events, engage in new experiences, peruse parks
and museums, and follow our natural curiosities. Informal learning
is especially critical for children as they explore, play, and make
sense of the world—they begin to conceptualize things like social
and cultural conventions, properties and processes of the natural
world, and spoken language vicariously through observation of
others. Somewhere within this spectrum we could make delineations,
such as semiformal learning, to define activities such as after-school
programs and summer camps; however, for the sake of simplicity,
we will use the formal–informal dichotomy, where informal learning
also encapsulates semistructured activities that occur outside of
school hours.

DEVELOPING LIFELONG LEARNERS

If you've ever watched someone play a videogame, hit a homerun, or drive a car, it becomes clear that the majority of what we do in our everyday lives was not learned in the classroom or in some structured environment. Rather, this learning occurrs in contexts based on personal interests and due to our own impetus—qualities associated with meaningful learning.[6] After a quick conversation with an art enthusiast or classic car guru, it is obvious that the learning we do outside of school seems to be more powerful and passionate than learning prescribed by a curriculum.

While most of us think of school as the place where students go to learn, in reality, the most common schoolhouse is our everyday lives. In fact, children ages 5 to 16 only spend about 18 percent of their waking hours at school,[7] leaving the "vast majority of all learning throughout the adult life course" to occur informally.[8] Moreover, the things we learn informally are not limited to hobbies and life skills. Instead, the majority of working individuals feel they developed most of the skills they use in their current occupation outside of school.[9] In essence, our informal learning skills dictate our ability to learn independently across the lifetime and thrive in the real world.

Despite the prevalence, effectiveness, and importance of informal learning, the majority of educational capital is targeted toward formal learning environments, as these environments are typically more controlled and defined. Moreover, the variability in students' personal lives creates a great challenge in encouraging an overlap between formal and informal education. It is difficult to teach and model to students strategies for answering their own questions outside of school without knowing what resources will be available at any given time. However, the recent proliferation of mobile devices has the potential to mitigate this challenge. There finally exists a pervasive resource that is not only appropriate for use both in and out of school, but is also robust enough to provide instruction for almost any domain. LeapFrog's director of learning, Jim Gray, feels, "Mobile devices help kids make connections between different spheres of their everyday world. It can help connect what they're doing in school with what they do in an afterschool program with what they do at home."[10]

But, while our curiosities might seem to come naturally, our knowledge of strategies for satisfying them do not. More importantly, as we have emphasized in previous chapters, we cannot assume our so-called digital natives are poised to use their mobile devices for learning independently[11]—despite the incessant presence of their devices. In fact, recent studies that analyze students' informal learning skills found students are only using a handful of apps for learning outside of school and need more instructional support to take advantage of mobile devices' capabilities.[12,13]

Unfortunately, the overlap between the personal and educational use of mobile devices manifests as obstructive as opposed to productive. For example, researchers found students are more likely to text during class rather than use their mobile devices for informal learning outside of school.[14] Therefore, there appears to be a great need for guided instruction that is directed at blurring the lines between formal and informal learning. The behaviors we want our students to engage in outside of school in order to develop lifelong learners must garner higher priority in more formal settings. Aside from the classroom, after school and summer programs provide a wonderful venue for modelling informal learning resources and behaviors, as these environments tend to closely align with the attributes of our daily curiosities. Ultimately, in order to develop lifelong learners, we need to take advantage of informal education to teach students how to teach themselves.

BRIDGING FORMAL AND INFORMAL LEARNING

In order to prepare learners for tackling informal learning independently, we must first identify common scenarios in which mobile devices might prove beneficial. Consequently, instructors can use formal educational settings to introduce students to particular resources and strategies for optimizing the learning experience outside of the classroom.

Supporting Informal Inquiry

What's the name of this song? How do I tie a bowtie? How many stitches are on a baseball? Why is the sky so dark this afternoon?

How do you play the guitar? Whether solving a particular problem, looking to learn a new skill, or simply looking to satisfy our curiosity, the plethora of apps available for download make our mobile devices a pocket guide to almost anything, and information on topics that do not have a specific app can likely be found through ebooks, podcasts, YouTube videos, or a simple Internet search.

However, not every reference tool is appropriate for every application or audience, although you would not guess this based on students' research habits. A recent study found 94 percent of teachers say their students are far more likely to simply use Google when finding information on their own, but also feel their students lack sophisticated research skills.[15] Introducing students to a variety of research tools—specific as well as general—can prevent them from falling into the information abyss as well as promote effective time management. For example, apps designed for reference within a specific domain expedite the process by narrowing the focus of search and are oftentimes vetted and more credible than information found through a Google search—especially for younger students. Educators can help students populate a reference folder on their devices filled with targeted apps like *The Elements*, *Dictionary.com*, *Wolfram Alpha*, *Speak & Translate*, *MyCongress*, or *MathRef*. But, as there is not a tool for every scenario, modelling best practices for navigating apps such as *YouTube*, *Podcasts*, *Wikipedia*, and mobile web browsers ensure students can effectively indulge all their informal education needs.

Like static apps for reference, dynamic sources of regularly updated content are another useful tool for informal learning. In fact, these ever-changing sources are often more engaging, as each visit can differ from the last, and the information is more likely to be relevant and novel. Up-to-date local, national, or global news headlines, sports scores, and weather reports are available in an instant. Similarly, more novel presentations of information, such as *Mental Floss* or *Pinterest*, also provide learning opportunities that might appeal to our humor or interests—while delivering a unique opportunity to get students reading. For younger students who might not be able to comprehend articles written for the greater public, student-centered news outlets are available. For example, CNN's student news, Go Go News, and NewsELA are wonderful resources for younger learners. For ESL/ELL students, 22 Frames takes a more visual approach to current events by helping students' comprehension through picture support.

In the case of more complex learning, we might need additional support beyond just the presentation of information to make sense of the world around us. Developmental psychologist and informal education researcher Katherine McMillan Culp explains, "Learning...is not a matter of being informed of something you don't yet understand ... rather, moving from not knowing to knowing requires gaining access to a series of insights—a type of relationship, a new pattern, a new possibility in the word—that was not previously available to you."[16] This can be especially true for younger children who have not yet mastered independent learning skills and cannot readily find (or realize they need to find) supplemental information or resources to truly comprehend the information they come across in their environment.

Students should be made aware of apps that support a direct input of information from their environment. Such apps immediately contextualize the data to provide a more clear and meaningful explanation of the question at hand. Consider the following example.

> Jessica, a 10-year-old girl, is currently studying astronomy
> in school. She has seen pictures of Venus in her textbook
> and online, but wants to see how the Earth's twin looks
> from her front yard. She tried to use her textbook and her
> dad's star chart, but both left her confused and unsure
> about where she was looking. Finally, Jessica brought up
> the augmented reality app *StarWalk* on her mobile device.
> With the app, she simply points the device to the night sky
> and the app readily identifies the stars, constellations, and,
> finally, Venus.

As this example shows, Jessica was able to benefit from the context-aware sensors embedded in her mobile device. Moreover, Jessica was able to observe Venus in an authentic and contextualized manner. By directly imputing information from her environment, there was little room for error, or even worse, misconception, which can be difficult to overcome. Similarly, many inquiry apps allow users to directly input information about their personal environment in order to identify various objects. Such apps include *Leafsnap* (flora and fauna), *Merlin Bird ID* (birds), *Shazam* (music), QR code scanners, *Google Maps*, and even *Compass*. For general inquiries, *Google Goggles* pulls from Google's expansive database and allows users to point their device toward a painting, landmark, barcode, QR code, printed foreign language, and even Sudoku puzzles to receive information about the object (or solutions to the Sudoku puzzle!).

Lastly, students should be directed toward apps designed to teach new skills. Instead of reading a static article online, these apps often come equipped with guided tutorials and lessons that more readily support understanding. There are interactive training apps for hobbies like creating origami (e.g., *Dollar Origami)*, tying knots, playing chess, or musical instruments (e.g, *Ultimate Guitar Tabs*); and apps for job or school-related skills like performing CPR, reading (e.g., *SAS Read Aloud*), computer programming (e.g., *Daisy the Dinosaur, Hopscotch*), and learning a new language (e.g., *Duolingo*).

Leveraging Popular Activities

Mobile devices also afford opportunities to demonstrate the educational value in activities students engage in on a regular basis—overtly overlapping personal and educational use. Therefore activities such as social media have been theorized to be an effective mechanism for connecting informal and formal learning and developing self-regulated, lifelong learners.[17] Other examples include bringing awareness to the fact that text messaging can be used to seek help or using *Minecraft* as a platform for modelling ancient civilizations.

Social Networking

According to a survey by Common Sense Media, approximately 75 percent of kids 13 to 17 years old had an account on a social networking website in 2012.[18] No surprise—students are more inclined to use their social media accounts to connect with friends rather than use them to find information. While we do not necessarily want youth to stop using these outlets for their intended purpose, there is great value in teaching students *how* to use their social media access for informal learning.

Twitter, for example, has garnered a lot of attention in the education world, but is particularly relevant within the realm of informal learning. The microblogging nature of Twitter allows users to view their own personal feed of short, concise messages that are easier to digest than a long article, thus providing an at-a-glance and up-to-date view of the topics you personally care about. In fact, Twitter has proven to be timelier than other news outlets. For example, people were posting to Twitter about the 2008 earthquake in China long before it was covered by the BBC news.[19] Moreover, the breadth of information on Twitter is infinite and allows users to find information about almost any topic, such as current events, miscellaneous facts, ideas and inspiration, or simply what your friends are up to today. However, by utilizing hashtags and hyperlinks, this broad overview can quickly turn into an in-depth investigation of a particular topic. Many tweets include hyperlinks that direct users to additional information, whereas hashtags filter the twitterverse, allowing users to only view tweets on a specific conversation.

One illustration of using social media as a means for productive informal learning is highlighted in a recent study that sought to understand the role Twitter can play in informal learning about current events. In particular, this study focused on the Occupy Wall Street (#OWS) campaign for social change. By analyzing various sets of tweets tagged with the hashtag #OWS, findings from the report indicated that the magnitude of user-generated content not only implied community engagement but also provided others with easy and instant access to "a number of different perspectives in multiple modalities, including text, video, audio, and image."[20]

Several other social media outlets, such as *Facebook*, *Instagram*, *Snapchat*, and *Vine*, distribute information in a similar manner. Users choose who they wish to share information with, create a feed of personalized headlines, and have the option to filter by hashtags. Therefore, the informal acquisition of knowledge via social media can take many forms, whether school-related (e.g., engaging in a hashtagged discussion about the president's state of the union address in real time) or otherwise (viewing an infographic on tricks for getting stains out of dirty laundry). Nonetheless, this mass posting of information provides an excellent opportunity for teaching students about who is an expert on a subject and, consequently, where to find sources for credible information. Students can be encouraged to follow experts or leaders in a certain field, conferences aligned to students' interests or class material, or even their instructor for immediate feedback during homework. Additionally, through the use of hashtags and user comments, students can often find a variety of perspectives on a single topic or details about the daily lives of individuals from other countries or cultures.

Game-Based Learning

With many buzzwords in education, game-based learning has a split reputation among educators and researchers. In general, it is hard to argue against the theory of game-based learning—capturing disengaged students' attention by couching instruction within games, an implicitly motivating and mesmerizing medium. Games researcher, Jordan Shapiro, argues the power of game-based learning lies in the observation that games can encourage educational risk-taking that would normally be hampered by a fear of failure. He notes that "kids spend hours learning the underlying system of a video game. These kids will die and hit replay thousands of times…They won't dive into learning about the real world in a classroom without being terrified of failing. That's terrible. Game-based learning can fix this."[21] Furthermore, a recent meta-analysis of 77 game-based learning studies conducted between 2000 and 2012 found an overall trend supporting the use of games in the classroom;[22] therefore, the question surrounding game-based learning should no longer be *if* games are good for learning, but rather *how* to optimize learning within games. In fact, it is estimated the game-learning market is expected to top $2.3 billion by 2017 with a great deal of this growth being attributed to mobile games.[23]

The game-based learning research community seems to agree that the theory of games for learning warrants their use, but developing such games is quite a challenging endeavor. Several camps argue that the power of games for learning lies in their ability to foster deep learning,[24] and programs that simply gamify instructional methods do not fulfill this standard.[25] Moreover, learning scientists developing games in academia have yet to produce a repertoire of promising solutions.[26,27] Games expert, James Gee, attributes this limitation to the fact that "We have good game designers who rarely communicate with academics and content people and then we have academics and content people who try to make their own games. They make terrible games, but the game designers make good games but they don't really speak to the kind of content, the way problem solving should work, when it's tied to a school-based topic."[28] Therefore, game-based learning research needs to continue to evolve and grow as researchers and game experts collaborate to investigate how to leverage games and game features for important tasks such as implicitly encouraging higher-level thinking, providing a means for assessing these previously elusive constructs, and developing professional development around this instructional method. Only through this continued investigation will games for the classroom finally shift from gamified quizzes to programs designed for long-term, multisession engagement similar to popular entertainment games today.

When considering developing or integrating games for learning into the classroom, it is important to consider the features of games that appear to not only trigger, but sustain engagement over time. In other words, games appear to be more effective when they explicitly integrate theoretical factors known to sustain interest,[29] such as creating adaptive challenge, contextualizing play within an engaging narrative, and emphasizing interactivity.[30,31] Also, in order to achieve deeper learning gains, games should require extended or multisession interaction—recent findings suggest an average of six hours of total interaction has beneficial results.[32] Successful implementations, such as Filament Games' *iCivics*, allows for this extended, multisession experience. In fact, fourth-graders interacting with the *iCivics* game suite during their civics curriculum twice a week for six weeks scored an average of ten points higher on their civics tests.[33] However, since integrating such an extended experience during school hours might be impractical, mobile devices are a great platform for providing students with access to the environment anytime, anywhere.

Alternatively, instructors have the option to repurpose popular entertainment games for educational purposes. As seen in the example below, Kristianna Luce, a high school math teacher, uses *Angry Birds* in her algebra classes to teach parabolas and the quadratic formula.[34]

> To begin, Luce had her students play the game. … Soon, she directed the conversation toward asking what would be the highest point for a bird. Such a point is called vertex of the parabola. Given our work here, let's find the highest point for a bird launched at 60 degrees. This occurs at $x = -b/2a$. For 60 degrees, a trajectory follows $y = 1 + 1.732x - 0.211x^2$. So, $a = -0.211$ and $b = 1.732$. The vertex occurs at $x = 1.732/(0.411) = 4.214$ at a height equaling $1 + 1.732(4.214) - 0.211(4.214)^2 = 4.552 …$

The basics of algebra can be covered through these discussions, and in playing a widely popular game. Luce even connected it to the state's standards, to further illustrate the usefulness of these concepts.[35] Through using an informal and popular game, Luce was able to connect with the students, and show algebra's connections with their real and digital worlds.

Similarly, teachers have developed lesson plans around other games. Lucas Gillispie, a district technology specialist in North Carolina, found ways to leverage *World of Warcraft* for poetry instruction by having students "study riddle poetry and share their notes within the guild. They write their own riddle poems based on Azeroth (the world in which World of Warcraft is set), edit and critique each other, then take their riddles into the wider game world to challenge outsiders."[36] Larger efforts, such as MinecraftEdu, have developed entire curricula around using the popular game, *Minecraft*, in the classroom. Equipped with lesson plans, resource guides, discussion forums, live chat, and a wiki for instructors, the MinecraftEdu campaign provides ideas for lessons and support across the content areas including science, history/geography, English language arts, and math.[37]

Beyond gameplay, providing instructors with an assessment engine, a teacher dashboard to monitor gameplay and generate reports with quantifiable learning outcomes, is a critical component. Games for learning should also come packaged with implementation strategies and lesson guides. Learning experiences using games should not be implemented in isolation; utilizing supplemental instruction for contextualizing play is key.[38] For example, a recent project by GlassLab, a game-based learning research group, situated the use of the popular game *SimCity* within environmental science instruction to not only assess content knowledge but also higher-order thinking skills such as systems thinking and problem solving.[39] Following a supplemental lesson guide, gameplay serves as an engaging vehicle for formative and summative assessment. In conjunction with a teacher dashboard or assessment engine, data points during gameplay are used to inform instruction. Moreover, by allowing access to a teacher dashboard on a mobile device, instructors are free to analyze the data while walking around the room, monitoring and scaffolding gameplay as needed, and as identified by real-time metrics. As we see both mobile technologies and games proliferate in the classroom, collaboration between these two fields seems like a natural fit.

Field Trips

Guided exploration outside of the classroom through events like field-trips offer great opportunities for teaching students how to use their devices in a contextualized manner. Many museums and other points of interest offer companion apps to add a level interaction to the traditional museum excursion, and can be implemented while still preserving informal behaviors.[40]

For added engagement, apps like *Tale Blazer*, and the British Museum's *A Gift for Athena*, turn a field trip to the museum into an adventure. Equipped with their mobile devices, scavenger hunts are presented, and students are tasked to complete a variety of activities using information found throughout the museum exhibits. Also, augmented reality apps bring objects in the real world to life, making what used to be a static exhibit into an interactive space. For example, the Royal Ontario Museum's *ROM Ultimate Dinosaurs* transforms a collection of dinosaur bones into a fully fleshed, breathing animal transporting students back to the prehistoric age. Similar efforts have been created in Europe at France's Cité de L'Espace aerospace museum and Greece's Acropolis Museum. The museums' companion apps allow visitors to point their devices toward exhibits to either see crumbing ancient statues in their original form or watch a rocket take off into space. These efforts also incorporate storytelling elements to further engage and help museum visitors understand how the exhibits fit into the historical timeline.[41] And don't forget about the bus ride. *Google Field Trip* uses GPS to gather relevant information for students as they travel to their field-trip destination. From estimated time of arrival to historical sights and landmarks along the way, this field-trip companion app allows teachers to utilize every minute of the trip for learning.

Moreover, apps can be used to differentiate users' visits by accommodating special needs. To date, most museums have little to offer visitors with visual impairments. The majority of exhibits are primarily visual, with rotating exhibits and tricky floor plans, museums can be extremely difficult to navigate for this population. However, mobile devices not only enhance the experience through multimedia supplemental material, but also take advantage of interactive maps, voice over, and Bluetooth beacons to aid navigation. For example, the NC Museum of Natural Sciences Guide app (*NC NatSci*) integrates audio content (data that would traditionally be housed on an audio guide or audio wand) within an interactive, accessible map of the museum (that produces a more personalized experience – allows user to see all dinosaur exhibits, etc.). Going one step further, the Palmer Museum of Art at Penn State University plans to start using low-energy, navigational iBeacons that transmit Bluetooth signals throughout the space.[42] They communicate with mobile devices running a companion app that is aware of the visitor's location (similar to how we use GPS for outdoor navigation). Therefore, the device can automatically identify where the visitor is standing and play the corresponding audio track or supply key information about a piece of artwork. This system can also guide users around the museum from their current location to points of interest as well as exits, restrooms, and elevators. iBeacons are a huge area for potential growth in the museum and mobile device world and something that we are very excited to see come to fruition.

Lastly, field trips are not just limited to museums and other landmarks. Students are also leaving the classroom being exposed to real-world experiences, such as observing flora and fauna, collecting data, and shadowing working adults—all of which can be enhanced with mobile devices. For example, consider the following illustration.

Mrs. Johnson's seventh-grade class is practicing different styles of writing. This week, the students are practicing descriptive writing, and Mrs. Johnson has asked her students to describe their school and the surrounding property. Before they begin, she asks the students to do a little research and document characteristics of the school by taking pictures that they can then use to support their writing. Mrs. Johnson divides students into groups and assigns them an area to take pictures with their devices. Some children go outside, some go to the gymnasium and cafeteria, while the others roam the hallways. Finally, she asks the students to upload their pictures to Instagram using the hashtag #SchoolSearch. Consequently, students have access to a collaborative scrapbook from which they can pull as they draft their essays.

Whether students are taking water samples from a local pond using *EcoMobile* or helping a nurse monitor her patient's pulse, guided exploration outside of the classroom provides a wonderful opportunity to show students how mobile devices are so much more than a source of entertainment or a way to connect with their friends.

CONCLUSION

Humans are curious by nature. And while we identify schools as the place we go to learn, we actually do the majority of our learning informally outside of the classroom. Also, informal learning generally aligns better with the way we learn. Our own curiosities and interests often guide it, and it occurs in context, which makes it seem more relevant than the material presented formally in the classroom. As we conduct daily activities like driving and cooking, meet new people, pick up new hobbies, or simply observe the world around us, we are always taking in new information. However, it is what we do with this information that can result in learning.

It is there, where information meets knowledge acquisition, that mobile devices serve to enhance our informal learning experiences. Instead of asking yourself, "What kind of flower is that?" on your morning walk, mobile devices provide you an opportunity to research and find the answer to your question immediately. So, instead of simply wondering, you have now learned another type of flower.

But, our ability to strategically use mobile devices to feed our curiosities does not come naturally. Therefore, to optimize students' informal learning, we must first teach them how to ask their own questions and effectively seek their own answers. Formal classroom learning at school provides a great opportunity to do that. Simulating daily activities and challenging students to solve real-world problems have not only been shown to encourage deeper engagement with the material, but also give students a chance to use a variety of tools and resources in a supervised setting. This way, instructors can guide students and ensure they do not flounder in the mass of available apps and information on the Internet. As a result, students learn their mobile devices are so much more than a means to communicate with their friends and update their social media accounts. Instead, they are a powerful tool for indulging curiosities individually. In short, by teaching how to use mobile devices in informal settings, we are teaching students how to be lifelong learners.

NOTES

1. H. Eshach, "Bridging In-School and Out-Of-School Learning: Formal, Non-Formal, and Informal Education," *Journal of Science Education and Technology* 16, no. 2 (2007): 171–190.

2. L. B. Resnick, *Education and Learning toThink* (Washington, DC: National Academies Press, 1987).

3. Eshach, "Bridging In-School and Out-of-School Learning."

4. J. Osborne and J. Dillon, "Research on Learning in Informal Contexts: Advancing the Field?," *International Journal of Science Education* 29, no. 12 (2007): 1441–1445.

5. K. W Lai, F. Khaddage, and G. Knezek, "Blending Student Technology Experiences in Formal and Informal Learning," *Journal of Computer-Assisted Learning* 29, no. 5 (2013): 414–425.

6. J. Lave, *The Culture of Acquisition and the Practice of Understanding* (Palo Alto, CA: Institute for Research on Learning,1988): 259–286.

7. Osborne and Dillon, "Research on Learning."

8. D. W. Livingstone, "Exploring the Icebergs of Adult Learning: Findings of the First Canadian Survey of Informal Learning Practices," Centre for the Study of Education and Work, 1999, https://tspace.library.utoronto.ca/retrieve/4451.

9. Microsoft Partners in Learning, The Pearson Foundation, Gallup, "21st Century Skills and the Workplace: A 2013 Microsoft Partners in Learning and Pearson Foundation Study," 2013, www.ferris.edu/HTMLS/administration/academicaffairs/extendedinternational/ccleadership/alliance/documents/21stCenturySkills.pdf.

10. Carly Shuler, "Pockets of Potential: Using Mobile Technologies to Promote Children's Learning," Joan Ganz Cooney Center, New York, January 2009, www.joanganzcooneycenter.org / wp-content / uploads / 2010 / 03 / pockets_of_potential_1_.pdf.

11. B. Gurung and D. Rutledge, "Digital Learners and the Overlapping of Their Personal and Educational Digital Engagement," *Computers & Education* 77 (2014): 91–100.

12. Y. A. Rahim, A. N. Che Pee, and M. A. Othman, "Observation on the Uses of Mobile Phones to Support Informal Learning," *International Journal of Interactive Mobile Technologies* 6, no. 4 (2012): 43.

13. I. M. Santos and N. Ali, "Exploring the Uses of Mobile Phones to Support Informal Learning," *Education and Information Technologies* 17, no. 2 (2012): 187–203.

14. Gurung and Rutledge, "Digital Learners."

15. Pew Research Center, "How Teens Do Research in the Digital World: A Survey of Advanced Placement and National Writing Project Teachers Finds That Teen's Research Habits Are Changing in the Digital Age," www.pewinternet.org/2012/11/01/how-teens-do-research-in-the-digital-world/.

16. Katherine McMillan Culp, "Possible Worlds Creator: Developers Should Focus on Function over Aesthetics," Games and Learning, www.gamesandlearning.org / 2014 / 05/12/possible-worlds-creator-developers-should-focus-on-function-over-aesthetics.

17. A. Kitsantas and N. Dabbagh, "The Role of Web 2.0 Technologies in Self-Regulated Learning," *New Directions for Teaching and Learning* 126 (2011): 99–106.

18. "Social Media, Social Life: How Teens View their Digital Lives," Common Sense Media, Summer 2012, www.commonsensemedia.org/research/social-media-social-life-how-teens-view-their-digital-lives.

19. Clay Shirky, "How Social Media Can Make History," 2009, www.ted.com/talks/clay_shirky_how_cellphones_twitter_facebook_can_make_history.

20. B. Gleason, "# Occupy Wall Street: Exploring Informal Learning About a Social Movement on Twitter," *American Behavioral Scientist* 57, no. 7 (2013): 966–982.

21. "Shapiro: Games, Not Gamification, Can Help Solve the Education Crisis," Games and Learning, March 28, 2014, www.gamesandlearning.org/2014/03/28/shapiro-games-not-gamification-can-help-solve-the-education-crisis/.

22. Douglas Clark, Emily Tanner-Smity, and Stephen Killingsworth, "Digital Games, Design, and Learning: A Systematic Review and Meta Analysis," *SRI International*, 2014, www.sri.com/work/publications/digital-games-design-and-learning-systematic-review-and-meta-analysis-brief.

23. Lee Banville, "Driven by Mobile, Edu-Games Market Expected to Top $2.3 Billion by 2017," Games and Learning, October 26, 2013, www.gamesandlearning.org/2013/10/26/driven-by-mobile-edu-games-market-expected-to-top-2-3-billion-by-2017.

24. Lee Banville, "Research Shows Games Have Significant Impact on Student Performance," Games and Learning, October 1, 2013, www.gamesandlearning.org/2013/10/01/research-shows-games-have-significant-impact-on-student-performance/.

25. "Shapiro: Games,"

26. L. Alfieri, P. J. Brooks, N. J. Aldrich, and H. R. Tenenbaum, "Does Discovery-Based Instruction Enhance Learning?," *Journal of Educational Psychology* 103, no. 1 (2011): 1–18.

27. R. E. Mayer and C. I. Johnson, "Adding Instructional Features That Promote Learning in a Game-Like Environment," *Journal of Educational Computing Research* 42, no. 3 (2010): 241–265.

28. Lee Banville, "Newsmaker: James Gee on Why the Power of Games to Teach Remains Unrealized," Games and Learning, February 10, 2014, www.gamesand learning.org/2014/02/10/newsmaker-james-gee-on-why-the-power-of-games-to -teach-remains-unrealized/.

29. Clark, Tanner-Smity, and Killingsworth, "Digital Games."

30. D. A. Bergin "Influences on Classroom Interest," *Educational Psychologist* 34, no. 2 (1999): 87–98.

31. M. Mitchell, "Situational Interest: Its Multifaceted Structure in the Secondary School Mathematics Classroom," *Journal of Educational Psychology* 85, no. 3 (1993): 424.

32. Clark and others, "Digital Games."

33. Games and Learning, "Study Highlights Effectiveness of iCivics at Raising Test Scores," February 21, 2014, www.gamesandlearning.org/2014/02/21/study -highlights-effectiveness-of-icivics-at-raising-test-scores/.

34. Tim Charier, "Frustrated with Math? Try Angry Birds," *Huffington Post,* June 11, 2012, www.huffingtonpost.com/tim-chartier/frustrated-with-math-try-_b_1581042.html.

35. Ibid.

36. Ann Doss Helms, "Popular Video Games Integrated into K–12 Learning," *Education Week*, January 22, 2013, www.edweek.org/ew/articles/2013/01/23/18games.h32 .html.

37. MinecraftEdu, www.minecraftedu.com.

38. Clark, Tanner-Smity, and Killingsworth, "Digital Games."

39. GlassLab, "Psychometric Considerations in Game-Based Assessment," www.institute ofplay.org/work/projects/glasslab-research/.

40. Yoon, S. A., Elinich, K., Wang, J., J. B. Schoonveld, and E. Anderson, "Scaffolding Informal Learning in Science Museums: How Much Is Too Much?.," *Science Education*, 97, no. 6 (2013): 848-877.

41. Yannis Ioannidis, Olivier Balet, and Dimitrios Pandermalis, "Tell Me a Story: Augmented Reality Technology In Museums," *The Guardian*, April 4, 2014, www .theguardian.com/culture-professionals-network/culture-professionals-blog/2014/ apr/04/story-augmented-reality-technology-museums.

42. Katie Jacobs, "A Day at the Museum," Penn State: IT News, October 21, 2014. http:// news.it.psu.edu/article/day-museum?utm_content=buffer66d84&utm_medium =social&utm_source=twitter.com&utm_campaign=buffer.

CHAPTER **13**

Engaging Young Users: Apps for Preschoolers

M obile devices offer an intuitive, simple interface that provides many benefits for all populations. For preschoolers, children from ages one to five, these benefits enable them to use mobile devices with an ease that often surprises their parents and teachers, and opens doors to new, rich educational experiences. With the increasing prevalence of mobile devices among parents and adults, preschoolers have access to this technology at unprecedented levels. Therefore, there is a burgeoning market for educational apps targeted toward preschoolers, leaving parents and teachers with many options and little guidance on how to choose quality apps for children. Moreover, app developers need to be in tune with what preschoolers are capable of and need to learn. This chapter will address these concerns.

It's an understatement to say there are a lot of preschool apps to choose from. Of the top-selling 200 educational apps, 58 percent are for toddlers and preschoolers,[1] a statistic that mirrors the Cooney Center's in-depth analysis in late 2010.[2] The market is responding to the increased demand from this demographic. More parents currently have smartphones and tablet devices than ever before and preschool-aged children, looking to emulate their parents' behaviors, have an unprecedented level of access. There is a tremendous opportunity to use these devices for good. That is, they can be used to teach children the skills they need for kindergarten in a fun, engaging, and effective way. It's an important time to reach young learners; positive learning experiences set them up for future academic success and lifelong learning. However, due to the market saturation and the often fuzzy line between pure fun and educational activities, it's vital that users figure out how to choose a good app and that developers develop useful apps. Providing good information to developers on what preschoolers need and desire, as well as providing information to parents on how to choose the best apps in a saturated market, are vital to making the most of mobile learning for this group. Issues, such as privacy, security, and screen time (the amount of exposure permitted to mobile devices) are important considerations to determine which apps to use and how much time with them should be allowed.

KEY SKILLS FOR PRESCHOOL APPS

When students enter kindergarten, teachers look for proficiency in certain areas, skills that prime young children for future learning. Parents are increasingly taking on the role of teacher (or facilitator) in the preschool years to ensure that their children are developing a strong foundation in a number of areas that prepare them for future academic success. Tablets are making their way into many homes, and they provide a new opportunity for preschoolers to learn these prerequisite skills in a fun, engaging way. Many preschool apps are developed and marketed with these capacities in mind, and these areas should certainly be used as a guide for parents in selecting apps (see Figure 13.1).

Language and Literacy

The ability to read and write is seen as a cornerstone skill for kids; both are used in all other subjects and without them, a child can quickly fall behind across the board. Providing quality instruction at the emergent-reader level has been identified as a powerful technique for mitigating reading difficulties later in development.[3] According to the

Figure 13.1 Key Skill for Preschool Apps

2013 National Assessment of Educational Progress (NAEP), on average only 42 percent of U.S. fourth graders read at or above the proficient level; the majority of students were not considered proficient readers.[4] These national statistics highlight the importance of creating valuable literary experiences for children during the emergent and early reader phases (preschool through third grade), and mobile devices afford a great opportunity to do this.

Emergent Reading Skills

Emergent reading skills—namely, written language awareness and phonological awareness—are quite critical for later reading development and performance.[5] Phonological awareness encompasses a child's knowledge of spoken language (e.g., phoneme identification and manipulation), whereas written language awareness involves an understanding of print concepts (e.g., letter and word identification, print conventions).[6] Given the predictive power of these skills, encouraging literacy behaviors at a young age is widely recommended.[7]

Two excellent ways to develop reading readiness translate well into the app space: shared book reading and drill and practice activities. Shared book reading is a tried and true means of developing reading readiness that precedes mobile learning by centuries. But mobile devices provide a level of interactivity not afforded by print materials. Creating apps that allow the users to read a book, or listen to a book being read to them, with print highlighting is a way to convey phonological awareness and written language awareness to the emergent reader. Another key way to develop reading readiness is through drill and practice apps for letter identification, letter sounds, and phonological awareness.

Of course, while emergent reading activities are valuable, the utility of the session as an instructional tool is dependent on the quality of the interaction.[8] It is important, when developing and using these emergent reader applications, that the mobile device not be thought of as taking the place of the parent. Parental involvement is advised and can enhance the outcomes further. The mobile device and reading app allow for a richer reading experience for both the parent and the child, and the opportunity for more frequent reading experiences.

Fine Motor Skills

Fine motor skills are a vital part of education. Writing and drawing, coloring within the lines, cutting using scissors, and playing a musical instrument are all activities that require strong fine motor skills. Handwriting is an important fine motor skill that is still very relevant, despite the growing use of technology in classrooms. Handwriting is a foundational literacy skill that enables learning of other skills. Children spend a substantial amount of their school day writing and performing other fine motor skills, and "difficulty in this area can interfere with academic achievement."[9] The inability to clearly and quickly take notes interferes with the acquisition of other skills, such as spelling, and impacts learning in every subject area. "Children with handwriting problems typically have difficulty keeping up with the volume of written work required during the elementary school years, which may impede academic progress and lead to lowered self-esteem and behavioral problems."[10] Even in today's classrooms with the widespread use of computers and mobile devices, handwriting remains a crucial developmental skill for a child to master.[11]

Mobile devices offer several opportunities to improve a preschooler's fine motor skills, which improve only through practice.[12] While apps can't afford student practice with scissors, glue, writing utensils, or other physical objects (yet!) they can support skills for coloring, staying in the lines, tracing, writing, connecting dots, and other fine motor skill development activities, with touch or using a stylus. The *Little Writer* app gives the preschooler guidance while tracing a letter shape, showing the correct way to make the letter, and forcing the user to stay within the letter shape.[13] Apps like this allow mobile devices to digitally scaffold the process of learning fine motor skills. A major benefit is that it's easy to start over; the child doesn't need to get a new piece of paper or dwell on mistakes. Additionally, tablets offer a direct transfer of skills; tracing a letter shape with your finger or a stylus is very similar to writing the letter on a piece of paper. The transferability of tracing using a mouse on a PC, for instance, is not nearly as high. Fostering strong fine motor skills early in the learning process sets the preschooler up with foundational skills upon which to build future learning.

Spatial Skills and Math

STEM (science, technology, engineering, and math) careers are in high demand and there is an increasing focus on cultivating these skills in students. A national effort is being made to expand participation in STEM subjects. Math proficiency denotes a broad set of competencies. In the preschool years, learning numbers and operations, measurement and analysis, algebraic thinking, and spatial reasoning are key subsets that lay the foundation for future academic achievement in mathematical areas.[14] Tablet and mobile devices hold promise to enhance a preschooler's early math skills, especially spatial skills and number fluency.

While advanced mathematical operations are typically beyond the reach of preschool-aged children, a strong foundation for mathematical aptitude can also be enhanced through developing basic numerical concepts. Ultimately, numerical literacy enables a person to move from performing a direct computation to an automated computation that requires few cognitive resources (see Chapter 2 for more on automaticity and other the psychological processes involved in learning). At the preschool level, this involves identifying numbers, recognizing amounts (1, 2, 3) without counting, comparing quantities, estimation, identifying and copying patterns, sorting and classifying objects, and performing operations on numbers.[15] The *SAS Math Stretch* app features many games that facilitate this number fluency and practice that lays the foundation for higher order mathematics.

Spatial skills are an important component of STEM and have been linked through extensive research with success in STEM careers. Spatial thinking concerns shapes, the locations of objects, the potential paths they might take to move, and their relation to other objects.[16] Excellent spatial thinkers are able to easily conceptualize movement and manipulation. While almost everyone thinks using verbal, mathematical, and spatial skills, research suggests those with an increased aptitude for spatial thinking are more inclined to pursue an interest in STEM subjects.[17] Numerous studies have shown that spatial skills begin developing in children at a very young age, but can be improved at all stages in a person's life through practice.[18] Indeed, the earlier these skills are fostered in children, the better. For the preschool crowd, this means using apps as a play space to teach skills like counting, number recognition, shapes, colors, spatial-relevant terms (i.e., in front of, behind, etc.), pattern recognition, and creation.

Unfortunately, most K-12 schools don't teach and assess spatial skills explicitly and leave it up to activities outside of the classroom to compensate for this lack of instruction. Given the interactive, hands-on nature of mobile technologies, there are many opportunities for valuable spatial skill development. For example, research has shown playing games like Tetris can lead to improvements in players' spatial skills, with one study concluding that regular Tetris playing leads to long-term improvement of spatial skills and was generalized to other spatial tasks, and even improved academic outcomes.[19] These results are not limited to just Tetris; other video games have been linked to similar results.[20]

How do we teach spatial and math skills to preschoolers? In the years before a child enters kindergarten, children often do the majority of their learning and development through play. With a balance of instruction and play, a child can develop a strong spatial skill set. Activities like putting together a jigsaw puzzle, using maps, and block building all challenge children to reason about the world in terms of spatial relations. Activities like these can easily be simulated in the appspace. For instance, in the *Toca Doctor* app, young users are challenged to guide a marble through simulated arteries to reach the heart. It also gives the child gears in different shapes and the user must find the right fit to make the mechanical "brain" start turning.

Social Skills

Social skills are an important skillset for getting preschoolers ready for kindergarten. Kindergarten readiness often entails the ability to listen, follow directions, play cooperatively, display empathy and emotional intelligence, and respect others. These skills can be fostered through time on mobile devices. In the popular press, some social skills are thought to be stunted by device exposure. However, research generally shows the opposite to be true. Through mobile play, preschoolers are developing several key social skills including communication of feelings, empathy, patience, interpersonal relations, and respect. The ability to regulate and communicate their emotions enables them to better interact with grownups and other children, as well as understand and control their own feelings. They figure out they can use communication to drive environmental changes to help regulate emotion. Furthermore, empathy enables them to recognize how others feel and act to improve others' situations. Beyond the emotional skills that are closely tied to the development of social skills, specific abilities, like following instructions and interacting with others, allow preschoolers to seamlessly transition to the structure of the classroom.

Historically, technology has enabled simulating situations for children to practice tasks such as social interaction, empathy, and following directions. The Next Generation Preschool Math grant focuses on creating and testing iPad apps in the preschool setting, noting the many instances of unprompted social sharing that take place among its users.[21] In several noted instances, one child will successfully complete a task or figure out how to do something and immediately look up to share this with his neighbor. Additionally, some apps allow for several people to play, which teaches turn taking and collaborative skills.

Other apps, like *Toca Tea Party*, encourage interpersonal relationships to take place off screen. This app allows the user to set an augmented reality tea party with drinks, treats, music, and customizable décor. The user can invite friends (or stuffed animals) to drink tea and eat treats, leaving plenty of room for imagination and social learning off screen.[22] Many educational apps that convey social skills are less obvious to parents; *Toca Tea Party* doesn't teach the alphabet or counting or any obvious reading and math skills. However, it is play-based and encourages the child to imagine and interact socially on and off screen.

Creativity

The Partnership for 21st Century Skills, a prominent advocate for empowering students with the skills necessary to succeed in the information economy, identifies creativity as one of the critical learning and innovation skills.[23] A critical part of thinking creatively is instilling strategies in students for when they are wrong. Being wrong is often a necessary step in creating original solutions and products.[24] It is important that students learn to "elaborate, refine, analyze, evaluate ideas to improve and maximize creative efforts."[25] Further, the Partnership for 21st Century Skills stresses the ability to work creatively with others and to produce tangible outcomes from creative thoughts.[26]

Preschoolers predominantly practice creative work with others through play. Play is a broadly important concept in learning, especially for young children. But play also has unique contributions to the development of creativity. The informal structure of play, as opposed to more strictly formal settings, allows for risk-free exploration and experimentation. Children are free to make mistakes without penalty. Consequently, preschoolers are provided with opportunities to refine and elaborate their ideas and mistakes to cultivate strategies relevant for lifelong learning. Exploring the intersection of imagination and reality through play, either individually or collaboratively, has tremendous value in the development of creativity.[27]

Great mobile apps need to incorporate and support the interesting, creative thoughts of preschoolers. This includes everything from idea formation and refinement to supporting collaboration and dissemination. Widely, today's mobile apps provide tools for creative art exploration, learning, play, and practice. Students can play instruments, both real (such as the guitar, piano, and bass found in Apple's *GarageBand*) and fantastical instruments (such as those from Smule, like *Ocarina* which turns your iPhone into a musical instrument). Numerous photo, drawing, and painting apps are also available to scaffold student creativity. *SAS Gloss* provides drawing starters to help teachers demonstrate to students their own creativity and how creativity can lead to different results from different students.

Creating and sharing something is a big part of preschool life, as any parent or teacher with walls, refrigerators or office bulletin boards filled with art work can attest. Capturing students' creativity is important so that they or others can build on it. As we move deeper into the twenty-first century, the creative productions of preschoolers are increasingly becoming more and more digitized. Numerous mobile apps have already been designed to harness the disseminative potential of creative productions of all ages, including preschoolers. For instance, *Toca Tailor* lets children choose fabrics in various colors and patterns, dressing their model in whatever way they want. When they're done, they can take a picture (a screenshot) within the app and save it to share with others, preserving their creative endeavor.

What Do Preschoolers Want to Learn in Your App?

- Language and literacy skills, specifically fine motor skills that enable writing and emergent reading skills (such as letters, sounds, and sight words), presented in a fun way to make reading a positive experience from the beginning.
- Spatial skills and early math activities are important to develop the child's budding analytical skills.
- Certain social skills can be developed through apps that cultivate emotional skills (like empathy) and necessary skills for socialization, like listening and obeying instructions.

- Creativity should be involved wherever possible, allowing the preschooler to use imagination and ingenuity.
- An opportunity to try something and recover from failure in a positive environment (which might include the use of verbal cues and encouragement).

WHAT MAKES AN ENGAGING PRESCHOOL APP?

A good preschool app is, above all, engaging. To retain preschoolers' relatively short attention span and educate them, an app must make sure that it grabs and maintains their interest. While many of these principles for preschool app design and development hold true across the educational domain, they're amplified in importance for preschool. Preschoolers come to the table with less developed literacy and mathematical skills and a short attention span, so it's vital that any app marketed to this age group understand these differences in ability.

There are several ways apps can engage this group, but a primary focus for the development of any concept for preschool educational apps should be play-based learning. The connotations of the term "play" should not undermine its educational importance. In fact, play is regarded as one of the most powerful methods of instruction during early childhood. Einstein knew the value of play when he said, " ... play seems to be the essential feature in productive scientific thought," and researchers are in universal agreement that play provides a strong foundation for intellectual growth, creativity, and problem solving.[28]

The app developer's challenge then, is balancing humorous and playful aspects with enriching content.[29] Finding a fun concept in which to embed the educational content is key. At some point, peeling back the play to expose just how much innate learning was occurring will help children develop efficacy for future learning, because they become aware of how learning was applied for enjoyment and growth. Additionally, they'll have positive connotations with learning. While learning doesn't always have to be hidden—some apps are very explicitly teaching an academic skill—it is one hallmark of preschool apps. The literature on student engagement is vast. In our experience, there are several relevant components of student engagement as they apply to preschool-aged children.

Motivation

Motivation is a powerful force: it drives humans to act.[30] Extrinsic and intrinsic motivations, discussed in Chapter 2, are two contrasting forces that compel us to act. For preschoolers, it's important to use both, but focus on cultivating intrinsic motivation. Intrinsic motivation refers to engaging in a behavior because it is inherently interesting.[31] The behavior is undertaken solely for the challenge it poses, the enjoyment it yields, or the curiosity it satisfies; the act has some internal utility. Intrinsic motivation is favored because it has been associated with quality learning and creativity.[32] Further, it is believed that pedagogy that cultivates interest in a subject matter is more likely to lead to self-initiated learning beyond instructional experiences.[33] Intrinsic motivation is more challenging in the app space, however, as it is very difficult to measure. Malone and Lepper's taxonomy of intrinsic motivations consists of both individual and interpersonal factors.[34] The four individual intrinsic motivators—challenge, control, curiosity, and fantasy—are useful guides in engaging preschoolers.

For an app to be challenging, the tasks presented to the preschooler must be neither too easy nor unduly difficult. Either of the ends of the spectrum will foster little or no intrinsic interest and may lead to user boredom or frustration. Designing optimally challenging, leveled tasks will maximize the child's motivation and scaffold the learning experience by providing differentiated instruction based on performance. This means that the app cannot require a child to master too many new functions to play. It is difficult to develop for this group, and this is a primary reason why. Continually refreshing content, integrating leveled content, and knowing your intended audience well are key practices in ensuring that your content is challenging.

Providing some level of control to the child is another way to promote intrinsic motivation. Humans have a basic tendency to want to have a hand in their own fate. Providing mechanisms that allow children to manipulate the learning experience results in a sense of power and choice. Tablet devices inherently offer this control, if the child is given free rein over which app he wants to play. (This may be restricted by the parents or teachers.) Another way to offer control to young users is within the app: activity choice. *Toca House* lets learners choose from several activities in different areas of the house.

Children are innately inquisitive, and apps can stoke this curiosity and use it to stimulate interest. Student interest can be maintained by controlling an optimal level of discrepancy between the student's current knowledge and skills and the expected knowledge and skills following engagement in particular activities. *Dinosaur Train Mesozoic Math Adventures* teaches math but sets these skills in a dinosaur world. Contextualizing concepts can often be a way to invoke curiosity in a different subject. For instance, in *Mesozoic Math*, the user collects, groups and counts fossils, learning to make bar charts and developing statistical problem solving skills.[35] Relating concepts to something students are interested in encourages them to seek deeper understanding and identify how it relates to their interest.

Fantasies can evoke intrinsic motivation and interest in ways that otherwise are unavailable to the student in reality. Apps should enable students to develop mental models of imaginary situations. A great example of a fantasy-based app is *Toca Pet Doctor*, in which children see injured pets and apply bandages, ointments, and give them food, in the imaginary setting of a veterinarian's office. Through the fantastical setting, children learn actual ways to help animals. One important challenge to note with using this type of motivation is to ensure that the app finds mechanisms to help learners translate knowledge to real-world situations. *Toca House* offers several opportunities for users to practice early math skills by doing chores within the virtual house, like sorting, matching, comparing and measuring.

While developing intrinsic motivation in preschoolers is most desirable because of its close relationship to their innate eagerness to learn, children don't always have this motivation for all tasks. Young children exhibit some intrinsic motivation for certain tasks (choosing an outfit or putting on shoes independently, for instance); however it is possible to use rewards to enhance intrinsic motivation. Instilling feelings of competency is one way to do this. A major way to motivate preschoolers uses rewards strategically and methodically, which can provide the external scaffolding to autonomous educational tasks.

When incorporating rewards, it is important to understand what your target audience in fact perceives as a reward. Rewards for an adult are often vastly different from what preschoolers see as a reward. Simple acts such as providing clear goals and encouraging feedback are often sufficient for motivating younger audiences. For instance, in guessing "Which shape is a triangle?" providing positive reinforcement and tips to direct the child to the correct answer after an incorrect answer is a good idea. ("A triangle has three sides, try again!")[36] And finally, rewarding and acknowledging productive effort, as opposed to correct answers alone, is important. For instance, the *Super Why!* app encourages players by awarding stickers after the successful completion of a module, holding their interest longer.[37] It could, however, be something less concrete, even a trumpeting sound or exuberant animation could be a reward for a success in an app.

Interest

There are several important considerations to be aware of regarding preschoolers' interest in apps. To effectively engage this age group, the app needs to have developmentally appropriate content to be interesting.[38] It is important to carefully delineate content so it is easy to find developmentally appropriate material. Consider apps with multiple levels, or using a standardized leveling system for content. Caretakers, parents, and teachers should be able to easily assess the appropriateness of an app for their preschooler. For developers, this means having a strong understanding of the exact age group being developed for; one year olds and four year olds have substantially different abilities and interests. Test your app on these age groups to have a solid grasp on how they interact with the app and what makes sense to them. The skills mentioned earlier in this chapter (reading readiness, spatial skills, and so on) are a good starting place in determining what the user knows and needs to know.

Consider your audience and how much new content they can attend to at one time. A valuable method is to segment the content into chunks.[39] For instance, preschoolers are more engaged with books that have fewer sentences and words per page, and wouldn't be as engaged with a long paragraph. Use similar principles to divide up the content into manageable pieces, colocating it with contextually relevant media. This is of particular importance to preschoolers since they tend to process information holistically.[40] According to developmental psychologist Jean Piaget's seminal work, children progress through a series of stages of cognitive development, and the majority of preschoolers cannot think logically or abstractly. So, what might be an easy problem for an adult to solve in his head is often very difficult for a preschooler. A common example is conservation. Imagine two containers: one is tall and skinny like a beaker, and one is short and wide like a baking dish. Even after pouring the same amount of water into each of the containers in front of a preschooler, the child will often claim the tall, skinny container contains more water than the short, wide container. The idea that the quantity is the same, or conserved, regardless of the shape of the container is not readily apparent to a very young child. In light of such psychological differences, developers should ensure that features or activities within the app involve explicit and straightforward content and presentation. Developers should take advantage of the mobile medium to provide the user with several models and visual aids as opposed to relying on the child to remember or process multiple concepts in working memory.[41]

Apps that keep users coming back are ones that have fresh and dynamic content and offer users predictable but new experiences each time. Preschoolers often embrace seeing the same movie again and again, and there is value to repetition. However, having content that expands or increases in complexity as children master the previous content, or even simply content that is refreshed periodically for new exploration, is critical to retain a learner's interest.

Interface

While there are best practices to apply when developing apps for any user group, such guidelines take on a special importance for preschool-aged children since they often have shorter attention spans as well as limited literacy skills and dexterity. (We outline our design principles for educational apps in Chapter 9.) Simple is almost always better, and the following principles for developing a user-friendly interface are suggested. Apps for preschoolers should offer a responsive interface, consistency, clarity of purpose, and simple interactions.

It is important to develop a responsive app that quickly loads and performs functions when instructed. No one likes to wait for an app to load, and preschoolers are even less patient than the rest of us.[42] When developing an app, it's therefore important to consider how long the content will take to load and, where possible, preload some content. Content should be threaded to improve processing efficiency. While the app is loading, give the user an indication that it is loading and will only take a moment; a progress bar or icon can usually accomplish this. Additionally, when the user presses a button, the app should provide immediate feedback. If an app is too slow to respond, the initial reaction is to hit more buttons or, ultimately, quit the app and move on.

The role of color, the sizes of buttons and shapes need to be considered and applied consistently throughout the app. When designing the elements of an app, all should contribute directly to the communication of function within the app, and be purposeful and consistent. If a red exit button is used throughout the app, don't use a red enter button on a certain screen to indicate a different action. Use larger buttons to dictate primary actions and smaller buttons for options, settings, or secondary, less common actions. Since most of the preschool audience cannot read, developers should rely on conventions (green means go/launch, red means stop/exit) and screen placement for intuitive use. Use concepts like flashing or flickering the button to draw attention to indicate the next step.[43] Given preschoolers' developing dexterity, larger buttons should be used.

In a preschool app, everything on the screen should have a purpose. This criterion is an important one for parents to use in evaluating which apps to purchase or download, and for developers to keep in mind while designing their apps. If the goal of an app is to hold educational value or lead to a specified educational outcome, then apps should remove content and graphics that are extraneous and do not directly contribute to the learning goals. There is certainly a fine line between making the learning environment visually interesting and providing clear guidance on the app's use. While it is important to make the learning environment visually interesting and fun, it should not be so busy that it detracts from the content or interferes with correct use.

Provide simple interactions by relying on intuitive gestures. Preschoolers' dexterity varies greatly, but big buttons are always best. Easy gestures are also preferable to more nuanced ones. For instance, in iPad apps, tap, swipe, and drag gestures are intuitive. Pinching, tilting, and double tapping aren't as instinctive for this group and should be avoided.[44] The sophistication of the touch functions and buttons should be scaled to the users' expected fine motor skill level.

Tips for Making an Engaging Preschool App

- Keep it playful. Play-based learning is an important concept for the preschool user, as play is the primary way this age group learns.
- Test your app with children. It is vital to watch a preschooler interact with the device and your app to ensure you're producing something engaging and effective.
- Use Malone and Lepper's four intrinsic motivators as guides: challenge, control, curiosity, and fantasy.
- Be sure the content in the app is leveled to the user's age, abilities, and interests.
- Adhere strictly to principles of good design, especially focusing on consistency and simplicity, as young users cannot read commands.

CHALLENGES

Developing apps for preschoolers also comes with its share of challenges, as shown in Figure 13.2. Parents and teachers are completely in control of the buying and usage patterns for preschool apps, even more so than with older children. Growing concerns over screen time and privacy are also under scrutiny and changing quickly for the preschool demographic.

Figure 13.2 Challenges for Preschool Apps

Parents as Gatekeepers

One key challenge in developing apps for preschoolers is the lack of direct access to the target audience. Children under five generally do not find and purchase their own apps and are often secondary users of a parent's mobile device. They're not always given free rein over the device, nor are they given unlimited time to play and learn. If children are given a choice of which apps to play, it's likely to be limited by the parent in some way. Since the parents are gatekeepers to this group—enabling or preventing their use of the device and apps—developers have an added responsibility when creating apps for preschoolers to make it attractive to parents, too. Making apps that address parents' questions, concerns, and objectives is an added challenge in developing apps for preschoolers.

A common concern among parents is that too much time with the device can lead to "physical and academic lethargy."[45] This view assumes that the time spent on the device is not enhancing the child's education but rather reducing the child's potential in some way. In a survey of parents conducted by the Cooney Center at Sesame Workshop, this was the number one reason that parents restricted the use of the technology for their children.[46] Unfortunately, this view is not necessarily unfounded. There are many noneducational apps, and not all apps designed for learning are equal in their educational value. However, there are also many educational apps that are enriching and well worth the time and effort invested by the child and his or her parents. It is essential that the parent take an active role in helping choose apps with their children that are both educational and engaging. To that end, developers need to make parents feel comfortable with the app by providing details on the educational skills to be taught through play in the app. Parents witnessing the educational value through their child's interaction with it is a key in their willingness to allow their child to continue to use the app.[47]

Apps and app developers have an additional responsibility in aiding parents who want to know how to best guide and teach certain skills to their preschool-aged children themselves. When you ask parents how to teach a very young child mathematical thinking, for instance, they may not be sure where to start. However, through use of an app, parents might pick up that number sense encompasses simple addition, numerical comparisons, counting, and numeral recognition, and see specific activities within the app that are teaching these skills to their child. *Endless Numbers* is an app that teaches these skills in a fun setting, verbally reinforcing the skills. Now the parents can continue this learning outside of the app, further developing a positive educational home environment.[48]

Involving the parents is an essential step in preschool apps, as parental guidance during media consumption has been found to positively impact a child's learning, promoting language development and increasing engagement.[49] Sesame Workshop notes that a best practice they use is to include information for parents under the Help icon. Since preschoolers typically could not read a detailed how-to guide on the use of the app, this section is essentially for the parents.[50] While mobile devices possess engaging and powerful ways to enhance the way a child learns essential preschool skills, parents are an invaluable part of the equation. It is the parents who must help the child make connections between the game and the world around them, engaging in discussions about the activity and participating.[51]

Passback

An increasingly common exposure model for preschoolers to gain access to mobile devices is what the Cooney Center refers to as the passback effect, where parents lend their device to a child to keep them occupied.[52] The passback is marked by short sessions for the child to play and learn, and the parent will generally provide scaffolding on which apps and programs are accessed. The mobile device is often used as an entertainment source for the child while out and about—on the subway, in restaurants, and in the car, for example—and represents an opportunity for preschoolers to have access to mobile devices.[53] It is also a relatively new opportunity to learn. In scenarios when parents are busy, this is a chance for the child to engage in a learning task when otherwise there would be no direct stimulation or instruction.

Teachers as Gatekeepers

Preschool is another setting where mobile learning can be introduced, though this avenue hasn't been explored in preschool classrooms as much as elementary schools. To enable effective use of technology, equipment and support must be provided to teachers to ensure effective implementation. The Next Generation Preschool Math grant works to provide quality math-centered apps, supporting classroom activities that reinforce skills learned in the app, and a guide for teachers instructing them on how to integrate the technology.[54] Like parents, it can't be assumed that teachers automatically understand what makes an enriching app, or how to make the best use of it in their classroom. A 1:1 mobile-device program in a preschool is uncommon, so apps intended to be used in preschool classrooms might consider accommodating multiple players. Sharing is an important element of any preschool curriculum, and playing collaborative games also enables social learning for the child.[55]

Screen Time

While we know there are many benefits to early use of mobile learning devices and apps, there is also a great deal researchers don't know about the long-term effects of exposure to this relatively new media. "Screen time" is the term we use to describe how much time is permitted by the parents for the child to use mobile devices, television, and computers. The American Academy of Pediatrics (AAP) recommends no screen time for children under two. The standards, though updated in 2011, offer no distinction between passive television programming and interactive technology. However, touch-screen mobile devices and computers offer a substantially different experience from sitting on the couch watching a television show: interactivity. In 2014, Dr. Dimitri Christakis, a member of the executive committee of the AAP's Council on Communications and Media, published an opinion that all screen time is not created equal, and he sees major differences between interactive, mobile device use and television screen time. He says, to promote brain development and stimulate language development in young children, play should be interactive. His research found that play on interactive apps can produce the same effects (measured in cortisol levels in the brain) as playing with blocks.[56] "The question at hand then might well be: are interactive touchscreen technologies more likeable to passively watching a screen or to playing with blocks? My hunch is that they are more akin to block play and here is why: the one thing a child never says (or thinks) when he or she interacts with passive media is "I did it!" This is, of course, quite different than what might be experienced in the context of using a well-designed interactive app," Christakis says.[57]

We see technology as being on a continuum of interactivity, and each medium offers different benefits and disadvantages to children at different stages. On one end, a television program with little or no educational value provides a passive viewing experience. Not all television falls into this far end of the spectrum, as many educational programs now have more interactive opportunities, such as the pause, an innovation introduced by *Blue's Clues* that asks the viewer a question and pauses for his reply.[58] On the other end of the interactivity spectrum are tablet apps that facilitate collaborative and interactive learning with other humans. The technology is moving quickly toward more interactive and responsive features, which make this technology substantially more useful to preschoolers. While unrestricted use of mobile devices isn't recommended, we do see them as more valuable to the preschool set than technologies that have come before.

Christakis says he "believe(s) that judicious use of interactive media is acceptable for children younger than the age of two years."[59] There has been very little research done on this demographic regarding the use of mobile devices, but given the number of waking hours and the fact that play on an interactive mobile device will displace other productive learning experiences, Christakis advises a half hour to one hour as a good range for children under two years. [60] While there is a lot that seems uncharted and new about the educational mobile learning world, there is much that remains the same. Parental involvement and discretion is a key determinant in how effective the technology is.

Christine Zanchi, executive producer of Children's Media at the WGBH Educational Foundation, notes that "screen time isn't passive time, it can be a moment of active engagement," both individually and socially.[61] For example, they noticed a wave when groups of kids had their own iPads and freedom to choose from certain apps. "One child would open *Sara Skates* (an app developed by NGPM), and the child next to her would notice and do the same. Pretty soon all of the children at the table were playing the same game (until, of course, someone decided to switch games and the whole thing started over again)."[62] Completing a level in the app, making a character smile, or solving a problem will often result in the child showing his neighbor or teacher what he's done. And, what's more, apps can even promote more than one player and instill social skills through play.[63] This level of engagement and enjoyment in an educational activity holds tremendous value, in our view, and should not be discouraged categorically.

Privacy

As we discuss in Chapter 15, privacy is an area within the app world that is very intimidating and confusing for many users (and in this case, their gatekeepers). With older users, teaching digital citizenship is a primary defense against the inadvertent sharing of information or wandering outside of the approved areas of use within the app, but for users who can't read yet, developers need to be even more meticulous with the way the app is constructed and the gates put in place.

The "parental gate" is a common way to prevent a young user from straying within the app (often to an area of the app where purchases can be made, sensitive data accessed, or information shared through social networks). A parental gate requires an adult to input a code or perform a sophisticated task (e.g. a math problem or reading) to confirm user age.[64]

Developers of preschool apps should also think twice about what user data is collected, how it is used and be very rigorous on how it is stored and when it is destroyed. Only collect data that is necessary; for instance, don't collect video or location for this demographic due to their high sensitivity to privacy issues. Many free or lite versions of apps will come with advertisements, which pose an additional privacy concern for young users. Preschoolers are naturally less dexterous (and therefore prone to accidentally touch areas on the screen), and drawn to flashing or moving areas within the screen. Launching an advertisement often takes the user out of the app and out of the preschool learning space, so this is an important consideration for preschool apps. Developers should be aware that advertisements are notoriously ineffective for this demographic, as users cannot read and make purchases independently; it also ruins the user experience.

Further, apps for preschoolers should be clear and up-front with the disclosures about what information is being collected and how it is being used. Preschool apps are compelled to comply with the existing legislation (The Family Educational Rights and Privacy Act (FERPA) and Children's Online Privacy Protection Act (COPPA)), but there are additional lengths developers can go to in order to communicate privacy affordances to adults and ensure the online safety of the youngest users. Parents of this age group are particularly concerned about privacy issues, so we recommend that developers make every effort to clearly communicate their privacy policies and provide a safe area for young users to learn.

CONCLUSION

While there is a tremendous opportunity to provide an academic advantage to preschoolers using mobile devices and apps that develop key skills, it is important that parents and caregivers understand the power of the device. James Paul Gee says, "the point is not to keep digital and social media away from kids early, but to build on experiences with these media to create a pathway toward higher-order and complex thinking skills, talk, and texts, just as we want to do with books."[65]

For adults, mobile technologies play an increasing role in our daily lives, a fact that preschoolers won't fail to notice. It's incumbent on parents to determine the value of these technologies for their children. Passback or hold back? Should we treat mobile apps as junk food or nutritious vegetables? Some apps are clearly one or the other, and some apps seem to be a bit of both. Parents should be encouraged to share well-designed, age-appropriate apps with their preschoolers. Developers should strive to provide parents with the information necessary to make an informed choice to separate the good from the bad. By adhering to the principles of good app design and taking into consideration the unique psychological capabilities of very small children, developers can make their app a more acceptable choice.

NOTES

1. "Back to School: Apps for Primary School Children and Younger," *Adjust*, August 2014, www.adjust.com/assets/downloads/back-to-school-app-report-2014 -adjust.pdf.
2. Cynthia Chiong and Carly Shuler, "Learning: Is There an App for That? Investigations of Young Children's Usage and Learning With Mobile Devices," The Joan Ganz Cooney Center at Sesame Workshop, 2010, New York, http://pbskids.org/ read/files/cooney_learning_apps.pdf.
3. M. Senechal and J. LeFevre, "The Influence of Home-Based Reading Interactions on 5-Year-Olds' Reading Motivations and Early Literacy Development," *Early Childhood Research Quarterly* 17 (2002): 318–337.
4. National Center for Education Statistics, "2013 National Assessment of Educational Progress in Reading," United States Department of Education, May 1, 2014, http://nces.ed.gov/nationsreportcard/reading/.
5. A. G. Bus, , M. H. van IJzendoorn, and A. D. Pellegrini, "Joint Book Reading Makes for Success in Learning to Read: A Meta-Analysis on Intergenerational Transmission of Literacy," *Review of Educational Research* 65, no. 1 (1995): 1–21.
6. L. M. Justice and C. Lankford, "Preschool Children's Visual Attention to Print During Storybook Reading," *Communication Disorders Quarterly* 24, no. 1 (2002): 11–21.
7. Bus, van IJzendoorn, and Pellegrini, "Joint Book Reading."
8. B. A. Wasik and M. A. Bond, "Beyond the Pages of a Book: Interactive Book Reading and Language Development in Preschool Classrooms," *Journal of Educational Psychology*, 93, no. 2 (2001): 243–250.

9. Katya P. Feder and Annette Majnemer, "Handwriting Development, Competency and Intervention," *Developmental Medicine & Child Neurology* 49, no. 4, http://onlinelibrary.wiley.com/doi/10.1111/j.1469-8749.2007.00312.x/pdf.

10. M. D. Levine, F. Oberklaid, and L. Meltzer, "Developmental Output Failure: A Study of Low Productivity in School-Aged Children," *Pediatrics* 67 (1981): 18–25.

11. Katya P. Feder and Annette Majnemer, "Handwriting Development, Competency and Intervention," *Developmental Medicine & Child Neurology* 49, no. 4 (2007), http://onlinelibrary.wiley.com/doi/10.1111/j.1469-8749.2007.00312.x/pdf.

12. Teacher Renee, "Helping Children Develop Fine Motor Skills," *HubPages*, www.squidoo.com/helping-children-develop-strong-fine-motor-skills.

13. "Little Writer—The Tracing App for Kids," Innovative Mobile Apps, https://itunes.apple.com/us/app/little-writer-tracing-app/id515890480?mt=8.

14. "PBS Kids Ready to Learn, Ready to Learn Math Framework," http://pbskids.org/readytolearn/media/math_framework_final.pdf.

15. Betsy McCarthy, Linlin Li, and Michelle Tiu, "PBS KIDS Mathematics Transmedia Suites in Preschool Homes: A Report to the CPB-PBS Ready to Learn Initiative," *WestEd*, September 2012, www.wested.org/resources/pbs-kids-mathematics-transmedia-suites-in-preschool-homes-a-report-to-the-cpb-pbs-ready-to-learn-initiative/.

16. Nora S. Newcombe, "Picture This: Increasing Math and Science Learning by Improving Spatial Thinking," *American Educator* (Summer 2010): 29–35.

17. Ibid.

18. Doug Boari, Mike Fraser, Danae Stanton Fraser, and Kirsten Cater, "Augmenting Spatial Skills with Mobile Devices," *Proceedings of the SIGCHI Conference on Human Factors in Computing Systems* (New York: ACM, 2012): 1611–1620.

19. Melissa S. Terlecki, Nora S. Newcombe, and Michelle Little, "Durable and Generalized Effects of Spatial Experience on Mental Rotation: Gender Differences in Growth Patterns," *Applied Cognitive Psychology* 22, no. 7 (2008): 996–1013.

20. Boari and others, "Augmenting Spatial Skills."

21. "Next Generation Preschool Math Project," http://nextgenmath.org/.

22. Hanna Rosen, "The Touchscreen Generation," *The Atlantic*, April 2013, www.theatlantic.com/magazine/archive/2013/04/the-touch-screen-generation/309250/?single_page=true.

23. Partnership for 21st Century Skills, "P21 Framework Definitions," 2009, www.p21.org/storage/documents/P21_Framework_Definitions.pdf.

24. Sir Ken Robinson, *The Element: How Finding Your Passion Changes Everything* (New York: Penguin, 2013).

25. Partnership for 21st Century Skills, "P21 Framework Definitions."

26. Ibid.

27. R. A. Chávez-Eakle, "Creativity and Personality," in *Measuring Creativity*, ed. E. Villalba (Luxembourg: Publications Office of the European Union, 2009).

28. K. Hirsh-Pasek and R. M. Golinkoff, *Einstein Never Used Flash Cards: How Our Children Really Learn and Why They Need to Play More and Memorize Less* (Emmaus, PA: Rodale Press, 2003).

29. Christine Zanchi, "Producers and Researchers: Making Technology PreK Ready," SXSWEdu Session, March 6, 2013, https://soundcloud.com/sxswedu/producers-and-researchers.

30. Dale H. Schunk, Paul R. Pintrich, and Judith R Meece, *Motivation in Education: Theory, Research, and Applications,* 3rd ed. (New York: Pearson, 2013).

31. T. Malone, "Toward a Theory of Intrinsically Motivating Instruction," *Cognitive Science* 5, no. 4 (1981): 333–369.

32. R. Ryan and E. Deci, "Intrinsic and Extrinsic Motivations: Classic Definitions and New Directions," *Contemporary Educational Psychology* 25 (2000): 54–67.

33. A. Bandura, *Self-Efficacy: The Exercise of Control* (New York: Freeman, 1997).

34. T. W. Malone and M. R. Lepper, "Making Learning Fun: A Taxonomy of Intrinsic Motivations for Learning," in *Aptitude, Learning and Instruction III: Conative and Affective Process Analyses,* eds. R. E. Snow and M. J. Farr (Hillsdale, NJ: Erlbaum, 1987), 223–253.

35. Mesozoic Math Adventures, *Dinosaur Train Math,* https://play.google.com/store/apps/details?id=air.org.pbskids.dtmesozoicmath&hl=en.

36. Sesame Workshop, "Best Practices: Designing Touch Tablet Experiences for Preschoolers," December 26, 2012, www.sesameworkshop.org/assets/1191/src/Best%20Practices%20Document%2011-26-12.pdf.

37. Chiong and Shuler, "Learning: Is There An App For That?"

38. Ibid.

39. R. E. Mayer, *Multimedia Learning,* 2nd ed. (New York: Cambridge University Press, 2009).

40. M. Rose, G. M. Rose, and J. G. Blodgett, "The Effects of Interface Design and Age on Children's Information Processing of Web Sites," *Psychology and Marketing* 26, no. 1 (2009).

41. J. D. Ormrod, *Educational Psychology* (New York: Pearson, 2010).

42. Sesame Workshop, "Best Practices."

43. Ibid.

44. Ibid.

45. Chiong and Shuler, "Learning: Is There an App for That?"

46. Ibid.

47. Ibid.

48. McCarthy, Li, and Tiu, "PBS KIDS Mathematics."

49. S.M. Fisch, *Children's Learning from Educational Television: Sesame Street and Beyond* (Mahwah, NJ: Lawrence Erlbaum Associates, 2004).

50. Sesame Workshop, "Best Practices."

51. James Paul Gee, *The Anti-Education Era: Creating Smarter Students through Digital Learning* (New York: Palgrave McMillan, 2013).

52. Chiong and Shuler, "Learning: Is There an App for That?"

53. Ibid.

54. Next Generation Preschool Math, "About," http://nextgenmath.org/about/.

55. Next Generation Preschool Math, *Play Patterns and Game Mechanics* (video), http://nextgenmath.org/videos/.

56. Dimitri A Christakis, "Interactive Media Use at Younger Than the Age of 2 Years: Time to Rethink the American Academy of Pediatrics Guideline?," May 2014, http://archpedi.jamanetwork.com/article.aspx?articleid=1840251&resultClick=3.

57. Ibid.

58. Rosen, "The Touchscreen Generation."

59. Christakis, "Interactive Media Use."
60. Ibid.
61. Zanchi, "Producers and Researchers."
62. *Next Generation Preschool Math* blog, February 21, 2013, http://nextgenmath.org/.
63. Zanchi, "Producers and Researchers."
64. Apple: Developer, "Parental Gates," https://developer.apple.com/app-store/parental-gates/.
65. Gee, *The Anti-Education Era*, 201.

CHAPTER 14

Making Accessible Apps: Autism and Visual Impairment

INTRODUCTION

When it comes to mobile devices in education, they present a distinct opportunity to reach all students. Where certain populations might have been marginalized by past technologies or traditional classroom structures, mobile technology offers a new way to personalize and make learning accessible for those with special needs. In this chapter, we'll discuss the functions that set Apple's iOS apart as the market leader for accessibility and how this impacts two specific populations: those on the autism spectrum and students with visual impairments. We also present things to consider when making an app to ensure it is accessible to all users.

ADVANTAGES OF THE IPAD FOR SPECIAL POPULATIONS

Students with autism or with low or no vision face many challenges in traditional education settings, as do others with special behavioral and physical needs. Autism typically is diagnosed by the prevalence of three key symptoms: difficulty with social interactions, verbal and nonverbal communication, and self-regulation.[1] To participate in lecture-style classroom education, proficiency in these areas is key, so students with autism quickly fall behind or, often, require a separate classroom for learning. Students with visual impairments are most often mainstreamed, placed into typical classroom settings, but, depending on the severity of their visual impairment these students have different tools with which to learn. Audio, braille, and magnification are just a few ways to adapt existing classroom structures to be accessible to the visually impaired. For both students with autism and visual impairment, there are expensive and dominant accessibility and assistive communication devices.

After it hit the market in 2010, the iPad became very popular with special populations. Ed Summers, an assistive technology guru, says, "We love the iPad because it is a mainstream device with built in accessibility at no extra cost."[2] The iPad brought a few key advantages to students with visual impairments and students on the autism spectrum, and most other special populations, changing the face of assistive technology as show in Figure 14.1: affordability, a mainstream device, built-in accessibility features, and easy to use, effective design.[3,4]

Affordability

While iPads are not low cost, they do represent a large step toward affordability for special populations when compared to previous augmentative-communication devices. Prior to the iPad's release, the most popular and successful augmentative-communication devices to aid nonverbal individuals ran about $8,000. Certainly an iPad (even combining the cost of the device with a $219 app to give the needed functionality—*Proloquo2Go*, discussed below) offers a vast cost benefit, as well as improved functionality.[5] For instance, the flicker of screens in older computers, a factor that individuals with autism are hypersensitive to, is not an issue with the iPad. Likewise for the visually impaired, the iPad and its native functionality offers a substantially cheaper alternative to previous devices. Before the iPad, JAWS was the most prominent screen reader, and it cost around $1000 and provided a more difficult user experience. Even with a

Figure 14.1 Advantages of the iPad for Special Populations

Bluetooth braille-display attachment, the iPad offers a substantially more affordable option to previous accessibility tools.

Mainstream

The iPad also offers high levels of portability and prominence in social situations. Students in special-needs populations often find themselves distanced from their peers socially, if not in a different classroom altogether. The iPad offers an assistive technological device that is not different than their peers' mobile devices, which is important for reducing social alienation and promoting equity. Instead of carrying around a clunky, expensive augmentative alternative communication device, using something that doesn't set them apart as different.[6] "The small size and portability of the iOS devices allows [students with autism and visual impairments] to easily integrate into regular education environment without making anyone stand out or look different," according to Erica Roberts, a speech language pathologist specializing in assistive technology.[7]

Accessibility

Apple's iOS is the most accessible in the mobile market, making the iPad, iPhone, and iPod Touch the most accessible devices. The operating system's architecture and app-approval process automatically gives a developer about 80 percent accessibility, though there are still important design and coding exercises developers should be aware of to make their app fully accessible. There is a strict approval process for an app to be authorized for the App Store, which might require developers to make a few changes to fully comply with the accessibility guidelines. What this means is that *each app* in the Apple App Store has some level of accessibility, not just apps developed for a special-needs population. Android, the other prominent operating system for mobile devices, also provides guidance on developing accessible apps.[8] However, the accessibility checklist and measures for developers are optional. While, on an Apple device, a user with special needs can play virtually any app whether or not it's specifically designed for their access, Android's operating system is not innately as accessible. For this reason, apps on the iPad and iPhone are hugely popular among populations with special needs, and thus the primary focus of this chapter.

Individuals with motor skill challenges can utilize the Multi-Touch functionality, for more distinct controls, as well as Siri to access the features of the device. Guided Access can aid in educational use in general and for those with special needs in particular. This feature can help to minimize visual stimulation and retain attention on the task at hand by limiting user access to other apps (including disabling the home button).[9] Being able to zoom easily and change the contrast of text screens makes it more accessible to those with visual impairments. Apple provides this functionality as part of their iOS, meaning that most apps on the device will accommodate these features easily, if coded correctly. We discuss how to accommodate these features at the end of this chapter.

Usable and Effective

Mobile also presents myriad ways for the individual to socialize and communicate with peers using the device in a variety of social situations.[10] In the past, clunky and heavy devices (like the DynaVox for nonverbal individuals) required motivation and technological savvy to navigate difficult systems. The iPad offers a huge variety of apps to support educational and communication needs for students with special needs, as well as the device's ability to quickly connect to the Internet, take pictures, and use email gives iPads unprecedented utility. It is also innately easy to use, a huge benefit compared to difficult-to-use devices of the past. The usability and effectiveness of the devices is a huge advantage for special populations.

AUTISM AND AUTISM SPECTRUM DISORDERS (ASD)

Autism is often referred to as autism spectrum disorder (ASD), meaning that each individual will present certain symptoms to a varying degree. Individuals with ASD range from completely unable to communicate verbally (an estimated 25 percent) to high functioning and able to be placed in traditional classroom settings with or without learning intervention program support.[11] Symptoms present themselves at a young age, and most ASDs are diagnosed before the child enters school, or when "social demands exceed capacity."[12] ASDs are diagnosed by the presence and severity of three main symptoms: social reciprocity, communicative intent, and regulation of self, behaviors, and interests.[13,14] It is assumed that cognitive processing of individuals with an ASD is unaffected by their disease; it's primarily a disorder affecting behavior and communication abilities. The U.S. Centers for Disease Control and Prevention (CDC) reports that 1 in 88 American children register on the autism spectrum, over 2 million individuals.[15]

While communication and social interactions can be very difficult for individuals with ASD, many on the spectrum show propensity toward visual skills, music, math, and art.[16] Furthermore, it is believed that, with therapy, everyone on the spectrum, even individuals who are unable to verbally communicate, can be taught to communicate using other means (signing, technology, etc.).[17] Breaking through barriers to give these individuals the opportunity to communicate and investigate their interests helps teachers and caregivers better address their academic and social needs, which in turn enables people with ASD to live more normal and socialized lives.[18] The tablet, and the iPad specifically, are proving invaluable in reaching individuals with autism.

Mobile devices are being used in separate special education settings, in homes (administered by parents or caregivers), and to facilitate children with ASD to remain in mainstream classrooms. As the presence of mobile devices in classrooms continues to grow, use of these devices as an aid to mainstreaming students with ASD is a major benefit. In the following discussion, we address some of the very specific challenges faced by learners with autism and how the iPad and iOS devices help them to overcome those challenges.

Key Skills to Develop through App Usage

Computers generally, and mobile devices specifically, offer many benefits in teaching individuals with autism the skills they need to thrive academically and socially. Technology presents a predictable, controlled experience, something that day-to-day social interactions do not.[19] For teaching basic skills, this feature can be a huge benefit.[20] It is also a medium that presents perfectability, a big draw for individuals with autism who show propensity toward repetitive behaviors.[21] Studies have consistently shown that individuals with autism are more enthusiastic about learning using computers and technology and showed greater growth in the intended areas when these media were used.[22] Using iPads as a classroom tool for children with autism, as one teacher reports, improved "the children's willingness to socialize, and it enhanced their attention spans."[23] It also gives teachers a tool to better understand how to reach the student, since they're not always able to communicate their interests or abilities in productive ways.[24]

When considering which apps to use for individuals with autism, or which skills to focus on in development, keep in mind that each user on the spectrum has various needs and abilities.[25] Another benefit of today's technology is the ability to customize the experience to the users' abilities, or find apps with very targeted user skills.

Social Interactions

Individuals with ASD show varying levels of ability to read social situations and interpret what others are thinking.[26] Social reciprocity is a prime factor in the diagnosis of ASD, and one that can be problematic in day-to-day interactions for individuals with autism. Many with autism are unable to read subtle social cues, such as a smile, wave, grimace, and other facial cues that indicate meaning in conversation. Without these nonverbal methods of communicating, social interactions become difficult and bewildering.[27] Making eye contact in social situations, as well as emotion recognition and nonverbal social cues, are key social skills to be developed through apps.

For instance, the app *Look in My Eyes* was developed specifically for individuals with autism who struggle with this part of social interaction. This app employs a token economy and rewards users for looking into the eyes of the faces on the screen. Different settings, such as a restaurant, train station, or dinosaur landscape offer the ability to customize it to the user's unique and specialized interests.[28] Another app, *Training Faces*, poses social situations where users are asked to recognize and name the emotions displayed by the characters on screen (e.g., happy, sad, excited).[29]

Beyond the basics of social situations, diving deeper into social thinking is important to help individuals with autism adjust to everyday social interactions. Social thinking is our understanding of our emotions, the emotions of those we're interacting with, as well as the understanding that actions affect emotions of others.[30] Roberts notes that it's essential to understand why paying attention to someone's emotional state is important. For instance, Roberts suggests this example: "Mom looks mad right now, I probably shouldn't ask her to buy me that new video game right now."[31] Getting past the concrete social skills of looking at faces and eyes and into the deeper meanings is something that mobile apps also enable. *Social Skill Builder* is an app that shows the user videos of good and bad social interactions (e.g., children bullying another student, children taking turns and sharing) and asks the user to determine what happened that was good or bad. It further asks the user to determine how they know these things ("How do you know the girl was sad?").[32] Video modeling is a strategy some use, including Roberts, to teach "expected and unexpected social behaviors in our everyday environments."[33] Roberts notes that mobile devices enable ease of recording short videos of students. Then, in near-real time, the student and teacher can "go back and analyze how the student did in that social interaction. The student can see what he or she was doing, determine what type of impression he or she was making, and then make adjustments to behavior if needed the next time that type of social situation occurs to make a positive impression," Roberts says.[34]

What Apps Can Do to Develop Social Interaction Skills

Apps aiming to help individuals with ASD learn social skills should:

- Teach emotion recognition, as well as encourage a deeper understanding of why understanding others' emotions is an important exercise.
- Cultivate skills within the user on how to read and respond to others' emotions.
- Encourage socially customary behavior and interpretation of social cues.

Verbal and Nonverbal Communication

Limited or no verbal communication is another defining trait of the autism spectrum. With a quarter of those on the spectrum being completely unable to communicate verbally, there is high demand for ways to unlock these individuals.[35] While ASD shows a range of abilities, the most severe cases leave individuals without the ability to communicate.[36] Parents and caregivers note that these individuals can understand more than it might seem, and they are isolated by the fact that they are unable to take part in conversation with their peers, teachers, parents, and others.

Giving individuals with ASD the ability to converse and communicate what is inside them is an invaluable opportunity, and one that mobile devices are especially qualified to do. Almost all with a verbal communication impairment can learn to use spoken language, and all can learn to communicate through therapy; however, the strides seen through use of certain apps and mobile technology are broadly unprecedented.[37]

When selecting an app for communication, it is important to think about the student's unique language needs and abilities. "Many communication apps are complex and the language is organized in layers that require the student to navigate between many pages," says Roberts. Certainly a complex communication app would work for some students and not others, based on their cognitive abilities. "While I do not believe that there are cognitive prerequisites a student 'must have' in order to use AAC [augmentative and alternative communication]—every child has a right to communicate," says Roberts, "I do believe the language and cognitive skills of the child need to be carefully considered when selecting an app and that the features of the app be matched to the skills and needs of the child."[38] Identifying the right app for the student's needs and abilities is vital.

Apps like *Proloquo2Go* provide a voice for individuals who are unable to verbally communicate (a disability that goes beyond the autism spectrum, including ALS, Down syndrome, traumatic brain injury, and many other developmental or cognitive impairments affecting speech).[39] *Proloquo2Go* allows the user to construct sentences using many word badges to do simple tasks such as order dinner at a restaurant, or to communicate their needs with caregivers.[40]

Carrie Grunkemeyer, a speech language pathologist, works with students on the autism spectrum. In her first year of teaching, she struggled to reach a first grade boy, Johnny,[41] who had "literally never said a word." She worked for months to "get him to communicate with me, and finally by around February, I realized he loved computers and he loved to type and write." This breakthrough coincided with the district's iPad initiative for assistive devices, which allowed for the real breakthrough in Johnny's communication. "When Johnny was given his iPad and we started to work on *Proloquo2Go*, it was like a whole world opened up. He knew so many words. He could spell anything. He even asked for Skittles! I saw him smile for the first time! He is now able to write whole sentences and answer comprehension questions on his device." For Grunkemeyer, and Johnny, the device and the *Proloquo2Go* app made all the difference in enabling not only education, but simple communication, to take place.[42]

What Apps Can Do to Develop Communication Skills

- Provide an easy-to-use interface that allows users to quickly access what is used most frequently. This is critical for taking part in regular conversation.
- Provide a natural-sounding voice for natural use in conversation.
- Provide an intuitive interface to enable quick navigation, differentiated depending on the educational level of the user.

Self-Regulation

Self-regulation, the third category of characteristics denoting the autism spectrum, means "people's ability to adjust their level of alertness and how they display their emotions through their behavior to attain goals in socially adaptive ways."[43] A person with strong self-regulation is able to balance their sensory needs, emotions, and impulses in a socially appropriate way for their environment. Successful self-regulation incorporates "sensory processing, executive functioning and emotional regulation."[44]

According to *Zones of Regulation*, a popular curriculum among therapists treating students with these difficulties, self-regulation is a broad category, encompassing many behaviors of children on the autism spectrum (as well as other mental health disorders, such as attention deficit hyperactive disorder and Tourette syndrome, for example).[45] Sensory challenges are described by Greer Aukstakalnis, an occupational therapist, as "over- and under-responding to both environmental and internal sensations, as well as difficulty adjusting their responses to these sensations."[46] Executive functioning, another branch of self-regulation, denotes behaviors like planning and organizing, impulse control, internalization of speech and multitasking.[47] Emotional regulation difficulties could mean the child is unable to have proper perspective on the size a problem at hand and trouble understanding others' perspectives.[48]

Mobile technologies present an opportunity for individuals struggling with self-regulation. Features like Guided Access in iOS allow teachers, caregivers, or therapists to restrict the learner to only one app, disable the home button, and even disable certain areas of the screen.[49] This can be very useful for learners who engage in unproductive, repetitive behaviors or struggles relating to impulse control or focus. The iPad, and other mobile devices, offer a streamlined process for video modeling. As we described in this chapter, some therapists use the iPad for social interaction, though it can also be used to provide visual guidance for individuals with difficulty regulating their reactions to change. Aukstakalnis uses this method. "I had a preschooler who exhibited extreme behaviors when moving to structured activity." This student had difficulty with a verbal demand, such as 'pick up your crayon.' [The difficulty] completely resolved when I was able to quickly video model the expected behaviors for transitioning and show a proper crayon grasp using the iPad," Aukstakalnis said.[50]

For students with emotional regulation challenges, the *Relax Lite* app offers a guided deep-breathing exercise, an ideal exercise to help calm an emotionally volatile child who may be suffering from a disruptive episode.[51] Another useful app for emotional regulation and planning is *Breathe, Think, Do with Sesame*, by Sesame Street. The user gets to "help a Sesame Street monster friend calm down and solve everyday challenges."[52] Aukstakalnis likes this app because it helps with "learning deep breathing, developing strategies to deal with basic problems and recognition of emotions."[53]

What Apps Can Do to Work With Self-Regulation

- Limit animation and opportunities for overstimulation, or include functionality to easily turn off animation and sound.
- Foster skills for relaxation, emotion recognition, and problem solving.
- Offer a simple storyline or simple commands.

VISUAL IMPAIRMENT

The term "visual impairment" covers a broad range of medical conditions. In developing accessible apps and programs, students are generally separated into two categories for usability purposes: low vision and functionally blind. Low vision constitutes the majority of the visually impaired, including low visual acuity, loss of visual field or low peripheral vision, photophobia (inability to look at light), diplopia (double vision), visual distortion, perception difficulties, or color blindness.[54] Students with severe visual impairments have different needs. The difference between those with low vision and severe visual impairments often lies in how they are able to consume content. While persons with low vision will be able to make adjustments to devices to read (by enhancing contrast or text size, for instance), persons with severe visual impairment will use braille or audio to adapt.

Today, the vast majority of visually impaired students are educated in mainstream classrooms.[55] A major factor in their success in the mainstream classroom is mobile devices, specifically touch-screen tablets. The iPad provides an accessibility device that's also a popular, mainstream device, which is a huge factor in the mind of Ed Summers, a software manager for Accessibility and Applied Assistive Technology, who is severely visually impaired himself. The features that enable the child to learn in a classroom of their peers, being "built into a mainstream device, just like everyone else has, is huge. Not some big clunky device off to the side that says 'I'm different.' These kids with visual impairments, before the iPad, they had these big, expensive things on carts, sitting beside them in class, and the kids just felt like major dorks," Summers says, with a smile. Again, the iPad offers the assistive functionality for special populations without the distinctive and alienating devices that might make a student with special needs feel … different.

All the Tools in the Toolbox

The iPad and iOS provide an array of native functionality that give students with low or no vision the ability to participate in education much more easily. With all the touch screen functionality and audio cues, is it necessary to even learn braille? Since most users with visual impairment still have some vision, it's helpful to think of their ability to access and consume content as a toolbox. A student with a severe visual impairment might use braille at certain times, listen to an audio book with a screen reader, or use visual contrast and zoom settings to make better use of his or her own visual capabilities.[56] Mobile technology gives the visually impaired learner easier access to these tools. "I believe in using all the tools in the toolbox," says Summers. While current technologies provide ample options for the visually impaired, Summers suggests relying only on one won't be enough for the student to keep up with his peers intellectually. For instance, braille is essential for learning math and reading poetry, Summers says.

However, braille has its limitations, and in certain cases other methods of reading and communicating are more effective. "I could not imagine reading *Moby Dick* with my fingers, because they'd get tired and fall off," Summers says with a smile. Summers also notes a braille calculus book he has in two large boxes in his office, corresponding to a 12th-grade textbook. It is 36 volumes, "so you can't really just put it in your backpack," he says. However, punched volumes of books aren't the only manifestation of braille currently; refreshable braille displays that use Bluetooth technology to communicate with tablets are a practical way for the visually impaired to use their devices with or without a screen reader.[57]

It comes down to numbers, ultimately. Average reading speeds for students with normal vision in high school are around 250 to 350 words per minute (wpm). Braille gives the reader 115 to 150 wpm, on average. Large print provides 7 to 75 wpm, and audio (using compressed speech) allows for 350 to 550 wpm. With increases in comprehension as the student learns to read, the student can increase his or her listening speed.[58]

"You've heard the adage: before third grade you're learning to read and after that you're reading to learn. For kids with severe visual impairments, reading with your fingers is (equivalent to) learning to read," Summers says.[59] After these literacy skills are established early, using ears and eyes to fill in the gaps is more efficiently done. Summers says, "I can hear 600 words per minute, but I know how to read. I'm a huge proponent of learning to read with your fingers and then augmenting that with ears and eyes."[60]

So, for students with visual impairments, learning the accessibility affordances of mobile devices is essential to their education in a mainstream environment. In Summers's example, the mobile device *is* the toolbox, containing nearly all the tools a student needs to adapt the technology to meet his or her needs, as shown in Figure 14.2. It

Figure 14.2 All the Tools in the Toolbox for the Visually Impaired

can be used to read and write braille (with a refreshable braille-reader attachment), used to input information using dictation and speech to text functionality, used to read with the ears (using audio books and screen readers), and can be customized to allow the student's remaining vision to be optimized (using changed contrast, zoom, and large print.)

Key Accessibility Features for the Visually Impaired

Students with low vision and students with severe visual impairments will not necessarily benefit from the same apps. Apps and functionality for students with low vision allow for enhancements to visual cues, supported by some nonvisual functionality. Apps for blind students focus on auditory and sensory adaptations. The two groups aren't without overlap; certain functionalities may work for both populations.

"I feel strongly that people with disabilities don't want separate materials," Summers said. "We want to be able to access the same materials as everybody else, but in a way that adapts to individual needs."[61] Summers, working with a NASA scientist and curriculum specialist, recently helped develop a fully accessible ebook called *Reach for the Stars*. It is a 90-page book that explores the Tarantula Nebula using

Hubble Space Telescope images. It is an excellent example of a way to present material for all audiences.

Users with Low Vision

Built-in features like Voiceover, Siri, Speak Selection, and Dictation allow users with limited or no vision to use the phone and access most of the key features.[62] Making text bigger or changing the contrast of the screen is also simple, and a good way to use limited vision to navigate. In the same vein, the ability to zoom and magnify anything on the screen is a huge plus. All of these features come built in on Apple iOS devices.

Many of iOS's native apps are popular for low vision users: *Safari*, *Mail*, *iBooks*, and *Pages* all receive high marks for usability. *Read2Go* offers books in the huge Bookshare library (containing books for all reading abilities, and most books a student would read in high school).[63] *Join.Me*, a free screen-sharing app used in many classrooms, is great for accessibility as well, allowing the student to pull up the screen the teacher is showing, changing contrast and size easily.[64]

Diane Brauner, an orientation mobility specialist who trains teachers and students on how to use mobile devices for students with low vision or severe visual impairment, offers Maya as an example .[65] Maya was a high school student with low vision who was reading by using the zoom function. However, she had to enlarge it to the point where she had to scroll back and forth frequently, and the motion of the screen caused her to feel ill and have severe migraines. She was a smart student with college aspirations, but was falling behind in class and unable to keep up with her assignments. Because of all of these negative effects from academic reading, had never read a book for fun. "I put her on the iPad and encouraged her to use VoiceOver. She resisted initially, because she's not an auditory learner and was trying to use her eyes still." Brauner showed Maya how to use the VoiceOver function with a book. Maya asked to use the device over the weekend and excitedly came back Monday, having finished the book. "It was the first time she'd ever read a book for pleasure. That is life changing." Now Maya is able to get her textbooks on the iPad, keep up with assignments better, and complete reading tasks. "We see this over and over with children with low vision," Brauner says. "It's very typical for students with low vision to get migraines from eye fatigue," she notes.[66]

There are a few apps that aid those with low vision in navigating the world around them. The *LookTel Money Reader* enables users with low vision to scan currency and the app will read the denomination out loud.[67] *TapTapSee* provides an explanation of what is pictured. These sorts of apps provide the opportunity to do things independently, with the help of the touch device.

What Apps Can Do for Users with Low Vision

- Support key iOS accessibility features: ability to change contrast, pinch to zoom, adjust font size and style.
- Provide an uncluttered, simple user interface.
- Avoid using color alone to communicate something.
- Promote or allow independence for the user.

Users with Severe Visual Impairment

iOS provides many options for users to consume content using touch and audio. Users with severe visual impairment will almost always require a screen reader or braille display to interact with their device. VoiceOver is a built-in screen reader that, with a simple tap, enables the user to hear the contents of the screen.[68] This facilitates use of websites, email, and most native iOS apps.

This functionality can be paired with refreshable braille displays. If a blind student knows braille, this provides another tool for them to use these devices and for independence. Refreshable braille displays use Bluetooth technology to synch with a device. Highlighted text, such as a line on a website, is produced in braille on the touch pad. As the user navigates through the text on the page, the display changes to produce different text. It also has buttons to allow clicking, as well as the ability to type in Braille. These devices vary in size, with some the size of an iPhone and others the size of a typical computer keyboard.[69]

Another way to communicate media to learners with severe visual impairment is through *sonification*. The *Reach for the Stars* ebook is able to communicate the brightness and placement of stars using sound to a blind user via sonification. Using headphones, the user is able to hear the stars, which are represented using changes in pitch and changes in location of sound. To get a sense of the brightness of a star, the pitch varies when touched. "The brighter the star, the higher the pitch. The temperature of a star will be conveyed through either the left or right ear … Readers will hear about a cooler star through their left ear and hotter stars through their right ear."[70] Sonification is one innovative way to communicate a visually rich subject matter to those without sight, one that relies on mobile devices and their functionality.

 What Apps Can Do for Users with Severe Visual Impairment

- Code and test using VoiceOver to ensure content is taking full advantage of the benefits of Voiceover
- Provide clear and easy to navigate audio cues.
- Enforce consistency of button placement on screens within the app.

DEVELOPING ACCESSIBLE APPS

While iOS gives many affordances for those with special needs, achieving a high level of accessibility requires developers to pay attention to certain design principles and code to accessibility guidelines. We think there are simple ways developers can make their apps more accessible and more widely used. Indeed, if you are making an app for any broad use that you hope to be included in a curriculum or used by a very large audience, considering accessibility should be a priority. To make an app fully accessible, as shown in Figure 14.3, the developer must ensure that the code and auditory and visual cues are optimized for all learners. The following are some basic guidelines to consider in developing accessible apps.

Test It with All Populations

If you're developing an educational app and your goal is to enable that technology to be included in a standard curriculum or widely used, you must test the app with multiple populations of different

Figure 14.3 Developing Accessible Apps

kinds of leaners. It is vital that you think about all potential users and whether or not they'll be able to access your app. Brauner notes that with the growing use of online state and benchmark testing, there are many that are simply inaccessible to visually impaired students.[71] "The most frequent problems I have seen are that the buttons and images are not labeled properly, and words that are highlighted, underlined, or italicized are not coded to reflect these formats when read using a screen reader," Brauner says. For instance, If a question asks "define the underlined word," a learner using VoiceOver will not know how to answer the question if there's no indication when read aloud which word is underlined.[72] When developing an app, consider users with exceptional needs and, if possible, solicit feedback in the early stages from these learners and their teachers.

A best practice in testing your app for accessibility would be to test it not only using the native iOS features (like VoiceOver), but also testing it using popular accessibility devices, such as a refreshable Braille display. Consulting with experts on accessibility or users from special populations is also advised.

Think Auditory

For users with visual impairments, using apps with their ears is often the most efficient way, if not the only way, to use them. It is, therefore, important for developers to think about the user experience for some-one who might not be able to read the text on a button. For instance, in an app there might be a Next button to move to the next screen. If that button is not coded in a way that the button can sound spe-cific text in the button graphic (saying, for instance, "Next," "Yes/No," "Start," "Done"), a screen reader will simply say "Button," and the stu-dent using VoiceOver will be stuck.[73] When coding an app, be sure to define the role, state, value, and description for each item to get the highest level of accessibility for users with visual impairments.[74] Using auditory cues in this case is also the best practice, Brauner says.[75]

In an early iteration of the *SAS Flash Cards* app, Brauner noticed that the app was not totally accessible to her students. She met with the developers of the product and showed them the areas in the app that were not accessible to her visually impaired users. "One of the issues with *SAS Flashcards* was that the right/wrong answer was displayed visually; the next release added an auditory award sound or a wrong answer sound," says Brauner.[76]

Keep It Simple

For most special populations, and definitely for those on the autism spectrum and with visual impairments, a simple, uncluttered interface is a major factor in an app's usability. Following the design principles enumerated in Chapter 9 is a start. A lot of what makes an app sim-ple and easy to maneuver for the widest demographics—from children through adults and every unique learner in between—means making the interface as simple as possible. Big buttons, high contrast images, and minimal animation are all best practices that enhance the acces-sibility of an app.[77] Additionally, coding the app in a way that allows for users to use zoom on all text, shift to landscape mode, or change contrast provides even greater accessibility.

Navigation

For the user to navigate through the app successfully, we recommend a consistent user experience. This is especially important for users with special needs. The predictability of the Next button being at the bottom right of the screen in a book, for instance, is essential for a user with limited vision to be able to use an app through its completion. Each app doesn't need to invent its own placement for all of these things. Another navigational challenge developers should consider is that entering text takes time and is a challenge for some users; use drop down menus when possible.

For users with visual impairment, dragging is a difficult command to execute without the proper affordances. For instance, Brauner notes, a student with low vision can begin the drag but unless the app is programmed to indicate when the item has arrived where it should be dropped, the student won't be able to complete the task.[78]

CONCLUSION

Mobile learning presents new and exciting opportunities in education for educating special populations. By and large, the iPad and Apple devices present a consistent, natural user experience that opens doors that were otherwise closed to students with special needs. We discussed autism spectrum disorders and visual impairment in this chapter. However, these same technologies and design guidelines can enable developers to build apps to help many other special needs learners overcome obstacles. Learners with attention deficit hyperactivity disorder, degenerative diseases affecting dexterity or communication (like ALS), and hearing impairment are all populations with tremendous opportunity where mobile devices are concerned. We believe the ease of including affordances for these populations is an amazing, singular feature of iOS, and an important exercise in creating an app accessible to all users.

NOTES

1. Susan L. Hyman, "New DSM-5 Includes Changes to Autism Criteria," *AAP News*, June 4, 2013, http://aapnews.aappublications.org/content/early/2013/06/04/aapnews.20130604-1.

2. Ed Summers, senior manager of accessibility and applied assistive technology, SAS Institute Inc., interview with authors, January 23, 2014.

3. Carrie Grunkemeyer, speech language pathologist, Churchwell Museum Magnet Elementary School, Nashville, TN, interview with authors, September 2013.

4. Erica Roberts, speech language pathologist, Derry Township School District, interview with authors, January 9, 2014.

5. Lois Jean Brady, *Apps For Autism: A Must-Have Resource for the Special Needs Community*: (Arlington, TX: Future Horizons, 2011).

6. Ibid.

7. Roberts, interview.

8. Google, "Making Applications Accessible," http://developer.android.com/guide/topics/ui/accessibility/apps.html.

9. Apple, "Accessibility," www.apple.com/accessibility/ios/.

10. Kevin Michael Ayres, Linda Mechling, and Frank J. Sansosti, "The Use of Mobile Technologies to Assist with Life Skills/Independence of Students with Moderate/Severe Intellectual Disability and/or Autism Spectrum Disorders: Considerations for the Future of School Psychology," *Psychology in Schools* 50, no. 3 (2013).

11. CBS News, *Apps for Autism*, *60 Minutes*, October 23, 2011, www.cbsnews.com/video/watch/?id=7385686n.

12. Hyman, "New DSM-5."

13. Ibid.

14. Joseph Mintz, Corinne Branch, Caty March, and Stephen Lerman, "Key Factors Mediating the Use of a Mobile Technology Tool Designed to Develop Social and Life Skills with Autistic Spectrum Disorders," *Computers & Education* 58 (2012): 53–62.

15. "What Is Autism?," Autism Speaks, www.autismspeaks.org/what-autism.

16. Ibid.

17. CBS News, *Apps for Autism*.

18. Ibid.

19. Stuart Powell and Rita Jordan, *Autism and Learning: A Guide to Good Practice* (David Fulton Publishers: London, 1997).

20. Ayres, Mechling, and Sansosti, "The Use of Mobile Technologies."

21. Powell and Jordan, *Autism and Learning*.

22. Valerie Herskowitz, *Autism and Computers: Maximizing Independence Through Technology* (Bloomington, IN: AuthorHouse, 2009).

23. CBS News, *Apps for Autism*.

24. Ibid.

25. Brady, *Apps For Autism*.

26. "What Is Autism?"

27. Ibid.

28. *Look In My Eyes*, Fizzbrain LLC, https://itunes.apple.com/us/app/look-in-my-eyes-1 -restaurant/id349835339?mt=8&ign-mpt=uo%3D4.

29. *Training Faces*, Training with Gaming, https://itunes.apple.com/us/app/training -faces/id522989729?mt=8.

30. Michelle Garcia Winner, "What is Social Thinking?," *Social Thinking*, www.social thinking.com/what-is-social-thinking.

31. Roberts, interview.

32. Social Skill Builder, App Promo, www.youtube.com/watch?v=cHtZwCZNZKc.

33. Roberts, interview.

34. Ibid.

35. CBS News, *Apps for Autism*.

36. Ibid.

37. "What Is Autism?," Autism Speaks, www.autismspeaks.org/what-autism/symptoms.

38. Roberts, interview.

39. *Proloquo2Go*, AssistiveWare, https://itunes.apple.com/us/app/proloquo2go/id30836 8164?mt=8.

40. CBS News, *Apps for Autism*.

41. Names have been changed to protect the identity of the student.

42. Grunkemeyer, interview.

43. Leah M. Kuypers, *The Zones of Regulation: A Curriculum Designed to Foster Self-Regulation and Emotional Control* (San Jose, CA: Social Thinking Publishing, 2011).

44. Ibid.

45. Ibid.

46. Greer Aukstakalnis, occupational therapist, email correspondence, January 25, 2014.

47. Kuypers, *The Zones of Regulation*.

48. Ibid.

49. Apple, "Accessibility."

50. Aukstakalnis, email.

51. Kelly Stewart, occupational therapist, Derry Township School District, email correspondence, January 26, 2014.

52. *Breathe, Think, Do with Sesame*, Sesame Street, https://itunes.apple.com/us/app/ breathe-think-do-with-sesame/id721853597?mt=8.

53. Aukstakalnis, email.

54. Dr. Ananya Mandal, "What is Visual Impairment?" *News-Medical*, September 17, 2013, www.news-medical.net/health/What-is-visual-impairment.aspx.

55. Summers, interview.

56. Ibid.

57. Ibid.

58. Diane Brauner, orientation mobility specialist, interview with authors, February 3, 2013.

59. Summers, interview.

60. Ibid.

61. "News Release: Electronic Book for Students with Visual Impairments Reaches for the Stars," HubbleSite, January 9, 2014, http://hubblesite.org/newscenter/archive/releases/2014/02/full/.

62. Apple, "Accessibility."

63. Summers, interview.

64. Brauner, interview.

65. Names have been changed to protect the identity of students in examples.

66. Brauner, interview

67. *LookTel Money Reader*, IPPLEX, https://itunes.apple.com/us/app/looktel-money-reader/id417476558?mt=8.

68. Apple, "Accessibility," https://www.apple.com/accessibility/ios/voiceover/.

69. Summers, interview.

70. HubbleSite, "News Release."

71. Brauner, interview.

72. Ibid.

73. Ibid.

74. Summers, interview.

75. Brauner, interview.

76. Ibid.

77. Ibid.

78. Ibid.

CHAPTER 15

Balancing Power: Data Use, Privacy, and Digital Citizenship

Educational data, whether it comes from school systems, mobile applications, or other technology-based resources, has immense power to transform our education system for the better. The more we understand how students learn new concepts, retain information, and apply it in the future, the better able we are to prepare students for success. Rich, high-quality data is necessary for this transformation. In fact, a recent report estimates that the appropriate use of educational data could result in an annual added economic value of $1.2 trillion worldwide.[1] Educational data can be used to improve instruction, ensure more efficient management of administrations and financing, and match students to programs and employment, all resulting in positive economic outcomes. What's more, the high number of data points, often called Big Data, allows for statistical sampling to be a thing of the past; using all the data to analyze trends and make decisions is the new normal.[2] Data has become, in almost all sectors, an asset that holds the power to improve all aspects of operation.

The outstanding benefits of educational data are more than just hypothetical. For example, through the use of student data, New York City school districts learned that nearly four out of five high school graduates were not sufficiently prepared when beginning community college.[3] This insight allows the district to make changes to its practices in order to better student outcomes whereas prior to this data being collected, there was no indication that students were so poorly prepared. On a broad scale, educational data has the power to build powerful predictors and allow better analysis of the causal factors in the educational systems.[4] More and more, we're seeing this data used to populate early warning systems for predicting students who are likely to drop out or be retained to repeat a grade.[5] It can be used to identify factors that lead to academic and career success,[6] as well as highlight teachers who are particularly effective.[7]

On a more local scale, educational data allows individual educators to better understand the impacts of their teaching techniques. They can more easily identify topics that individual students struggle with and how effective different interventions are.[8] Developers can also use data they collect to paint a rich picture of student learning that can be used to automatically guide more effective instruction. This data helps developers to create apps that better meet the needs of students and educators.

While educational data in all its forms offers significant power to help students, educators, and administrators, this benefit comes at a cost: privacy. The high volumes of data collected provide ever more opportunities for misuse; personally identifiable information could be shared inadvertently, and vendors could take advantage of underage users' trust. And while there is little to no evidence that this abuse is happening,[9] there is still concern over the implications of all this data collection. In this chapter, we discuss privacy and the risks associated with big data in the educational setting. We also discuss digital citizenship and the teaching of responsible use, which is the primary defense users have against these threats.

PRIVACY

Privacy of student data has become an increasingly controversial topic in recent years. In a recent survey, 89 percent of adults expressed concern about the use of student's personal data for secondary means.[10] Furthermore, the majority of adults expressed a concern that they are not kept well informed about the details of how their students' data is being collected, accessed, and stored.[11] These parents felt that privacy of student data should be a primary concern and that more restrictions are needed at the school district and company levels. Surveys have also shown the primary concerns of parents are varied and have changed over time.

Privacy Concerns

There are many concerns relating to student data privacy, with some of these concerns having more validity than others. However, like many public-relations issues, if enough parents and educators *believe* there is a problem, the public's negative perception will start to grow. Below we address six of the top concerns related to student data privacy and how these fears are reflected in reality (pictured in Figure 15.1.)

Stranger Danger

When the Internet started to become more prolific in the lives of teens and young children in the early 2000s, one of the primary concerns of parents and adults was the presence of online predators who could take advantage of naïve youth. This concern led parents to limit technology use and monitor what their children were doing on the Internet.

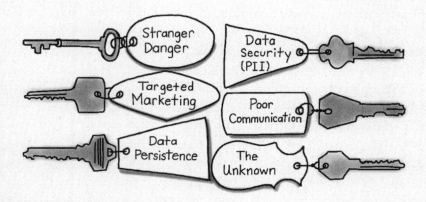

Figure 15.1 Privacy Concerns

Technology providers responded by providing tools that offer protection against these fears. For example, there are many social networks designed specifically for children with special safety measures in place, such as *Jabbersmack,* which keeps children from adding strangers as friends by requiring a code that has to be shared outside of the app.[12] These protections help allay many parental fears, though recent surveys suggest that 72 percent of parents are still concerned about interactions with strangers online.[13] However, while this still represents the majority of parents, other fears have recently taken center stage and concern a greater proportion of parents whose children use the Internet and related technologies.

Targeted Marketing to Children

Targeting marketing to users based on their behaviors and usage data is a practice that has been pervasive on the Internet for years. Simply look at the ads on Facebook or at the top of Gmail and you'll see obvious correlations with the content of your pages, pages you've visited, and messages you've received and sent. Many parents are angry at the practice of targeting of advertisements to children, with 81 percent showing concern that data being collected about their children may be made available to advertisers.[14] For example, an app that helps students manage sports practices and games could collect data that would be useful for sporting goods stores who could specifically market items at important times during the sport season. Alternatively, apps that gather data about student performance in class could be used to market tutoring services. These types of targeted advertising are seen as an invasion to individual privacy. While many of the fears parents have related to the Internet and their students' privacy are unlikely to occur, marketing based on data collected from students is very real and has been highlighted by large and prominent providers of educational technology.[15,16] Furthermore, a recent study shows that only 7 percent of school contracts with technology vendors explicitly restrict the sale of student data to third parties.[17] However, while the sale and use of this data may feel like a major breach in privacy, the types of data and analyses involved have little capabilities for malicious outcomes. In fact, recommendations for tutoring services or educational products in the exact area where a child needs further support could be a great benefit.[18]

Persistence of Data over Time

Another concern extends beyond what is being done with student data now and what could be done in the future. Many worry that data could be used in making future decisions about their students (e.g., college acceptance or career placement) that could be unfair. This is a concern that is growing both with the amount of data that is being collected and the sophistication of the analyses that can be applied to it. Social media in particular has been a major concern for parents who are worried about how their child develops an online reputation that is available to future employers. However, this concern now extends to applications that collect data in a more subtle manner, as apps often do. Privacy specialists warn that new technologies allow the classification of academic performance from low-level data (such as keystrokes) that would previously be perceived as harmless.[19] While this type of technology is still on the horizon and not yet in practice, the concern that this type of data could be used by colleges or employers to make admission or hiring decisions persists.

Security of Personally Identifiable Student Data

There is additional concern about the collection, storage, and access of personally identifiable information. Many parents are extremely concerned about their child's personal data being collected and stored, with or without their knowledge. The Children's Online Privacy Protection Act of 1998 (COPPA) requires many disclosures and parental consent to collect information, and also places parameters on how the company collecting the data must handle it (i.e., the procedures for storage and destruction, as well as reasonable security procedures to maintain confidentiality of the data it obtains).[20] However, though the law offers protection against the collection of personally identifiable information on minors, the rapidly expanding capabilities of technology stand to reduce the effectiveness of these restrictions.

The quantity of data that is being collected is driving parents' concerns. While many companies that collect data strive for anonymization, so that no data is personally identifiable, the sheer quantity of data collected about individuals makes it so that identifying information can be reverse engineered or exploited for strictly commercial purposes. In these cases "the data may not even explicitly seem like personal information, but with big-data processes it can easily be traced back to the individual it refers to."[21] As an example, consider the anonymized data Netflix has publicly released as part of their challenge for innovation,[22] which includes user ratings and viewing history. As a proof of concept, data scientists have demonstrated how this data can be used in conjunction with publicly visible review data on IMDB.com to identify individuals and link the two accounts, essentially de-anonymizing the data.[23] While these actions require a substantial amount of effort on the part of malicious individuals or companies, and the information would be difficult to come by, it is not completely implausible. Also worth noting, big-data sources are generally not the issue when discussing security; small data are the ones more prone to fraud and security breaches. A large educational database, the kind required for these kinds of analyses, will have strong security (firewalls, tiered access, and strong data-quality protocols), while something like a personal banking password isn't generally as strong, and is more prone to being hacked.[24]

The security of student data, while governed by tight restrictions, is still a valid area for concern. It is important for those who develop and market apps to be diligent and transparent about the data they're collecting. But the laws, rules, regulations, and common practices around collection of such data are constantly changing, and it is important for developers to stay informed of the most recent changes.

Poor Communication

The disclosures to parents under COPPA, often part and parcel of the lengthy privacy policy that requires a parent to click a button if they agree, are less than ideal. Apps are required to provide a privacy policy, but these are often lengthy and are not written in understandable terms. Therefore, these terms are seldom read and even less frequently understood by guardians.[25] Furthermore, parents, educators, and administrators often have a difficult time communicating with each other as well as developers, leading to many unanswered questions and increasing frustration.[26] So, while there are valid and strong regulations governing the collection of data for children under 13, there are also many gray areas for parents and educators on these practices, simply because of confusing communication practices. This concern is, we feel, warranted. Research into the practices of apps as they relate to privacy laws and disclosures has noted an appalling lack of transparency in the privacy policies of children's apps.[27] It represents a major area for improvement in the educational app market. Without proper communication, it is impossible for users and guardians to feel knowledgeable and comfortable about what data is being shared and how data is being used. These concerns can quickly escalate as users become afraid of hypothetical scenarios.

The Unknown

Perhaps the scariest privacy concerns are the ones that cannot be voiced. Many parents do not know exactly why it feels wrong to have their student's data collected, they just know that it feels creepy. And this fear is not without good reason. Some of the largest educational technology providers are collecting up to 100 million data points, per child, per day.[28] That's an astounding amount of data, and it's not clear what companies are using it for, or what they could use it for. While there isn't any clear evidence that this data is being used for malicious purposes,[29] the unknown allows imaginations to wander to the worst possible fears. Fears that cannot be articulated are often the most difficult to quell.

PRIVACY LEGISLATION

To help protect the privacy of student data, there are several pieces of legislation that have been put in place. The Family Educational Rights and Privacy Act (FERPA) was initially adopted in 1974, before many issues surrounding digital data arose. The key provision of FERPA is to establish students as the owners of their educational data, and educators and administrators as the custodians. It specifies how the educational records of students under 18 can be used and accessed. Primarily, it states that parents and eligible students have a right to view and request corrections to their records, since they are, in fact, the owners of these records.[30] Records can also be released for purposes related to evaluation, audit, and compliance. All other purposes require consent from the parent or eligible student. For example, teachers and federal officials can use data to understand student achievement and make policy changes. However, they are prohibited from using the data for marketing or advertisement.[31] FERPA has been amended many times since 1974 to address the latest technological concerns and data sharing practices, and it continues to evolve to address the ever-changing world of student data collection and sharing.

COPPA is designed specifically to protect the online data of children under the age of 13. Its primary goals are to increase parental involvement in children's online activities, protect the online safety of children, ensure security of children's personal information, and limit the collection of data from children without parental consent.[32] The primary requirements of COPPA are that website or online entities with users under the age of 13 require parental consent and notification about use and data collection policies. They are also expected to secure this data and dispose of it after a reasonable amount of time has passed. Parents are further given the right to revoke permissions at any time.

OPEN ISSUES

Unfortunately, the existence of these legislative measures is not enough to remove the issue of data privacy or allay many concerns, since there are many entities affected by it. One is a matter of compliance. For example, in 2012 the Federal Trade Commission conducted a survey of the top 960 apps for children in the Apple App Store and the Google Play Android Market.[33] The survey revealed startling information about the state of compliance in the children's mobile app market. In fact, "most apps failed to provide any information about the data collected through the app, let alone the type of data collected, the purpose of the collection, and who would obtain access to the data. Even more troubling, the results showed that many of the apps shared certain information—such as device ID, geolocation, or phone number—with third parties without disclosing that fact to parents. Further, a number of apps contained interactive features—such as advertising, the ability to make in-app purchases, and links to social media—without disclosing these features to parents prior to download."[34] These applications are using child data in a way that violates many parental expectations without proper notification.

Another issue is that even when privacy policies are provided they can often be difficult to read and understand and may not contain information of value to users in making decisions about their use of the app. For instance, a readability analysis of a sample of online privacy policies indicated that approximately 70 percent of policies were written at a level higher than what the average adult user of the Internet finds easy to comprehend, and an even higher proportion of policies were beyond the grasp of the general public.[35] In the FTC's study of the children's mobile app market, they found that of the few apps that provided a privacy disclosure (20 percent), many used external links to often-irrelevant information that was difficult to read. The disclosures often failed to alert parents to what types of data were actually being collected.[36] According to Dr. Aaron Massey, a post-doctoral researcher specializing in interactive computing at Georgia Tech University, "a lot of the privacy policies that are pretty detailed are mostly detailed in terms of the things that they [developers] are not doing for you. One of the common misconceptions about privacy policies is that if you have a policy then they are protecting privacy. That's not the case. You can have a privacy policy that says we're collecting all this information and selling it to third parties. ... There is no minimum standard of conduct that (developers) have to meet."[37] So, reading and understanding what a privacy policy says is more important than noting that an app has a privacy policy. This, unfortunately, is something most parents do not take the time to do, or, if they do read it, they don't know to look for.

In addition to issues of how users are notified of privacy policies, there are further issues related to parental consent. When interacting with digital technologies it is very difficult to verify that individuals are who they claim to be. This is especially important when apps are required to obtain parental consent before collecting and using student data. Often websites will simply ask users if they are over the age of 13 before they are allowed in. This is very easy to bypass without parental permission. Other forms of parental notification involve email or password checks that, again, do not guarantee the parental consent has truly been given. Under current COPPA guidelines, consent should be verifiable, by using signed consent forms, credit card account information, or phone or video conferencing staffed by trained personnel.[38] However, the numbers of organizations that use these techniques are still very few.

Another critical issue is that of recourse. If parents notice that a company violated their child's privacy and seek to take action, there are limited means for doing so. First, it must be something that explicitly violates the company's stated privacy policies, so even if the act is perceived as egregious to the individual, this not enough to prosecute a company. Furthermore, an individual alone is often not enough to begin any investigation by the FTC or legal entity. There often must be multiple complaints or publicity before a violation will be investigated.[39] For example, the successful suit against educational app provider 24x7 for unauthorized sharing of users' personal information to third parties was filed by Attorney General Jeffry Chiesa, on behalf of the state of New Jersey.[40]

One final issue relates to rapid changes in technology over time. While the government seeks to protect students and their privacy, the current technological landscape makes it very difficult to do so For example, when COPPA was first passed in 1998, approximately 3 million children under the age of 18 had access to the Internet. As of 2012, this number has risen to approximately 61.7 million children.[41] There are far more products being marketed to young children, and it is difficult to ensure that all entities are adhering to the law. Furthermore, data is becoming increasingly valuable to companies. They are now able to store, process, and use it much more efficiently, which increases incentives to collect it. Individual data is a highly valued commodity to developers and individual companies, as well as third-party entities. This leads to a difficult balance between what is appropriate to collect and use and what is not.

What You Can Do

In the challenging world of big data, with so much of our personal activity on the Internet stored in permanent data logs, what can you actually do to ensure the security of any one student's data? This depends a lot on your role: school faculty, caregiver of a student, or software developer. These tips are shown in Figure 15.2.

Privacy in School

School systems should be proactive and ensure they evaluate the software products they adopt, and maintain clear communications with parents and legislators. They have significant power to determine

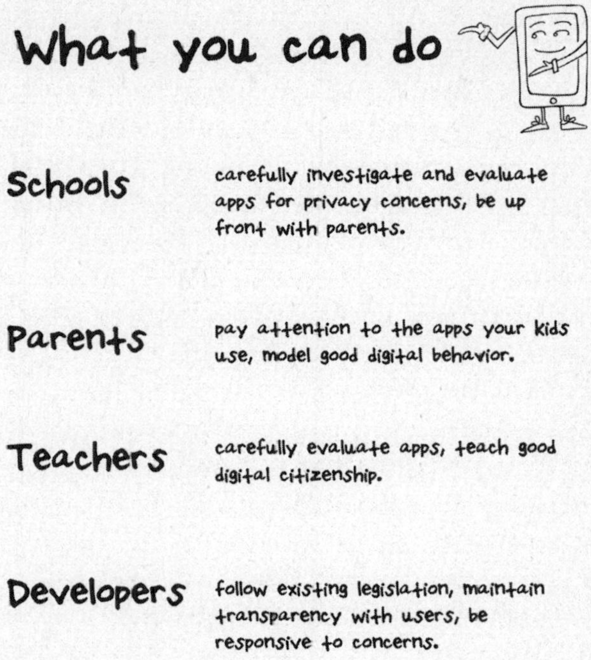

What you can do

Schools   carefully investigate and evaluate apps for privacy concerns, be up front with parents.

Parents   pay attention to the apps your kids use, model good digital behavior.

Teachers   carefully evaluate apps, teach good digital citizenship.

Developers   follow existing legislation, maintain transparency with users, be responsive to concerns.

Figure 15.2 What You Can Do

which apps are used and, consequently, what types of student data to collect and share. Schools often serve as intermediaries between parents and the technology providers.[42] They often act on behalf of parents and, in some cases, have authorization to provide consent. For that reason, schools should still be expected to do their own due diligence by investigating the companies they interact with and communicating with parents. The FTC recommends that schools and/or individual faculty members ask the following questions of any tech provider before engaging with them:[43]

- What personal information is collected?
- How is it used?
- Is the information shared in any way?
- Are there mechanisms in place for parental control of student data?
- How is the data kept secure?
- What are the retention and deletion policies?

Common Sense Media, an organization committed to promoting responsible media fluency for children and families, has also been leading initiatives to ensure that schools' policies are up to date and that all stakeholders are kept informed. In October of 2013, they launched the School Privacy Zone campaign with the goal of promoting national standards centered around the use of student data.[44] This campaign focuses on promoting three core principles: Student data should be used only for educational purposes, student data should never be used for targeted advertising, and schools and technology providers should adopt policies in line with these objectives.[45]

Many states have already begun advocating for stronger regulations of student data in their school systems. For example, the state of California enacted a law in 2014 that prevents the collection or use of student data for any reason other than for purposes intended by the school, or required for product maintenance. This is the strictest data regulation in the country.[46] These endeavors are important as school systems are often large disseminators of educational technology, and this responsibility will only increase as technology becomes increasingly pervasive in the classroom. As the prevalence of statewide longitudinal data systems continues to grow, these issues are becoming more relevant (and controversial) as states draw lines on what is acceptable use of student data.[47]

Privacy at Home

Parents should be aware of the apps used by their children and how these apps collect and use personal data. This involves reading privacy policies and making informed judgments about what level of data collection and usage they view as appropriate for their children. Unfortunately, as Dr. Aaron Massey points out, this is not an easy task. "It is very difficult to evaluate these things. Often it ends up … where success is a non-story and failure is a front page headline. … All that tells you as a consumer is 'that's one company I don't want to do business with.' It doesn't give you any information about who you should trust."[48] Massey goes on to recommend that parents talk with one another about their concerns. Often sharing information in this way is one of the best method for parents to stay informed about the apps their children are using and any privacy concerns that may warrant investigation.

Another important responsibility is to pay attention to requests for consent. Requests for children to use an app often come through email and may look like spam or may be otherwise easy to ignore. It is important that parents read the email understand what is being asked, and provide consent only when appropriate. Parents should also feel comfortable contacting the company for clarification if they are unsure about what data is being collected and how it will be used. By asking these questions, parents can communicate to companies that their privacy policies may need updating. Parents should also be aware that they have the right to view the information that is being collected about their student and withdraw consent at any time. Companies that comply with COPPA are required to provide a mechanism for this, though it may not be a simple task. However, if a parent is truly concerned, it is an available course of action.

Finally, we recommend that parents model good digital citizenship behaviors to their children so they can learn how to make these evaluations on their own. Parents should talk openly with their children about data privacy concerns and how to identify trustworthy apps or websites. The goal should be to teach students how to recognize when companies may be using their data and how to be proactive about managing their personal information.

Privacy for the Student

In many ways, digital dangers are like any other risk children face in their analog lives. "Swimming pools can be dangerous for children. To protect them, one can install locks, put up fences, and deploy pool alarms. All these measures are helpful, but by far the most important thing that one can do for one's children is to teach them to swim."[49] Similarly, the new digital landscape and associated privacy issues, lead many to be nervous about the safety of their children. However, when navigating the potentially scary waters of student privacy, it is important to consider one key component of keeping young children safe from having their data misused: teaching them to be digital citizens who can assess the risk associated with putting information on the

Internet and identify trustworthy software providers. As schools transition from outright bans on technology to policies of responsible use, it is imperative that students see mobile devices as tools for their everyday life and be taught the skills needed to guard secure information and evaluate threats.

DIGITAL CITIZENSHIP: TEACHING RESPONSIBLE USE

Instead of ignoring the issue by restricting students' use of technology, students should be explicitly aware of the dangers of digital media and instructed on how to make ethical choices to mitigate these threats. For example, Common Sense Media provides a comprehensive, free digital citizenship curriculum equipped with lesson plans, interactive tools, and assessments for K to 12 students. For elementary-age children, they also provide an interactive world equipped with games and videos that ultimately allows students to acquire their digital passport. Similarly, Project New Media Literacies provides a free curriculum for high school students, *Our Space: Being a Responsible Citizen of the Digital World*.[50] Through this lesson plan, students are exposed to activities designed to address privacy, identity, credibility, authorship and ownership, and participation.

Moreover, a case has been made for schools to replace the more typical acceptable use policy with the more appropriate responsible use policy that teaches students the dangers of mobile and how to use their devices responsibly.[51] This slight semantic adjustment shifts responsibility to the student to make responsible choices. In her book, *One-to-One Learning: Laptop Programs that Work*, Pamela Livingston describes a successful implementation of using the LARK (legal, appropriate, responsible, kind) framework for drafting responsible use policies.[52] Beyond teaching students how to use technology responsibly, Livingston explains how the LARK framework can also be used productively when violations occur. "They're considered opportunities for students to reflect on their actions both in light of LARK and in terms of their own reputations and membership in a community of learners," Livingston writes.[53]

Using some of these methods, Kelly Walsh, CIO at The College of Westchester and author of the EmergingEdTech blog, reports school districts across the country have opted to embrace and moderate as opposed to ignore and restrict when it comes to cellphones in the classroom.[54] Allen Independent School District in Texas established a productive use of cellphones by instating an acceptable use policy for technology and providing a guide for parents.[55] Katy Independent School District took a different approach and transformed students' devices into mobile learning devices by disabling texting and calling features. Also, the Oak Hills Local School District in Ohio believes in the benefits of mobile devices and has published a bring your own device framework, complete with lessons learned so other schools can successfully adopt a similar policy.

The fact is students are using and will continue to use mobile devices. Therefore, by restricting their use in schools, we are missing two valuable teaching points: the responsible use of mobile devices and the power of mobile devices for productivity and engagement. With respect to the former, students use mobile devices outside of the classroom, and this use is rarely monitored; therefore, by ignoring mobile in the classroom, students are not learning the potential dangers of their actions. Instead of fighting the inevitable and infinite battle of restricting use, educators should leverage students' desire to use mobile devices and introduce students to tools and strategies for making learning more efficient and effective. Teaching digital citizenship will ultimately lead to smarter use of technology and fewer security issues, as students internalize the principles for what is appropriate to share and how to make those decisions independently.

Privacy for the App Developer

In many cases, privacy concerns portray app developers as the villain. However, companies that put careful thought into how they manage student data and how they communicate with the public about their practices are increasingly viewed in a positive light. Furthermore, failure to take initiative in this arena could have disastrous consequences. For example, the software company inBloom was viewed as a well-funded educational powerhouse as it grew in 2011 to 2013, and many states chose its services. However, a failure to address the privacy concerns of parents and schools districts led states to pull out and ultimately resulted in the closing of the company in 2014, shortly after its inception.[56]

Developers must ensure that they are complying with the appropriate legislation. If an app has access to student educational records, this means complying with FERPA. Many apps must also comply with COPPA if they have material that is intended or may be used by children under the age of 13. The FTC has created clear guidelines for compliance that involve six key steps.

Step 1   Determine if your company is a website or online service that collects personal information from kids under 13.

Step 2   Post a privacy policy that complies with COPPA.

Step 3   Notify parents directly before collecting personal information from their kids.

Step 4   Get parents' verifiable consent before collecting information from their kids.

Step 5   Honor parents' ongoing rights with respect to information collected from their kids.

Step 6   Implement reasonable procedures to protect the security of kids' personal information.[57]

These steps are a bare minimum. We advise communicating and sharing as much as possible with users and responsible parties. Developers should strive to offer transparency in their privacy and data security practices, offering plain-text summaries of their legalese policies. Text should be at a level that is easy to read by the majority of the expected users. For example, Moms with Apps, an online advocacy group, recommends using an icon-based system to disclose policies to reduce the need to read complex texts in order to understand a company's privacy policy.[58] Companies should clearly disclose what they will and will not do with student data. LinkedIn.com, the networking site for professionals, does a commendable job with this.[59] They break each section of their privacy policy down to an unintimidating, colloquial sentence or two, and also provide a brief video explaining how they treat the information you share in your profile. They even give a few benefits to them using your data, like providing you with more relevant connections and personalized suggestions. It is important to show a use of the data that benefits users rather than allow them to assume their data is being harvested and stored somewhere to be used against them or to exploit them. The things that apps and developers do to safeguard user data and keep it secure, as well as new features to enable that, should be touted as any other updates would. It is also important to let users know what their rights and options are. How can they remove data about themselves? Who should they contact with questions and concerns? Treat privacy like a feature and discuss it openly; by showing it is something you take seriously, you make the users better informed and more comfortable. Massey recommends that companies take steps to facilitate communication among users and parents where privacy concerns can be voiced and addressed.[60] By supporting and addressing this type of dialog, a company can be aware of the needs of its users and demonstrate a clear commitment to transparency and respect of student privacy. Anything that can be done to demonstrate honesty and compassion towards user concerns is likely to be well received.

CONCLUSION

There are advantages and disadvantages to sharing data. It often feels as though keeping data private and choosing not to share usage patterns and location is a default practice: When in doubt, don't share. Sharing data for personalization and customized experiences within an app or website is certainly a tradeoff. Collecting detailed personalized data about students is the only way to offer truly customized instruction. But what are the risks associated with allowing this data collection and use? Dr. Aaron Massey, digital privacy researcher, notes, frankly, that "most people who are freaking out about this are concerned about a hypothetical that isn't reflective of what's really happening."[61] Perhaps the biggest issue surrounding data privacy and security is misunderstanding and the big scary unknown. Certainly there are many possibilities, but there's not much hard evidence (at this point in time) to point to actual malfeasance or misuse. The best defense educators and parents have against this threat is to be educated on their students' device use, questioning tech providers if something feels off. Educational tech companies can be up front and transparent, openly sharing their privacy policies in plain text. As the digital world continues to expand and mature at breakneck speed, it is vital, in our opinion, that all parties take a seat at the table and, without fear, shape the future of privacy.

NOTES

1. James Manyika, Michael Chui, Diana Farrell, Steve Van Kuiken, Peter Groves, and Elizabeth Almasi Doshi, "Open Data: Unlocking Innovation and Performance with Liquid Information," McKinsey & Company, October 2013, www.mckinsey.com/insights/business_technology/open_data_unlocking_innovation_and_performance_with_liquid_information.

2. Viktor Mayer-Schonberger and Kenneth Cukier, *Big Data* (New York: Houghton Mifflin Harcourt Publishing Company, 2013).

3. Anya Kaminetz, "Mass Collection of Student Data Raises Privacy Concerns," National Public Radio, May 26, 2014, www.npr.org/2014/05/26/316110345/mass-collection-of-student-data-raises-privacy-concerns?ft=1&f=.

4. Vasuki Rethinam, "Predictive Analytics in K–12: Advantages, Limitations and Implementations," *The Journal*, June 12, 2014, http://thejournal.com/articles/2014/06/12/predictive-analytics-in-k-12-advantages-limitations-implementation.aspx#0qwJQppfRl40cfYM.99.

5. Hansheng Chen, "Identifying Early Indicators for College Readiness," Research paper, www.gse.harvard.edu/cepr-resources/files/news-events/sdp-fellowship-capstone-chen.pdf.

6. Vasuki Rethinam, "Grade 9 Indicators Influencing High School Graduation and College Readiness in Montgomery County Public High Schools," May 2011, http://montgomeryschoolsmd.org/departments/sharedaccountability/reports/2011/Grade%209%20Indicators_5-25-11%20FINAL.pdf.

7. Laura Pappano, "Using Research to Predict Great Teachers," *Harvard Education Letter*, May/June 2011, http://hepg.org/hel-home/issues/27_3/helarticle/using-research-to-predict-great-teachers_501.

8. Data Quality Campaign, Infographic, "Ms. Bullen's Data-Rich Year," www2.dataqualitycampaign.org/files/Data-Rich%20Year%20Infographic.pdf.

9. Stephanie Simon, "Data Mining Your Children," *Politico*, www.politico.com/story/2014/05/data-mining-your-children-106676.html#ixzz34pis4dlx.

10. Student Privacy Infographic, Common Sense Media, http://cdn2-d7dev.ec.commonsensemedia.org/sites/default/files/uploads/about_us/csm-school_privacy-infographic_feb14-lores.pdf.

11. Ibid.

12. "Social Networking for Kids," Common Sense Media, www.commonsensemedia.org/lists/social-networking-for-kids.

13. Mary Madden, Sandra Cortesi, Urs Gasser, Amanda Lenhart, and Maeve Duggan, "Parents, Teens and Online Privacy," *Pew Research*, November 20, 2012, www.pewinternet.org/2012/11/20/main-report-10/.

14. Ibid.

15. Melissa Block, "Who's Using the Data Mined from Students?," *National Public Radio*, May 26, 2014, www.npr.org/2014/05/26/316110352/whos-using-the-data-mined-from-students.

16. Amy Gesenhues, "Google Says It Will No Longer Scan and Collect Data from Student Gmail Accounts for Ad Purposes," *MarketingLand*, April 30, 2014, http://marketingland.com/google-says-will-longer-scan-student-gmail-accounts-ad-purposes-82213.

17. Fordham University Center on Law and Information Policy, "Privacy and Cloud Computing in Public Schools (2013)," December 13, 2013, http://law.fordham.edu/center-on-law-and-information-policy/30198.htm.

18. Block, "Who's Using the Data?"

19. Natasha Singer, "Schools Use Web Tools, and Data Is Seen at Risk," *New York Times*, December 12, 2013, www.nytimes.com/2013/12/13/education/schools-use-web-tools-and-data-is-seen-at-risk.html?_r=2&.

20. COPPA, "Children's Online Privacy Protection Act," www.coppa.org/coppa.htm.

21. Mayer-Schonberger and Cukier, *Big Data*.

22. Elliot Van Buskirk, "How the Netflix Prize Was Won," *Wired*, September 22, 2009, www.wired.com/2009/09/how-the-netflix-prize-was-won/.

23. Mayer-Schonberger and Cukier, *Big Data*.

24. Executive Office of the President, "Big Data: Seizing Opportunities, Preserving Values," The White House, May 1, 2014, www.whitehouse.gov/sites/default/files/docs/big_data_privacy_report_5.1.14_final_print.pdf.

25. Carlos Jenson and Colin Potts, "Privacy Policies as Decision-Making Tools: An Evaluation of Online Privacy Notices," *Proceedings of the SIGCHI Conference on Human Factors in Computing Systems*, 2004, pdf.aminer.org/000/088/850/privacy_policies_as_decision_making_tools_an_evaluation_of_online.pdf.

26. Simon, "Data Mining."

27. Federal Trade Commission, "Mobile Apps for Kids: Current Privacy Disclosures are Disappointing," *FTC*, February 2012, www.ftc.gov/reports/mobile-apps-kids-current-privacy-disclosures-are-disappointing.

28. Simon, "Data Mining."

29. Ibid.

30. U.S. Department of Education, "Family Educational Rights and Privacy Act (FERPA)," www.ed.gov/policy/gen/guid/fpco/ferpa/index.html.

31. Joel Reidenberg, "Parents Worry Student Data Will Be Used for Marketing, Not Education," Fordham University Newsroom, January 23, 2014, http://law.fordham.edu/center-on-law-and-information-policy/32351.htm.

32. Bureau of Consumer Protection, "Complying with COPPA: A Guide for Business and Parents and Small Entity Compliance Guide," July 16, 2014, www.business.ftc.gov/documents/0493-Complying-with-COPPA-Frequently-Asked-Questions.

33. Federal Trade Commission, "Mobile Apps for Kids."

34. Ibid.

35. Jenson and Potts, "Privacy Policies."

36. Federal Trade Commission, "Mobile Apps for Kids."

37. Dr. Aaron Massey, post-doctoral fellow in interactive computing at Georgia Tech University, interview with authors, March 20, 2014.

38. Federal Trade Commission, "The Children's Online Privacy Protection Rule: A Six-Step Compliance Plan for Your Business," *FTC*, http://business.ftc.gov/sites/default/files/pdf/BUS84-coppa-6-steps.pdf.

39. Massey, interview.

40. Davis & Gilbert LLP, "Mobile App Developer Settles COPPA Suit," *DGLaw*, July 2012, www.google.com/url?sa=t&rct=j&q=&esrc=s&source=web&cd=1&cad=rja&uact =8&ved=0CDQQFjAA&url=http%3A%2F%2Fwww.dglaw.com%2Fimages_user %2Fnewsalerts%2FAdvMktngPromo_Mobile_App_Developer_Settles_COPPA _Suit.pdf&ei=-supU7PgJJTJsATFrICIAQ&usg=AFQjCNHRibfn2dmevQMf36DOxiv LkFGRMQ&sig2=cIeQvaR3ghMY8b_rDvRLxA&bvm=bv.69620078,d.cWc.

41. New Jersey Office of the Attorney General, "New Jersey Attorney General and Division of Consumer Affairs File Federal Suit against App Developer Accused of Collecting, Transmitting Children's Personal Information without Parental Notification or Consent," June 6, 2012, www.nj.gov/oag/newsreleases12/pr20120606a.html.

42. Bureau of Consumer Protection, "Complying with COPPA FAQ."

43. New Jersey Office of the Attorney General, "New Jersey Attorney General."

44. "Protect Students' Data: Schools Must be Privacy Zones," Common Sense Media, www.commonsensemedia.org/school-privacy-zone.

45. Ibid.

46. Sharon Noguchi, "California Legislature Passes Stiffest US Bill to Protect K–12 Students' Online Data," *San Jose Mercury News*, August 31, 2014, www.mercurynews .com/education/ci_26444107/online-privacy-california-passes-nations-stiffest -protections-k.

47. Jamie McQuiggan and Armistead W. Sapp, *Implement, Improve, and Expand Your Statewide Longitudinal Data System* (Hoboken, NJ: John Wiley & Sons, 2014).

48. Massey, interview.

49. National Research Council, *Youth, Pornography, and the Internet* (Washington, DC: The National Academies Press, 2002).

50. Project New Media Literacies and The GoodPlay Project, "Our Space: Being a Responsible Citizen of the Digital World," www.newmedialiteracies.org/our-space- being-a-responsible-citizen-of-the-digital-world/.

51. Carly Shuler, Niall Winters, and Mark West, "The Future of Mobile Learning: Implications for Policymakers and Planners," UNESCO, 2013, http://unesdoc.unesco.org/ images/0021/002196/219637e.pdf.

52. Pamela Livingston, *1-To-1 Learning: Laptop Programs That Work* (Washington, DC: International Society for Technology in Education, 2006).

53. Ibid.

54. Kelly Walsh, "Making BYOD Work in Schools—Three School Districts That Have Figured It Out," EmergingEdTech, December 16, 2012, www.emergingedtech.com/ 2012/12/making-byod-work-in-schools/.

55. Ibid.

56. Benjamin Herold, "inBloom to Shut Down Amid Growing Data-Privacy Concerns," *Education Week*, April 21, 2014, http://blogs.edweek.org/edweek/DigitalEducation/ 2014/04/inbloom_to_shut_down_amid_growing_data_privacy_concerns.html.

57. Federal Trade Commission, "Children's Online Privacy."

58. Moms with Apps, "Privacy Icon," http://blog.momswithapps.com/privacy-icon/

59. LinkedIn, "Your Privacy Matters," www.linkedin.com/legal/privacy-policy.

60. Massey, interview.

61. Ibid.

CHAPTER 16

Mobile Learning Today and Tomorrow

INTRODUCTION

The ability to create rich, meaningful, and engaging learning experiences for students has never been more attainable. With the proliferation of powerful devices and the significant momentum toward widespread access to broadband, the nuts and bolts are in place waiting for developers, educators, students, and other stakeholders to take the benefits of mobile learning from theory to practice. Trailblazers have already set the stage for this movement, creating and documenting best practices as well as failures. The potential for leveraging today's technologies for education has driven these leaders to take great risks and demonstrate unwavering perseverance. As more teachers on the front lines of education have positive experiences with mobile learning, more advocates and leaders are created to improve it.

The motivation behind mobile learning has never been about the devices themselves but rather the empowerment and opportunity they provide to the student. Few educators would argue that taking the SAT outdoors on an iPad represents mobile learning. Instead, mobile learning embodies those lessons that would otherwise be impossible without synergizing the affordances of mobile technologies. Using a mobile device to identify a bird by searching key features on a birding app, or sharing work in real time with others working on a group project are key differentiators for the mobile experience that facilitate deeper learning and a more engaging experience. These possibilities and new ways of connecting learning experiences are the essence of mobile learning, and embody more than a simple mobile learning device.

The leaders of the educational technology movement will forever remain as restless as technology developers, given "education and technology can and should co-evolve in mutually supportive ways."[1] As new ideas and functionalities arise, the potential for mobile learning experiences will evolve—just as the iPad allowed for experiences above and beyond those available through the Palm Pilot. So, while it is important to understand how to make mobile work today, it is equally as critical to keep an eye on the horizon. The mobile devices we discuss in this book are state of the art today; we fully expect in a few years that the technology will be radically different. What is most important when engaging in and developing apps for mobile learning is to embrace and try new technology as it enters the market.

MAKING MOBILE LEARNING WORK

We hold that mobile learning offers a unique and unrivaled learning opportunity, one that offers significant implications for teaching and learning; however, the shift from potential to realization is rife with challenges. Grounded in the research and analysis conducted in writing this book, we uncovered five critical themes for making mobile learning work: prioritizing pedagogy over technology; favoring tools over content; collaborative efforts in development and implementations; a strong feedback loop; and an openness to using mobile technology rather than a fear of the unknown.

From the development of apps to the student experience, we believe the success of mobile learning lies in communication and collaboration among all stakeholders. By being aware of these five themes, developers and educators alike can use mobile learning to improve education, not as an accessory or an afterthought. After all, a poor mobile implementation won't change any educational outcomes or increase enthusiasm about learning; it takes a concerted and pedagogically-grounded approach to successfully use mobile devices for learning.

Pedagogy Leads Technology

In our definition of mobile learning, we argue this experience cannot be simplified to learning with a mobile device. Instead, instances of mobile learning are defined by leveraging mobile devices and empowering students to actively transact with the curriculum in ways that align with the science behind how we learn best (Chapter 2). Therefore, mobile learning is not about novelty or cool apps, but rather redefining pedagogy to capitalize on the affordances of mobile devices to empower students. Mobile learning environments enable empowerment to take many forms: it lets students take control of their own learning, personalize their experience, pose an authentic problem, provide a meaningful purpose or audience, or connect with others.

When transitioning to a mobile classroom, leaders must encourage educators to consider the research behind learning and higher-order thinking. That is, we must think about how the affordances of mobile devices can be used to induce active, meaningful learning where students are charged with constructing their own meaning through deep engagement with the material. Educational models, such as the SAMR and TPACK models discussed in Chapter 4, suggest that mobile devices be wrapped with pedagogy to generate lessons not otherwise possible. In a recent interview, Scott Smith, chief technology officer at Mooresville Graded School District, said, "The technology is a tool. The technology gives us exponential potential to do things we haven't been able to do before. But the focus is on curriculum and instruction."[2]

App developers face a challenge in this respect too: it is simple to create an app version of an existing educational resource (say, an ebook version of a textbook or videos of lectures), but what will be most valuable is to break out of the familiar and create a different kind of experience, an opportunity for deeper learning.[3] While mobile devices significantly expand the opportunities for classroom activities, even less active instructional strategies, such as lectures, can utilize specific functionalities to encourage active engagement. Apps like *Twitter* or *Padlet* are great tools for backchanneling. Entry and exit tickets, or knowledge checks using Google Forms or *Poll Everywhere*, help to ensure engagement and monitor understanding. Furthermore, apps like *Educreations* and *Explain Everything* provide a perfect space to demonstrate deep understanding by having students show what they know as opposed to stating what you know with a simple quiz or test. Other strategies for enhancing instructional methods are detailed throughout Section 1.

In sum, pedagogy must lead technology. Both developers and educators should maintain awareness of the science behind optimizing learning. When designing apps or lessons, both parties should consider how an app can be used to enhance current instructional strategies. Dressing up previous resources in a digital costume is insufficient, as true mobile learning experiences lie in the potential for experiences previously impossible.

Tools over Content

In line with the previous discussion, apps that are tool based, as opposed to content based, tend to more closely align with creating the optimal mobile learning experience. The objective underlying most content apps is simply to teach students about a specific topic; thus, such apps are generally used to replace teacher-led instruction as opposed to redefine the way in which the lesson is presented. That being said, there is nothing wrong with additional practice. Drill and practice, exploratory, and game-based apps present wonderful opportunities for students to continue engaging with the material or develop automaticity for basic skills (for more information, see Chapter 2).

Nonetheless, we believe the promise of mobile learning lies in tool-based apps—apps that allow students to create, collaborate, and solve meaningful problems. Such apps can often be used in several different ways across domains to encourage higher-order thinking and construct their own meaning. Moreover, practice with and exposure to such apps more closely aligns to the way mobile devices are used in the real world, both in our careers and for lifelong learning. These are the skills—efficiency with using devices to solve our own problems, answering our own questions, and communicating with others—in which employers are most interested. Content- and job-specific knowledge can be, and often is, taught through training.

Therefore, while it is important for students to learn about the events leading up to World War II, for instance, students are better served when this subject is taught in ways that that charge students to practice and develop skills associated with conducting research, critical analysis, and communication. Using this example, apps designed to help students filter through information, analyze primary and secondary sources, and demonstrate and communicate deep levels of understanding often are in greater demand than a World War II content app. Just because a video or textbook is presented on an iPad does not make it mobile learning.

Collaborative Effort

Mobile learning efforts cannot be achieved in a vacuum. This applies both to the developer side—in that an interdisciplinary team is ideal—and in the education setting. Implementing a mobile learning plan requires adequate staff and expertise, and wide support for the initiative.

From a development point of view, apps for education should stand on a solid pedagogical foundation. As highlighted in Chapter 8, best practices emphasize interdisciplinary teamwork to be sure the app meets the needs of educators and is grounded in the science of learning. Effective teams generally require not only programming expertise, but also careful, user-centered design in terms of instruction, usability, and design. For example, button size and placement might have different requirements for preschoolers versus adults. Lastly, rigorous testing can determine whether your app sinks or swims in the education market. Apps that do not withstand weak network strength or significant load do not accommodate the demands of in-school use.

A similar story applies to integrating mobile devices into the classroom. Administrators, teachers, students, IT staff members, curriculum specialists, and parents must work together to get the most out of a mobile initiative. As many teachers can attest, an inferior infrastructure can quickly ruin perceptions of the benefits of mobile and turn believers into doubters. Moreover, without adequate training, many teachers are left overwhelmed with the daunting pressure of creating instructional magic with mobile devices. Buying the devices and ramping up the Wi-Fi network is only the beginning. Providing professional development and helping teachers create a supportive personal learning network helps get the creative juices flowing.

Feedback Loop

Once an app has been released, the development process still continues. As in the planning and initial development phase, we believe the most integral components for creating mobile learning experiences are teachers and students in the classroom *today*. These are the individuals who know exactly what their objectives are, what engages their students, and what they need to achieve. With the recent pace of educational policy changes, even the newly retired teacher might not be able to provide the most accurate feedback and direction. Therefore, close partnerships with in-service teachers round out the expertise needed on a development team.

Further, developers need to be sure their app is engaging to students, if that is their audience. Engagement is a key tenet of pedagogy: "If kids don't like it, then it doesn't work. It's as simple as that," says Bjorn Jeffrey of Toca Boca.[4] Taking students' perspective into account is important because an app can be cool to developers, and hit all the key educational standards, but if the kids don't enjoy it and aren't engaged by it, it won't be effective. This aspect can be easily lost in the mix, and it is worth remembering.

Educators should be aware of this need for two-way communication. Software development models emphasize the importance of user feedback, and the best companies are indeed seeking such guidance. Teachers should not just accept what's out there. We encourage teachers to get involved in the process by communicating with developers on what the app did or what is making the experience less than perfect. It's an iterative process, and this input is critical. In our experience, working with in-service teachers has yielded invaluable expertise to our development process. Understanding not only what teachers and students need, but also the constraints in which they operate has greatly influenced the development of SAS Curriculum Pathways's products. Similarly, informing educators about the latest and greatest in the mobile technology field has inspired wonderful ideas of innovation. This partnership is instrumental for advancing the field of educational technology.

Leverage It, Don't Fear It

Initially, when one suggests letting students use cellphones in class, the reaction might be mixed. In the recent past, many students had their own mobile devices and used them for off-task texting or inappropriate posting to social media sites or even, in some cases, cheating on exams. Much as students in previous generations used passing notes for the same purposes, some students use mobile devices to disrupt learning in the classroom. Often, the school's response is to ban the devices, and hopefully, ban the actions that students are taking part in. However, our suggestion is different: incorporate mobile devices into learning to leverage their ubiquity and engaging qualities. In fact, successful BYOD implementations have found that allowing students to use their devices actually decreases misuse.[5]

Through training teachers, developing guidelines, and, ultimately, relinquishing control, mobile learning initiatives can become a reality—a reality that will likely exceed expectations. Like any other resource, setting appropriate guidelines and teaching responsible use has proven successful in many districts. Even large districts with high rates of poverty and disciplinary infractions have devised workable models for mobile learning implementations.

Almost every best-practices resource for mobile learning emphasizes the importance of mindset, buy-in, and teacher training. Best practice guides typically include advice for communicating the need for mobile devices, addressing common concerns, budgeting, preventing and managing misuse, and preparing infrastructure. With such a comprehensive set of well-known obstacles, it is easy to see why schools might resist implementing a mobile program. However, we believe fearing mobile devices does not save teachers from headaches and behavior management; fearing mobile simply poses a significant disservice to today's learners. Digital media specialist, Mimi Ito, argues "We tend to see [mobile devices] as a distraction from learning because adults aren't participating in [formalizing the process] ... It's a bit of a chicken or the egg problem. They're not participating in shaping the kind of influence these devices [could have]. By embracing mobile devices in our classrooms, we empower students in the learning process."[6]

While BYOD and school-provided initiatives are on the rise, a surprising number of schools still subscribe to a strict no-cellphone policy. For many mobile learning pioneers, fears were common, but many were short lived. In a recent interview regarding the essentials of mobile learning, BYOD expert, Tim Clark, "noted that it's natural for schools to worry about the technical aspects of a rollout, but the novelty of the devices wears off quickly and when it does, the whole school community can become even more focused on how to use the devices to offer the best learning opportunities possible."[7] Similarly, for skeptical districts where fear outweighs perceived benefit, consider educational technology specialist Michelle Bourgeois' experience. In her schools, she found that "once devices were in the hands of teachers and students there was far more potential for creativity and student empowerment than district officials had imagined. The district has been working to get out of the way of that generative energy."[8] There are clear benefits and possibilities that mobile learning enables; however, states and districts must play their part in setting fair and open guidelines to facilitate mobile learning.[9] This means states need to not only ensure their laws aren't overly restrictive (such as no-cellphones in school) but are geared toward finding innovative and progressive ways to use mobile learning to teach kids. In Chapter 1, we offered an example of a teacher in a Cary, NC middle school who, by her school's policy, was compelled to have an app downloaded onto all of the school's 90 devices before being able to test it. After working with the school's policies and the person responsible for the iPad carts, she was able to help create a policy that enables new apps to be downloaded and updated more regularly, and for the devices to be more useful. This sort of organic, teacher-led change is a common way for mobile learning initiatives to better meet the needs of their users and evolve over time.

Teaching digital citizenship is a necessary companion to any mobile learning initiative. While there are certainly many things to be wary of in the digital age, there are also many useful and robust resources that can help students. Embracing the enormity and unpredictability of the digital age as a resource is a necessary step, and teaching students how to navigate this world as it continues to grow and evolve is important. Through mobile learning programs, students can also learn when, where, and why mobile devices are appropriate, learning how to use them for productivity, knowledge, and communication, as opposed to simply informal communication and gameplay. Class discussions can develop on unfavorable outcomes (be they abuses of the acceptable use policy or a search that yielded a noneducational outcome), where students learn how to avoid them in the future. Teaching students to be responsible digital citizens also encompasses teaching good judgment about sharing on social media sites, the reading of privacy statements, and evaluating the security and validity of websites.

THE FUTURE

The future adoption of mobile learning and the success of such efforts require continuous awareness and integration of new technologies and functions. Thus, as we have emphasized before, the leaders of mobile learning must stay informed of the latest changes to these devices. The landscape of mobile learning has shifted dramatically just in the past five years with the advent of the iPad and the proliferation of other tablet devices; we have no doubt this momentum will continue at an equally rapid pace. As we continue to be part of the mobile-learning world, we are monitoring a few areas very closely.

What Can We Do with All This Educational Data?

Collecting usage and user data enables all kinds of possibilities in personalization of the educational experience, as well as insight into how students learn in the digital world. A personalized learning environment has been discussed for years among educational technologists and teachers, but with the rich datasets provided through use of mobile devices in classrooms—both by students and teachers—the dream of personalized learning is closer to realization than it has ever been. Harvesting the huge amounts of data that are available, both from one student and from other users, it is possible to make connections and suggestions for each student based on patterns of performance for large numbers of students.

Further, using educational data for embedded, summative assessment has the potential to revolutionize the way we currently assess learning. Embedded, or stealth, assessments use a variety of data points to gauge students' understanding in real time while completing a lesson or game, which provides feedback to the teacher on how well the students are grasping the material and what concepts might need to be reframed. We are beginning to explore these possibilities with apps like *Poll Everywhere*, that poll a classroom for general understanding, but we believe there are big gains to be made in the area of personalized learning and embedded assessment.

Educational data also present a huge opportunity for fostering accountability among teachers and schools, with data tracked about effectiveness in the classroom. Combined with a potential move away from formative assessments, there will be more voluminous and more accurate data points to judge teacher and school performance.

Ultimately, using these mobile devices to harvest more valuable data and turn that data into actionable information leads to better educational decisions. An abundance of contextualized data that users can parlay into directed actions in the classroom is a huge step for education as a whole. Decisions are made all the time in the classroom; providing educators with data to make those decisions even better just makes good sense, and is something that mobile devices can make a reality.

The Continued Shift in the Way We Think of Education

As we have discussed, fear is one of the biggest obstacles schools face when pursuing a mobile implementation. Fear of distraction and misbehavior, fear of failure, fear of the unknown. Many of these are valid concerns. However, with the increasing number of success cases in districts ranging in socioeconomic status, academic achievement, geographic location, and the like, it is time for districts to face these fears.

Case studies, research investigations, and anecdotal evidence continue to surface leaving skeptics with few points to debate. As the trend of smartphone and tablet ownership becomes ever more ubiquitous, we believe their presence in the classroom will become as common as backpacks and students themselves. Parents, administrators, teachers, and students are beginning to realize restricting the use of mobile devices in the classroom is like giving Archimedes a calculator and telling him not to use it. These devices touch every other aspect of our lives, and schools provide the perfect environment to teach students responsible and effective use for thriving in today's connected society.

Exciting Research

While it might seem surprising, at the time of writing the book, the iPad is only five years old, schools are only now beginning to support widespread use, and the price points on smartphones and tablets are only recently becoming affordable for the general public. That being said, the field of mobile-learning research is only starting to take form. While mobile learning devices have been around for a while (e.g., books, cameras, voice recorders), the capabilities of today's smartphones and tablets have revolutionized the concept of mobile learning. Similarly, although the theoretical foundations behind mobile learning remain relevant (e.g., constructivism, problem- and project-based learning, etc.; see Section I), synthesizing the research within this scope has yet to be fully articulated.

Several important research questions remain unanswered, questions that have significant implications for how developers go about making apps, as well as how educators integrate mobile devices within their curriculum. How pervasive should mobile use be within the curriculum? What concepts and skills are most benefited by mobile devices? How can we scale or generalize integration techniques? What professional development has the most success among teachers? What concepts and skills must be taught that are not already covered by the curriculum? Beyond the classroom, it will be interesting to see the longitudinal effects mobile deployments have on students' college and career readiness. Do mobile device implementations truly blur the lines between formal and informal learning? Do students see connections about how devices can be used similarly both inside and outside of school? In other words, how can we quantify the benefits of mobile devices and measure the return on investment?

In mobile learning, we see a world full of data just waiting for research to make connections. While there is currently no official and acknowledged theory of mobile learning, the field is wide open and full of interesting insights.

Increased Connectivity

Although there is great interest among educators to invest in a 1:1 mobile initiative, many schools simply do not have the infrastructure to support it. A survey conducted in 2014 by the Consortium for School Networking (CoSN) found that only "Forty-five percent of school districts indicated they do not have the capacity to deploy a 1:1 initiative."[10] Even though the report notes there are substantial financial and logistical hurdles for schools in increasing their bandwidth and connectivity, they are improving.[11] In 2014, the Federal Communications Commission (FCC) approved "an additional $5 billion for Wi-Fi over the next five years"[12] giving high priority to providing sufficient connectivity across the country.

Furthermore, as one of the goals of 1:1 or BYOD implementations is the opportunity for anytime, anywhere learning, schools must also be concerned with access to the Internet outside of school. As of 2013, approximately 70 percent of American households had Internet connections at home, leaving a significant number of students without access.[13] Fortunately, an increasing number of public locations now offer free Internet connections. Over 15,000 libraries across the country provide free Wi-Fi. The same free Wi-Fi can increasingly be found in commercial establishments such as Starbucks and McDonalds, with 7,000 and 12,000 connected locations respectively as of early 2013.[14] Public parks and city centers have also started to extend the mesh of connectivity bringing anytime, anywhere learning for everyone closer to a reality.

Better Integration and Better User Experiences

With 90 percent of American adults owning a cellphone and 58 percent owning a smartphone, it is no surprise that we find ourselves going to our mobile devices more and more to accomplish everyday activities.[15] As of 2012, 86 percent of smartphone users reported using their device to do tasks such as coordinate meetings, solve unexpected problems, find information to settle an argument, read the news, navigate through traffic, and get help in an emergency.[16] As features continue to be added to the repertoire of mobile devices' abilities, additional data about our everyday lives are being integrated. The hardware and software that mobile devices offer will continue to become more intuitive and user centered, and apps will necessarily become more mature.

The current movement in the mobile market is toward integrated packages, like Apple's medical, fitness, and home kits. Offering compatibility among apps that are all geared toward one purpose to gain a more holistic image of something, whether it is the user's medical health or fitness, is a key trend to keep an eye on. Wearable technology and other accessories that extend the reach and features of mobile devices are also on the cusp and can enable a fuller mobile-user experience. Google Glass also has many promising features that could impact education in the near future.

Equalizing Effect on Education

One of the great features of mobile devices, as discussed in Chapter 1, is their relative affordability. As mobile technology continues to grow, we see it as a major force in opening educational doors to underserved populations, equalizing opportunity among the haves and have nots. Compared with the prevailing classroom technology that came before, the laptop, a tablet is a bargain. Outfitting a classroom, or a school, with these lower-cost devices is much more doable. As the other pieces of the puzzle begin to fall in place—the loosening of restrictions on device use, improvement of Wi-Fi networks and connectivity, the continuing improvement of devices and apps—we think that more widespread use of mobile devices can have an equalizing effect on education. There are many positive effects the use of mobile devices can have on children's learning and opportunities, such as the ability to take online classes that aren't offered at their school; access to more books than their school's library holds; apps that teach math in a way that speaks to that student's interests and abilities; or a way to create something that doesn't require any additional supplies. Mobile devices teach students a suite of skills that are in high demand in the workplace and the world, and as these devices become common in all schools, irrespective of socioeconomic level, students will receive a more equal and useful education. It is our belief and fervent hope that widespread access to mobile learning can improve educational opportunity for all students. We feel the benefits of mobile technology are within reach of the majority of the population, and that these exciting possibilities are closer than they've ever been.

CONCLUSION

Investing in mobile learning, both financially and as an educational tool, requires a mind that is open to change. This open mind is what paves the way to positive changes in the educational system, as it has become clear that in today's digital world, doing it the way it's always been done is no longer an effective option. Being in tune with what the technology, in this case mobile devices, can do to better educate kids is essential for educators. Education is evolving—it must evolve to give students the skills they need—and being open to the newest technologies is essential for educators.

If we had written this book 15 years ago, it would have been about laptops, and surely in another 15 years there will be another as yet unthought-of technology to revolutionize the field. The nature of technology is that it is constantly changing; it is important that schools do not shy away from technology simply because it presents technical and social challenges. It is a necessary investment of time and resources to update curriculum and methods, to update devices and tools, all with the eventual goal of giving students a more relevant and engaging education. With broader implementation, technology will continue to prove its utility in engaging students and enhancing education and, we think, will come to be thought of as invaluable to the classroom experience.

And, make no mistake—the changes will continue to come. It may seem impossible to imagine what devices and apps will look like in even a few years. These changes will start happening at an even faster pace once the children who were the first generation of mobile learning students become the next generation of mobile developers. To think we are currently in the infancy of the mobile learning movement is truly exciting, as the issues we explore and decisions we make will influence the field for decades to come.[17] Developers and educators alike have the duty to continue looking forward and considering new innovations as they arise.

In the end, mobile devices are great, but mobile learning is less about the cool new gadgets, and more about what and how those gadgets enable children to learn. The ability to unlock the potential of the 10 factors that make mobile learning revolutionary, as detailed in Chapter 3, is the ultimate benefit to any mobile learning implementation, app, or activity. As early adopters in the mobile learning movement, you—the educators, developers, and learners—are pioneers, navigating the new and often rough landscape, paving the way for generations to come. There are still many roadblocks for mobile learning to overcome, but with intelligent and thoughtful conversation, passionate advocacy and support, and the spirit of adventure, we are certain mobile learning will become the dominant form of education in the coming years.

NOTES

1. Carly Shuler, Niall Winters, and Mark West, "The Future of Mobile Learning: Implications for Policymakers and Planners," UNESCO, 2013, http://unesdoc.unesco.org/images/0021/002196/219637e.pdf.

2. Katrina Schwartz, "5 Essential Insights About Mobile Learning," *KQED Mind/Shift*, July 15, 2014, http://blogs.kqed.org/mindshift/2014/07/5-essential-insights-about-mobile-learning.

3. Justin Reich, "Ed Tech Start-Ups and the Curse of the Familiar," *Education Week*, November 20, 2013, http://blogs.edweek.org/edweek/edtechresearcher/2013/11/edtech_start-ups_and_the_curse_of_the_familar.html.

4. "Björn Jeffrey on Why Toca Boca Won't Be Selling to Schools," Games and Learning, March 17, 2014, www.gamesandlearning.org/2014/03/17/bjorn-jeffrey-on-why-toca-boca-wont-be-selling-to-schools/.

5. Forsyth county schools document.

6. Mimi Ito, quoted in "Mobile Devices for Learning: What You Need to Know," Edutopia, www.edutopia.org/mobile-devices-learning-resource-guide.

7. Schwartz, "5 Essential Insights."

8. Ibid.

9. Jennifer Fritschi and Mary Ann Wolf, "Turning on Mobile Learning in North America," UNESCO, 2012, http://unesdoc.unesco.org/images/0021/002160/216083E .pdf.

10. COSN, "COSN's Second Annual E-Rate and Infrastructure Survey," 2014, http://cosn.org/cosns-second-annual-e-rate-and-infrastructure-survey.

11. Ibid.

12. FCC. News Release, "FCC Modernizes E-Rate Program to Expand Robust Wi-Fi Networks in the Nation's Schools and Libraries," July 11, 2014, www.fcc .gov/document/fcc-modernizes-e-rate-expand-robust-wi-fi-schools-libraries.

13. "Broadband Technology Fact Sheet," *Pew Research*, September 2013, www .pewinternet.org/fact-sheets/broadband-technology-fact-sheet/.

14. Anton Troianovski, "The Web-Deprived Study at McDonald's," *Wall Street Journal*, January 28, 2013, http://online.wsj.com/news/articles/SB10001424127887324731 304578189794161056954.

15. Pew Research, "Broadband Technology."

16. Ibid.

17. Shuler, Winters, and West, "The Future of Mobile Learning."

APPENDIX **A**

List of Apps
by Chapter

A complete list of the apps mentioned in this book, in order of their mention within the chapter.

Chapter 1: Changing Education with Mobile Learning

- *Evernote* is an organizational, tool-based app that enables users to create and search lists. By Evernote. Free.
- *Socrative* is a student response system, enabling student participation via smart phones, tablets, and laptops. By Socrative. Free.

Chapter 2: The Science of Learning

- None.

Chapter 3: What Is It about These Devices?

- *Remind* is a way for teachers to send text messages to students and parents and keep all phone numbers private. By Remind. Free.
- *Google Drive* provides cloud-based storage, making it great for taking notes and having access from anywhere. By Google.

- *Dropbox* allows access to documents and photos from anywhere, secure sharing, and collaborative editing capabilities. By Dropbox. Free.
- *Nearpod*. Facilitates interactive mobile presentations. By Nearpod. Free.
- *Join.me*. Classroom app shows the teacher's screen on a mobile device and allows invited users to join and interact with the content. By LogMeIn. Free trial with cost for more features.
- *Showbie* is a tool enabling teachers to easily "assign, collect and review student work in the tablet classroom." By Showbie Inc. Free.
- *Comic Touch 2* Take user photos and add filter, texture, and words in the style of a comic strip. by Plasq. Free with in-app purchases.
- *SAS Gloss* can facilitate paperless workflow in a classroom setting, as well as the opportunity to creatively construct notes and drawings. By SAS Institute Inc. Free.
- *Dictionary.com app* allows offline word look up. By Dictionary.com LLC. Free.
- *SAS Reading Records* is a tool for teachers to administer reading proficiency tests by using a variety of passages. By SAS Institute Inc. Free.
- *Cicada Hunt* allows the user to take an audio recording of their surroundings, determine if cicadas are present, and report the data back to the New Forest Cicada Project. Developed by RareLoop. Free.
- *Ocarina* turns your phone into an ancient flute; you make music by blowing into the microphone. By Smule. Premium.
- *Pocket Trumpet* simulates a trumpet. The user blows into the microphone and uses valves to play real songs. By 10 Startups. Premium.
- *Real Clarinet* simulates a clarinet. The user blows into the microphone and plays notes by placing fingers on specific positions. By Mauro apps. Premium.

- *Leafsnap* is an electronic field guide that helps users identify tree species using visual recognition software on user photos. By Columbia University, University of Maryland, and Smithsonian Institution. Free.

- *acrossair* is an augmented reality browser that provides context for users when navigating in real time, providing points of interest around the user. By acrossair. Free.

- *Elements 4D* conceptualizes chemistry in an augmented reality, story- and game-based activity. By Augmented Dynamics. Free.

- *Companion apps for Smithsonian American Museum of Natural History*. These apps provide an additional way to interact with the museum's exhibits, providing a content-specific experience. *The Power of Poison: Be a Detective, Pterosaurs: Flight in the Age of Dinosaurs*, and *Creatures of Light* (exploring light-producing organisms) are all examples of their apps that dive deep into exhibit topics, with their offerings changing frequently. By American Museum of Natural History. Free.

- *Google Earth* enables users to "fly around the planet with a swipe of your finger," using Google's Street View images and aerial shots. It also shows 3D recreations of certain cities. By Google. Free.

- *Driver Feedback* gives users scores based on their driving (using the accelerometer and GPS hardware), and offers suggestions to improve driving habits and safety. By State Farm. Free.

- *Twitter* is a microblogging social networking site, allowing users to interact with one another via tweets. By Twitter Inc. Free.

- *Instagram* facilitates taking, editing photographs and sharing. By Instagram. Free.

- *Facebook* is a website and app that enables users to connect socially, share photos, and report updates. Free for all operating systems. By Facebook. Free.

- *Minecraft (Pocket Edition)*. Minecraft is a popular, multiplayer, social computer game about "placing blocks and going on adventures." By Mojang. Premium.

- *iBooks* is Apple's ebook reader application. By Apple. Free.

- *To The Brink* provides all of the information in the National Archives and JFK Library and Museum's exhibit about the Cuban Missile Crisis for users who are unable to visit the exhibit, or want to dive deeper. By National Archives and Records Administration. Free.

- *Edmodo* is an app to facilitate teachers and students collaboration and engagement. By Edmodo. Free.

- *WolframAlpha* powers a suite of apps offering "deep computational knowledge in specific educational, professional and personal areas," including algebra, calculus, physics, and astronomy. By WolframAlpha. Free.

- *Numbers* is a robust spreadsheet app. By Apple. Premium.

- *Keynote* is a robust presentation app. By Apple. Premium.

- *Fetch! Lunch Rush!* Is an augmented reality game where users help Ruff Ruffman, a cartoon character keep lunch orders straight for a movie crew. By PBS Kids. Free.

- *Merlin Bird ID* provides a tool to instantly identify 400 North American birds. By The Cornell Lab. Free.

- *StarWalk* is an "interactive astronomy guide," identifying celestial objects for users. By Vito Technology. Premium.

- *Google Maps* provides interactive maps with local attractions identified, to aid navigation. By Google. Free.

- *Find my iPhone* enables a device to use another device to locate a missing iOS device and control data loss. By Apple. Free.

- *MyFitnessPal* is a tool for users to track calories and physical activities. By MyFitnessPal, Inc. Free.

- *ThingLink* lets users make more dynamic and informational images by adding links, music, notes to them. By ThingLink. Free.

- *Math Chomp* is an app suitable for all ages that teaches basic mathematics using a cartoon crocodile. By Mike Irving. Premium

- *Pocket Law Firm* has users match clients and lawyers up, challenge cases and grow law firms. By iCivics and Filament Games. Free.

- *Stack the Countries* teaches world countries, capitals, landmarks, and geography, allowing users to manipulate continents and achieve new levels within the app. By Freecloud Design, Inc. Premium.

- *Rocket Math* is an app (backing up to an established curriculum) designed to teach quick addition skills in students. By Rocket Math. Free.

- *Animoto Video Maker* enables the creation of videos and slide shows using media on the user's device. By Animoto, Inc. Free.

- *ClassDojo*. Realtime classroom management tool to track participation and behavior; enables sharing data with parents and students. By Class Twist Inc. Free.

- *Poll Everywhere* allows real-time audience participation via SMS voting in polls. By PollEverywhere. Free.

- *SAS Flash Cards* is an app that allows users to upload decks of informational flashcards, sharing them with other users, and be quizzed on the information. By SAS Curriculum Pathways. Free.

- *Explain Everything* is an app that facilitates presentation building through inclusion of multimedia elements. By MorrisCooke. Premium.

- *SAS Reading Records* is a tool for teachers to administer reading proficiency tests, using a variety of passages. By SAS. Free.

- *SAS Data Notebook* is a data management tool that allows students to track their own educational goals and progress, as well as take and organize class notes. By SAS Curriculum Pathways. Free.

- *Popplet* is a tool to capture and collaborate on ideas using sharable mind maps. By Notion. Premium.

- *EcoMOBILE. (Ecosystems Mobile Outdoor Blended Immersive Learning Environment)* is a virtual representation of a pond ecosystem that lets students collect and analyze clues to solve an environmental mystery. By Ecomobile. Free

- *SAS Math Stretch* teaches elementary math skills, such as operations, telling time, pattern identification, and comparing numbers. SAS Institute Inc. Free.

- *Duolingo* teaches Spanish, French, German, Portuguese, Italian, and English, providing a fun experience with levels and competition among friends. By Duolingo. Free.

Chapter 4: Creating the Mobile Classroom

- *Evernote* is an organizational tool-based app that enables users to create and search lists. By Evernote. Free.
- *Google Drive* provides cloud-based storage, making it great for taking notes and access from anywhere. By Google.
- *inClass* is an organization app that allows students to keep their notes, schedules, and assignments in one location. By inClass. Free.
- *Join.me*. Classroom app shows the teacher's screen on a mobile device and allows invited users to join and interact with the content. By LogMeIn. Free trail with cost for more features.
- *GoSoapbox* offers a web-based clicker system to allow student response and increase student engagement in lectures. By Go Education, LLC. Free.
- *Poll Everywhere* allows real-time audience participation via SMS voting in polls. By PollEverywhere. Free.
- *Socrative* is a student response system, enabling student participation via smart phones, tablets, and laptops. By Socrative. Free.
- *Padlet* enables the creation of walls and collaboration among students by organizing and sharing information and multimedia, and allowing for student creativity. By Padlet. Free.
- *ShowMe* is a tool that allows for simple creation and viewing of tutorials on the iPad. By ShowMe. Free.
- *Knowmia Teach* is a tool enabling easy lesson planning, video recording, and sharing among students and teachers. By Knowmia. Free.
- *Educreations* is an interactive whiteboard app that allows annotation, animation, and narration of any type of content. By Educreations, Inc. Free.

- *Video Note* allows screen and audio capture of sketch drawings. By TopLineSoft Systems. Premium.

- *Frog Dissection* offers a more economical, greener alternative to dissection in biology class. By Emantras. Premium.

- *3D Brain* allows users to interact with and learn about different brain regions, as well as explore brain injuries and functions. By Cold Springs Harbor Laboratory. Free.

- *TimeMaps* show a sequence of interactive maps, illustrating the different stages of history. For instance, *The Rise of the Roman Empire* shows Rome's expansion. Available for other regions and time periods. By TimeMaps. Premium.

- *Google Maps* provides interactive maps with local attractions identified, to aid navigation. By Google. Free.

- *Things to Think About* offers prompts or writing and discussion lessons to encourage conversation about ideas and issues relevant to kids. By Jackson County Intermediate School District. Free.

- *SAS InContext* is a web-based language arts tool that allows students to explore new terms, topics, and definitions. By SAS Curriculum Pathways. Free.

- *SAS Writing Reviser* is a web-based tool that provides assistance for revising student writing. By SAS Curriculum Pathways. Free.

- *Popplet* is a tool to capture and collaborate on ideas using sharable mind maps. By Notion. Premium.

- *EcoMOBILE. (Ecosystems Mobile Outdoor Blended Immersive Learning Environment)* is a virtual representation of a pond ecosystem that lets students collect and analyze clues to solve an environmental mystery. By Ecomobile. Free.

- *Leafsnap* is an electronic field guide that helps users identify tree species using visual recognition software on user photos. By Columbia University, University of Maryland, and Smithsonian Institution. Free.

- *Mentira* is a place-based augmented reality game, offering informative text and Spanish dialog that guides students through a murder mystery. By University of Wisconsin-Madison. Free.

- *Elements 4D* conceptualizes chemistry in an augmented reality, story- and game-based activity. By Augmented Dynamics. Free.

- *StarWalk* is an "interactive astronomy guide," identifying celestial objects for users. By Vito Technology. Premium.

- *FaceTime* is the iOS video calling app, facilitating collaboration over wireless networks. By Apple. Free (on iOS devices).

Chapter 5: Higher-Order Thinking Skills and Digital Fluency

- *EcoMOBILE. (Ecosystems Mobile Outdoor Blended Immersive Learning Environment)* is a virtual representation of a pond ecosystem that lets students collect and analyze clues to solve an environmental mystery. By Ecomobile. Free.

- *Exploriments.* Offers simulation-based, interactive learning for deeper conceptual understanding of science and math concepts. By IL&FS Education and Technology Services Ltd. Premium.

- *Socrative* is a student response system, enabling student participation via smart phones, tablets, and laptops. By Socrative. Free.

- *Padlet* enables the creation of walls and collaboration among students by organizing and sharing information and multimedia and allowing for student creativity. By Padlet. Free.

- *Keynote* is a native iOS app for creating presentations. By Apple. Premium.

- *Evernote* is an organizational tool-based app that enables users to create and search lists. By Evernote. Free.

- *Google Drive* provides cloud-based storage, making it great for taking notes and having access from anywhere. By Google. Free.

- *Skype* enables free video calls on computers and tablets. By Skype. Free.

- *Screenr* allows the user to record and share screencasts, capturing screen and voice. By Articulate Global, Inc. Free.

- *Dropbox* allows access to documents and photos from anywhere, secure sharing, and collaborative editing capabilities. By Dropbox. Free.

- *Poll Everywhere* allows real-time audience participation via SMS voting in polls. By PollEverywhere. Free.

- *Celly* enables creation of private social networks (cells) of groups of family members, friends, classes, or teammates. By Celly. Free.

- *StudyBoost* allows students to study using text messaging. By StudyBoost. Free.

Chapter 6: Instructional Management and Levels of Technology Access

- *Find my iPhone* enables a device to use another device to locate a missing iOS device and control data loss. By Apple. Free.

- *Apple Configurator*. Facilitates mass deployments of Apple devices. By Apple. Free.

- *Keynote* is a native iOS app for creating presentations. By Apple. Premium.

- *Safari* is a web browser. By Apple. Free.

- *Brushes 3* is a painting app that provides a suite of tools for the creation and sharing of art. By Taptrix. Free.

- *Puppet Pals* facilitates the creation animated puppet shows with audio. By Polished Play, LLC. Free.

- *Dropbox* allows access to documents and photos from anywhere, secure sharing, and collaborative editing capabilities. By Dropbox Free.

- *GoogleDocs* is a website and app to facilitate creating and sharing documents. By Google. Free.

- *Showbie* is a tool enabling teachers to easily "assign, collect and review student work in the tablet classroom." By Showbie. Free.

- *Groupboard Collaborative Whiteboard* allows users to draw and chat in real time. By Group Technologies Inc. Free.

- *ClassDojo*. Realtime classroom management tool to track participation and behavior; enables sharing data with parents and students. By Class Twist Inc. Free.

- *SlideStory* allows users to present pictures with recorded narration. By nanameue, Inc. Free.

- *SAS Data Notebook* is a data management tool that allows students to track their own educational goals and progress, as well as take and organize class notes. By SAS Curriculum Pathways. Free.

Chapter 7: Mobile Technology's Defining Features

- *Google Maps* provides interactive maps with local attractions identified, aiding in navigating. By Google. Free.

- Apple *Maps* offers maps and directions to aid in navigation. By Apple. Free.

- *UrbanSpoon* enables users to find restaurants nearby and see reviews. By UrbanSpoon. Free

- *FourSquare* provides a personalized search for area attractions and restaurants, and allows users to check in on their social networks. By Foursquare Labs, Inc. Free.

- *Instagram* facilitates taking and editing photographs and sharing. By Instagram. Free.

- *Facebook* is a website and app that enables users to connect socially, sharing photos and updates. Free for all operating systems. By Facebook. Free.

- *Firefly Counter* is an app that crowdsources the monitoring of firefly populations, allowing users to log sightings. By Clemson University. Free.

- *Evernote* is an organizational tool-based app that enables users to create and search lists. By Evernote. Free.

- *SAS Flash Cards* is an app that allows users to upload decks of informational flashcards, sharing them with other users, and be quizzed on the information. By SAS Curriculum Pathways. Free.

- *Sensor Kinetics* uses the iPhone's gyroscope and accelerometer sensors to measure the effect of gravity, among other physics concepts. By INNOVENTIONS, Inc. Free.
- *StarWalk* is an "interactive astronomy guide" that identifies celestial objects for users. By Vito Technology. Premium.
- *Leafsnap* is an electronic field guide that helps users identify tree species using visual recognition software on user photos. By Columbia University, University of Maryland, and Smithsonian Institution. Free.
- *GarageBand* allow users to use simulated instruments to record music. By Apple. Free.
- *ThingLink* lets users make more dynamic and informational images by adding links, music, and notes to them. By ThingLink. Free.
- *SAS Data Notebook* is a data management tool that allows students to track their own educational goals and progress, as well as take and organize class notes. By SAS Curriculum Pathways. Free.

Chapter 8: The Educational App Development Process

- *SAS Flash Cards* is an app that allows users to upload decks of informational flashcards, sharing them with other users, and be quizzed on the information. By SAS Curriculum Pathways. Free.
- *SAS Data Notebook* is a data management tool that allows students to track their own educational goals and progress, as well as take and organize class notes. By SAS Curriculum Pathways. Free.
- *SAS Read Aloud* provides books that are read aloud to the user, with word by word highlighting. By SAS Curriculum Pathways. Free.

Chapter 9: Design and User Experience

- None.

Chapter 10: Data, Evaluation and Learning Analytics

● *SAS Flash Cards* is an app that allows users to upload decks of informational flashcards, sharing them with other users and be quizzed on the information. By SAS Curriculum Pathways. Free.

● *SAS Reading Records* is a tool for teachers to administer reading proficiency tests, using a variety of passages. By SAS. Free.

Chapter 11: The Business of Educational Apps

● *Explain Everything* is an app that facilitates presentation building through inclusion of multimedia elements. By MorrisCooke. Premium.

● *Endless Reader* is an app for early readers, introducing sight words and sentence construction with fun characters and animation. By Originator, Inc. Freemium.

● *Proloquo2go* allows nonverbal users to create sentences by sequencing symbols to take part in conversations and communicate needs. By AssistiveWare. Premium.

● *Hopscotch* is a programming app "for everyone" that allows manipulation of characters through code. By Hopscotch Technologies. Free.

Chapter 12: Informal Learning

● *The Elements: A Visual Exploration* is an app that provides an engaging experience, a new way to understand the elements. By Touch Press. Premium.

● Dictionary.com *app* allows offline word look up. By Dictionary.com LLC. Free

● *Wolfram Alpha* powers a suite of apps offering "deep computational knowledge in specific educational, professional and personal areas," including algebra, calculus, physics, and astronomy. By Wolfram Alpha. Free.

- *Speak & Translate* turns your mobile device into an instant interpreter, detecting and converting speech into one of 100 foreign languages. For iOS and Android. By Appic Fun. Free.

- *MyCongress* provides a portal for users to find and see communications from their elected officials, and contact them directly. By Objective Apps, LLC. Free.

- *MathRef* is a quick reference to over "1,400 formulas, figures, and examples to help you with math, physics, chemistry, and more." By Happy Maau Studios, LLC. Premium.

- *YouTube* is a website and app that enables users to search, watch, and share videos. By YouTube. Free.

- *Podcasts* facilitates finding, subscribing to and playing podcasts. By Apple. Free.

- *Wikipedia Mobile* is a robust encyclopedia, "the most comprehensive and widely used reference work humans have ever compiled." By Wikimedia Foundation. Free.

- *Mental Floss* is filled with eclectic material for the user: stories, lists, quizzes about math and history, and pop culture articles By The Week Publications, Inc. Free with magazine subscription.

- *Pinterest* is a website and app that allows users to discover and pin items of interest, curating and organizing boards of ideas for anything at all. By Pinterest, Inc. Free.

- *Leafsnap* is an electronic field guide that helps users identify tree species using visual recognition software on user photos. By Columbia University, University of Maryland, and Smithsonian Institution. Free.

- *Merlin Bird ID* provides a tool to instantly identify 400 North American birds. By The Cornell Lab. Free.

- *Shazam* is a tool that identifies music from a small sound byte. By Shazam Entertainment Ltd. Free with upgrade available.

- *Google Maps* provides interactive maps with local attractions identified, aiding in navigating. By Google. Free.

- *Compass* is an app that displays true north and aids in navigation. By gabenative. Free.

- *Google Goggles* allows users to search using photographs (including QR codes, barcodes, and images of the world around them). By Google. Free.

- *Dollar Origami* shows the user how to make various origami creations out of a dollar bill using visual cues. By LEARN2MAKE. Premium with in-app purchases.

- *Ultimate Guitar Tabs* offers a "catalog of songs with guitar and ukulele chords, tabs, and lyrics." By Ultimate Guitar. Paid.

- *SAS Read Aloud* provides books that are read aloud to the user, with word by word highlighting. By SAS Curriculum Pathways. Free.

- *Daisy the Dinosaur* teaches the basics of computer programming, using drag and drop for kids of all ages. By Hopscotch Technologies. Free.

- *Hopscotch* is a programming app "for everyone" that allows manipulation of characters through code. By Hopscotch Technologies. Free.

- *Duolingo* teaches Spanish, French, German, Portuguese, Italian, and English, providing a fun experience with levels and competition among friends. By Duolingo. Free.

- *Minecraft* (Pocket Edition). Minecraft is a popular, multiplayer, social computer game about "placing blocks and going on adventures." By Mojang. Premium.

- *World of Warcraft Mobile Armory* is a tool to keep track of the users' characters, adventures, and guild activities. By Blizzard Entertainment. Free.

- *SimCity* allows users to create simulated cities. By Aspyr Media. Premium.

- *TaleBlazer* is an augmented reality game platform, enabling users to create games. By MIT STEP Lab. Free.

- *A Gift for Athena* is an augmented reality scavenger hunt that guides users through the British Museum. By British Museum. Free.

- *ROM Ultimate Dinosaurs* uses augmented reality to bring dinosaurs to life, from the (now closed) special exhibit at Royal Ontario Museum. By Royal Ontario Museum. Free.

- *Google Field Trip* provides contextualized, local information to guide the way on trips in new cities. By NianticLabs@Google. Free.

- *NC NatSci* app is a digital guide for visitors to the North Carolina Museum of Natural Sciences in Raleigh, NC, allowing users to filter exhibits by topic and location and to receive additional audio and visual aids. By North Carolina Museum of Natural Sciences. Free.

- *EcoMOBILE. (Ecosystems Mobile Outdoor Blended Immersive Learning Environment)* is a virtual representation of a pond ecosystem that lets students collect and analyze clues to solve an environmental mystery. By Ecomobile. Free.

Chapter 13: Engaging Young Users: Apps for Preschoolers

- *Little Writer* is a tracing app that shows young users how to properly write letters, numbers, shapes, and three- and four-letter words. By Innovative Mobile Apps. Free.

- *SAS Math Stretch* teaches elementary math skills, such as operations, telling time, pattern identification, and comparing numbers. SAS Institute Inc. Free.

- *Toca Doctor* is an app geared toward young users, where they're challenged with many puzzles taking place in the human body to cultivate fine motor skills. By Toca Boca. Premium.

- *Toca Tea Party* allows young users to choose the place settings and refreshments for their tea party, and facilitates social play with others (real or make believe). It ends with washing the dishes. By Toca Boca. Premium.

- *Toca Pet Doctor* for preschoolers simulates 15 different animals that need help. Users simulate feeding, playing, and taking care of animals. By Toca Boca. Premium.

- *GarageBand* lets you use simulated instruments to record music. By Apple. Free.

- *Ocarina* turns your phone into an ancient flute, making music by blowing into the microphone. By Smule. $0.99.

- *SAS Gloss* can facilitate paperless workflow in a classroom setting, as well as the opportunity to creatively construct notes and drawings. By SAS Institute Inc. Free.

- *Toca Tailor* is a kid-friendly app where the user designs and constructs clothes. By Toca Boca. Premium.

- *Toca House* lets learners choose from several chores in different areas of the house. By Toca Boca. Premium.

- *Dinosaur Train Mesozoic Math Adventures* teaches early math and science skills using characters from the popular PBS cartoon. By PBS Kids. Premium.

- *Super Why!* Uses the characters from the popular PBS television show to teach users spelling, letter sounds, and early reading skills using a reward system. By PBS Kids. Premium.

- *Endless Numbers* focuses on early numeracy skills (number recognition, sequences, quantity, patterns, and simple addition). By Originator Inc. Freemium.

Chapter 14: Making Accessible Apps: Autism and Visual Impairment

- *Proloquo2go* allows nonverbal users to create sentences by sequencing symbols to take part in conversations and communicate needs. By AssistiveWare. Premium

- *Look In My Eyes*, designed for users with autism who struggle with social interaction. Employs a token economy that rewards users for making eye contact with faces on the screen. By FIZZBRAIN LLC. Premium.

- *Training Faces* teaches emotion recognition and is geared toward individuals with autism or other special needs. By Training With Gaming. Premium.

- *Social Skill Builder* shows the user videos of good and bad social interactions (e.g., children bullying another student, children taking turns and sharing) and asks the user to determine what happened that was good or bad. By Social Skill Builder, Inc. Premium.

- *Relax Lite* offers a guided deep-breathing exercise, perfect for a student who struggles with self-regulation and who needs a few minutes to calm down. By Saagara. Free.

- *Breathe, Think, Do with Sesame* teaches users to stay calm, solve everyday problems, and recognize emotions in others. By Sesame Street. Free.

- *Safari* is a web browser. By Apple. Free.

- *Mail* is Apple's email application. By Apple. Free

- *iBooks* is Apple's ebook reader application. By Apple. Free.

- *Pages* is a word processing app for Apple devices. By Apple. Premium.

- *Read2Go* offers books in the huge Bookshare library (containing most books a student would read in high school). Excellent for low vision and blind users. By Benetech. Premium.

- *Join.me*. Classroom app showing teacher's screen on mobile device, allowing invited users to join and interact with the content. By LogMeIn. Free trial with cost for more features.

- *LookTel Money Reader* enables users with low vision to scan currency and the app will read the denomination out loud. By IPPLEX. Premium.

- *TapTapSee* provides an audio identification of what is pictured. By Image Searcher. Free.

- *Reach for the Stars*. Ebook designed for the visually impaired, providing audio and pitch-based cues to facilitate the exploration of the Tarantula Nebula. By SAS Institute. Free.

- *SAS Flash Cards* is an app that allows users to upload decks of informational flashcards, sharing them with other users and be quizzed on the information. By SAS Curriculum Pathways. Free.

Chapter 15: Balancing Power: Data Use, Privacy, and Digital Citizenship

- *Jabbersmack* is an app and website that provides a "safe and secure social playspace" for kids to interact with other kids. Google Play App. Free.

Chapter 16: Mobile Learning Today and Tomorrow

- *Twitter* is a microblogging social networking site, allowing users to interact with one another via tweets. By Twitter Inc. Free.

- *Padlet* enables the creation of walls and collaboration among students, organizing and sharing information and multimedia and allowing for student creativity. By Padlet. Free.

- *Poll Everywhere* allows real-time audience participation via SMS voting in polls. By PollEverywhere. Free.

- *Educreations* is an interactive whiteboard app, allowing annotation, animation, and narration of any type of content. By Educreations, Inc. Free.

- *Explain Everything* is an app that facilitates presentation building through inclusion of multimedia elements. By MorrisCooke. Premium.

The Great App Checklist

In our conversations with educators, one of the biggest gray areas we found was how to determine which app is a good one. Many teachers rely on colleagues or word of mouth, or go with the first app they find that meets their needs. There's no denying that the educational app marketplace is full of options, but this poses the problem of how to find and choose good apps. With the high volumes of apps available in app stores, and numbers only increasing, there is a strong need for ways to clearly differentiate apps and guidance on how to decide which should be downloaded and which should be used in the classroom. It's an important discussion because there simply isn't time to download and try each app that might seem to meet the needs of the user. Learning how to swiftly and accurately judge an app without investing a lot of time (and, if it's not a free app, money) is essential to the mobile classroom. For educators the challenge of finding a good app is surprisingly hard.

Developers have a different problem: standing out in a crowded market. This is certainly an exciting and active sector of development and technology to be involved with, and one that we feel will continue to raise the bar on the caliber of educational technology available and demanded in the classroom. However, this also means that making an app that stands out and meets the needs of the educational market and your intended audience is even more important.

We offer this checklist as an answer to these issues, as a way to help educators zero in on what app they need, and to judge how well it performs. This rubric can also inform developers as to how educators choose apps—the types of information that would be helpful to someone in this audience, things to mention in the app store summary, and functionality that is essential.

HOW TO USE THIS CHECKLIST

To fully evaluate an app using our checklist, downloading the app will be necessary. Therefore, some judgment will need to be exercised based on the app summary and ratings. While exploring the app's supporting materials, app store description, and user reviews you can learn some information, but the best way to determine an app's ultimate use and value is to try it out. The following checklist is designed to guide educators through the process of determining if the app they've chosen is good for their purposes, in their classroom. The list is a meta-analysis, based on several popular app checklists[1,2,3,4] as well as our own contributions.

This checklist is designed to be completed in sequential order. Ultimately, we feel the purpose, what the educator's need is, will guide the evaluation. For instance, if a teacher needs a note-taking app for general use, or if he needs a game that offers a chance for his students to practice math concepts, very different lessons and learning objectives are at play in each. We urge educators to first consider their purpose for the app and evaluate the app within that context.

These questions are also designed to steer the person choosing the apps—the teacher or technology specialist—toward thinking about how an app should be evaluated; with the breadth of educational apps out there it is impossible to create a checklist that addresses all possible apps and their value in different settings. Therefore, the answer need not be yes for each question for an app to be great.

And finally, when evaluating apps, search for answers, but if the information isn't apparent, consider reaching out to the developer with the question. Developers should strive to make this information accessible to users and potential users. Further, communicating with app developers is certainly something educators shouldn't shy away from.

THE GREAT APP CHECKLIST

Purpose
☐ Does this app meet my needs, as an educator, for the lesson at hand?

Alignment
☐ Does it fit into my school's standards?

☐ Does it relate to the curriculum?

☐ Is it leveled appropriately for my students?

Pedagogical Framework
☐ Does the app provide appropriate and immediate feedback?

☐ Does it provide a properly scaffolded learning experience?

☐ Does the app facilitate higher-order thinking skills?

☐ Does it provide an authentic experience that mirrors the real world (e.g., a note-taking app with the same processes as the way students take notes with pencil and paper)?

☐ Does it facilitate or enable collaboration?

☐ Does it make the task at hand more efficient?

☐ Does it make the task more engaging?

Personalization
☐ Does the app enable (or require) students to create logins?

☐ Does the app offer a different experience for students based on their interest?

☐ Does the app allow for differentiation and challenge based on the student's ability and knowledge?

Sharing and Access to Work

☐ What happens to work created in the app? Can it be exported or shared on social media sites?

☐ Does their work live on the cloud? Can it be accessed using computers?

☐ Can I see reports of my students' usage?

Ease of Use

☐ Is the app well designed? Can my students figure this out without guidance?

☐ Is navigating logical and simple?

☐ Does the app offer intuitive support?

Privacy

(We suggest searching the app's privacy policy, if one exists, to answer these questions. If the answers aren't obvious, contact the developer.)

☐ Does the app have a privacy policy?

☐ Is student data shared, sold, or kept private?

☐ Is the student data that the app collects stored and maintained in a responsible manner?

App Citizenship

☐ Is the app priced reasonably or free? Based on what it offers, does the app provide good bang for the buck?

☐ Does my school's network support the classroom-wide use of this app?

☐ Is the size of the app appropriate?

☐ Does it provide support or ideas on how to integrate with lesson plans?

☐ Is the app updated frequently?

☐ Is it ad free? If not, are the ads appropriate for students?

Accessibility

☐ Is the app available on the necessary platform(s) to accommodate the devices in my classroom?

☐ Does the app allow the accessibility framework on the mobile devices to be used (i.e., manipulation of font size, contrast, use of voiceover, etc.)?

☐ Is language support necessary and available?

NOTES

1. Tony Vincent, "Ways to Evaluate Educational Apps," *Learning In Hand*, March 4, 2012, http://learninginhand.com/blog/ways-to-evaluate-educational-apps.html.
2. Kathy Schrock, "Critical Evaluation of a Content-Based IPAD/IPOD App," 2014, www.kathyschrock.net/uploads/3/9/2/2/392267/evalipad_content.pdf.
3. Jeff Dunn, "The Must-Have App Review Rubric," *Edudemic*, November 22, 2011, www.edudemic.com/app-review-rubric/.
4. eSpark, "Unpacking the Common Core with iPad Apps: Middle School, Webinar (and evaluation rubric)," www.esparklearning.com/blended-learning-webinars/unpacking-common-core-middle-school.html.

About the Authors

Scott McQuiggan leads SAS Curriculum Pathways, an interdisciplinary team focused on the development of no-cost educational software in the core disciplines at SAS Institute Inc. He received his PhD in computer science from North Carolina State University, where his research focused on affective reasoning in intelligent game-based learning environments. McQuiggan also holds an MS in computer science from North Carolina State University and a Bachelor of Science in computer science from Susquehanna University. He developed his first app, *SAS Flash Cards*, in 2010.

Lucy Kosturko is a research scientist and curriculum specialist for SAS Curriculum Pathways in Cary, North Carolina. She holds a PhD in educational psychology (2013) and a Master's in computer science (2010) from North Carolina State University. She received a Bachelor of Arts in computer science and psychology (2008) from Rhodes College in Memphis, Tennessee. Kosturko's research interests include reading comprehension, self-regulated learning, and educational technologies.

Jamie McQuiggan is a writer for SAS Institute Inc. She earned her Master's degree in technical communication from North Carolina State University in May 2011. She earned a Bachelor of Arts in corporate communication from Susquehanna University in Selinsgrove, Pennsylvania, with a minor in writing. She also co-authored *Implement, Improve and Expand your Statewide Longitudinal Data System: Creating a Culture of Data in Education* in 2014.

Jennifer Sabourin is a research scientist and a software developer at SAS Institute Inc. She received a BS (2008), Masters (2012), and PhD (2013) in computer science from North Carolina State University, where she graduated as valedictorian. She is a recipient of the U.S. National Science Foundation Graduate Research Fellowship award. Her research focuses on educational technologies and data analytics.

Index